Evangelization of Hispanic Young People

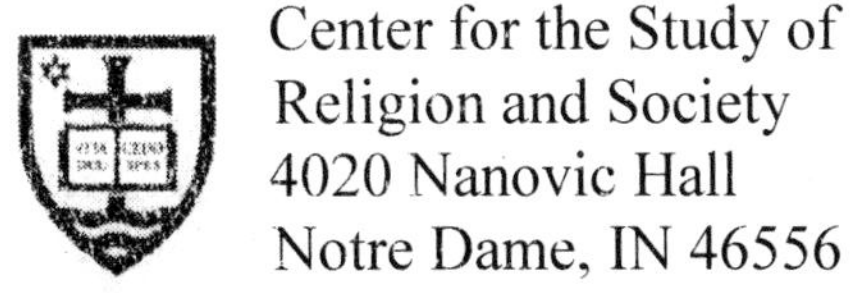

Prophets of Hope

Volume 1

Hispanic Young People and the Church's Pastoral Response

Volume 2

Evangelization of Hispanic Young People

Profetas de Esperanza

Volumen 1

La Juventud Hispana y la Respuesta Pastoral de la Iglesia

Volumen 2

Evangelización de la Juventud Hispana

Prophets of Hope

Volume 2

Evangelization of Hispanic Young People

Prophets of Hope Editorial Team

Saint Mary's Press
Christian Brothers Publications
Winona, Minnesota

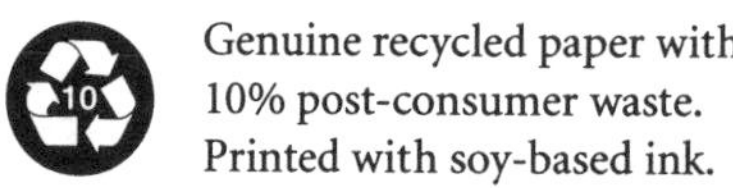
Genuine recycled paper with
10% post-consumer waste.
Printed with soy-based ink.

The publishing team for this volume included Eduardo Arnouil, Pedro Castex, and Yvette Nelson, development editors; Charles Capek, consulting editor; Rebecca Fairbank, copy editor; Amy Schlumpf Manion, production editor and typesetter; María Alicia Sánchez, illustrator; Jayne L. Stokke of Romance Valley Graphics, cover designer; Francine Cronshaw, indexer; pre-press, printing, and binding by the graphics division of Saint Mary's Press.

Saint Mary's Press wishes to give special acknowledgment to the ACTA Foundation, for funding that helped to subsidize this publication.

The permissions are on page 286.

Printed in the United States of America

Printing: 9 8 7 6 5 4 3 2 1

Year: 2003 02 01 00 99 98 97 96 95

ISBN 0-88489-327-8

Library of Congress card catalog number: 94-066205

Prophets of Hope Editorial Team

General Editor: Carmen María Cervantes, EdD

Writers: Alejandro Aguilera-Titus
Eduardo Arnouil
Carlos Carrillo
Pedro Castex
Carmen María Cervantes, EdD
Juan Díaz-Vilar, SJ
Juan Huitrado, MCCJ

Consultants: José Ahumada, CSC
María de la Cruz Aymes, SH, PhD
Rigoberto Caloca-Rivas, OFM, PhD
Rev. Ricardo Chávez
Juan Cruz, PhD
Gelasia Márquez
William McDonald
Isabel Ordoñez, STJ
Angeles Pla-Farmer
Elisa Rodríguez, SL
William Sousae
Carmencita Villafañe
Isabel Vinent

Translator into English: Richard Wood

Secretaries: Aurora M. Dewhirst
María Teresa Macías

Contents

To young leaders, youth ministers, and pastoral agents
who are giving their lives to carry Christ to Hispanic young people
in the United States

Preface

1 Every year, the Catholic church in the United States includes more Hispanic (or Latino) members, nearly half of whom are less than twenty-five years old. These young people and young adults represent both a challenge and a hope for us, our church, and our society. They provide us with a challenge because millions of them are not receiving adequate pastoral attention. They give us hope because by incarnating the Gospel in their lives, these young people can help renew our church, transform cultural values, and build the Reign of God. To confront this challenge and make this hope a reality, we need Hispanics—both young people and adults—who fulfill their mission as Christians in the world.

2 In 1987, Saint Mary's Press in Winona, Minnesota, joined the effort to provide foundation and direction for Hispanic youth ministry by developing materials for publication. To identify the most urgent program needs, Saint Mary's Press representatives consulted with Hispanic pastoral leaders throughout the United States. This research led to the development of a bilingual series for the evangelization of youth and young adults and to the hiring of Dr. Carmen María Cervantes as director of the publishing program for Hispanic materials.

3 The need to have a pastoral-theological framework that would provide consistency and direction for these publications gave rise to the first draft of this book. In August of 1988, Saint Mary's Press hosted a discernment meeting about this framework and about related Hispanic publications. Twenty-four pastoral agents, representing eleven different Hispanic groups and their diverse ministries, attended that meeting. These pastoral agents established the foundations of the project, planned the materials to be published, and revised the first draft of the framework. A month later, participants of the discernment meeting and Saint Mary's Press representatives developed an editorial board that has played a crucial role in planning and revising publications and in identifying appropriate people to write materials.

4 Thirty people from around the country, whose careful analyses and suggestions proved invaluable, reviewed the second draft of the framework. The third draft was translated into English and refined through bilingual consultation. The final manuscript emerged from this bilingual consultation.

5 Developing and writing the pastoral-theological framework was complex and exciting. The broad pastoral-theological vision shared by the editorial team took root in the reality of Hispanic young people and became a source of direction for their evangelization, but only after many hours of reflection, prayer, and sharing of experiences. Seven persons wrote significant pieces of the manuscript, and several others contributed with their advice and editing skills, making a truly collaborative work of what came to be the Prophets of Hope Editorial Team.

6 Consultations in Spanish and English with experts in different fields, pastoralists, pastoral agents, young leaders—Hispanics and non-Hispanics—provided the comprehensive perspective needed in a publication that was dealing with the reality of Hispanic young people in the United States and attempting to provide a pastoral-theological framework for their evangelization. Two surveys were conducted in areas of key importance for the evangelization of Hispanic young people. The first one identified the reality of Hispanic youth ministry in the country. The second one provided insight on who Jesus is, what the process of evangelization is, and what the church means for Hispanic young people.

7 The reflections and input by Richard Wood, the translator, and the editors in English were extremely valuable. The translation was bicultural, meaning that several concepts, theories, and philosophical and theological approaches identified as hard to understand or easy to misunderstand by a non-Hispanic reader were clarified. The respectful, sensible, and careful reactions of Yvette Nelson, Charles Capek, and Rebecca Fairbank, who were not familiar with Hispanic culture and religious life, helped the editorial team tremendously in two ways: to see and value the many points of unity between the mainstream and the Hispanic pastoral approaches and to further clarify the differences between them. This cross-cultural dialog gave origin to new sections in the framework that reinforce the identity and pastoral-theological vision of Hispanics in the United States who are faced with honest questions and the desire to learn from American pastoral agents of non-Hispanic background.

8 The complexity of the reality of Hispanic young people and the need to provide a pastoral-theological framework for their evangelization led Saint Mary's Press to publish two volumes of Prophets of Hope. The first volume focuses on Hispanic young people and the church's pastoral response. The second volume focuses on evangelization of Hispanic young people.

9 In a very special way, the editorial team wants to express our deep gratitude to Saint Mary's Press for making the publication of these two books possible; to Br. Damian Steger, FSC, president of Saint Mary's Press, for his patience and encouragement; and to Stephan Nagel, for his constant support and direction as editor-in-chief. We also want to thank those persons who helped to shape the manuscript with their valuable insights and all the other people who made the books in the Prophets of Hope series possible.

Introduction

Jesus, Prophet of Hope
Yesterday, Today, and Always

1 About two thousand years ago, after Jesus had been baptized by his cousin John and had prayed in the desert for forty days, he returned to Galilee. There, in the land of his childhood, Jesus began to preach in the Jewish synagogues. All who listened with an open heart praised him, and his fame spread throughout the region.

2 Jesus arrived in Galilee full of the power of the Spirit and began to carry out his mission. His experience of baptism, when the Holy Spirit revealed that he was the beloved Son of God, the Chosen One, had forever changed his life. To each and every one of us Christians, God has said the same thing: "You are my beloved son, my beloved daughter. I have chosen you to receive my message, and I give to you the power to follow the path begun by Jesus, who is my Son, your brother, and prophet of the Reign." This experience of God's love should forever change our life, as it changed Jesus' life.

3 After arriving in Nazareth, where he had been raised, Jesus went to the synagogue on the Sabbath, as he was accustomed to doing:

> He stood up to read, and the scroll of the prophet Isaiah was given to him. He unrolled the scroll and found the place where it was written:
>
> "The Spirit of the Lord is upon me,
> because he has anointed me
> to bring good news to the poor.
> He has sent me to proclaim release to the captives
> and recovery of sight to the blind,
> to let the oppressed go free,
> to proclaim the year of the Lord's favor."
>
> And he rolled up the scroll, gave it back to the attendant, and sat down. The eyes of all in the synagogue were fixed on him. Then he began to say to them, "Today this scripture passage has been fulfilled in your hearing." (Luke 4:16–21)

4 This first proclamation, as surprising as it was grandiose, occurred in a synagogue in Jesus' hometown, in a meeting of a *small community of believers* who awaited the arrival of the Messiah.

> All spoke well of him and were amazed at the gracious words that came from his mouth. They said, "Is not this Joseph's son?" He said to them, "Doubtless you will quote to me this proverb, 'Doctor, cure yourself!' And you will say, 'Do here also in your hometown the things that we have heard you did at Capernaum.'" And he said, "Truly I tell you, no prophet is accepted in the prophet's hometown. . . ." When they heard this, all in the synagogue were filled with rage. They got up, drove him out of the town, and led him to the brow of the hill on which their town was built, so that they might hurl him off the cliff. But he passed through the midst of them and went on his way. He went down to Capernaum, a city in Galilee, and was teaching them on the sabbath. They were astounded at his teaching, because he spoke with authority. (Luke 4:22–32)

5 We also have been called to proclaim the Good News of the Reign of God. Our message centers on sharing our faith in the Risen Jesus present in the ecclesial community, in order to give new life to the poor, imprisoned, blind, and oppressed.

6 Our mission is an adventure that is worth beginning with passion, because it is God's will; it is the same mission God gave to Jesus. Today Jesus is calling us to continue his mission, inviting us to return to our own Nazareth in Galilee: our people, our neighborhood, our community. This Scripture passage is fulfilled in our hearing when—as Jesus did—we disciples accept our mission of being *prophets of hope*, carrying the Good News to young people who suffer economic or educational poverty, to captives in physical or psychological prisons, to the blind who have not found the way of life, and to those oppressed by their own sinfulness or the sins of society.

7 Just as Jesus chose the disciples who formed the first Christian community, Jesus personally chooses and invites each young person to be his disciple. The power of their vocation and mission is rooted in this divine calling. In the past, when Jesus chose his disciples and sent them out to proclaim the Gospel, he instructed them to give freely what had been given freely to them. Today God contin-

ues giving his love and his life freely and asks us, as members of the Body of Christ, to share his love and life freely with others.

8 In the past, Jesus Christ proclaimed the Gospel in Jewish synagogues, on the roads and byways of ancient Israel, in the countryside, and on lakeshores. Today Jesus proclaims the Gospel through his church, in small ecclesial communities, in parks and schools, in factories and family celebrations—wherever people gather together to share life.

9 In Jesus' day, many people doubted him and had no faith in him; his disciples were challenged and written off by many. Today as well, Christians who want to preach the Good News often face rejection. But just as Jesus fulfilled his mission, and just as the first Christian communities carried the Good News to the ends of the world they knew, today we must never cease evangelizing.

10 Now is the time of favor of the Lord. Jesus is calling his young disciples to be prophets of hope, to evangelize, to proclaim true freedom. In and through their own communities, with the power of the Holy Spirit, young people will be prophets of hope who proclaim the resurrected Jesus Christ, "the same yesterday and today and forever" (Heb. 13:8); the fullness of the Gospel; and the Good News of the Reign of God incarnate in the history of all who receive it and make it their own.

Prophets of Hope

11 Prophets of Hope is a two-volume series that proposes a pastoral and theological vision for ministry with Hispanic young people and young adults in the United States. This work brings together the social analysis, pastoral priorities, vision, and spirit of Hispanic youth ministry inspired by the three Encuentros Nacionales Hispanos de Pastoral, the *National Pastoral Plan for Hispanic Ministry*, and the call to a New Evangelization for America made by Pope John Paul II and ratified in 1992 at the Fourth General Conference of the Latin American Bishops in Santo Domingo.

12 The analysis of reality, reflection, guidance, and concrete suggestions for action that give substance to the pastoral and theological vision of Prophets of Hope is divided into the two volumes as follows:

- **Volume 1,** *Hispanic Young People and the Church's Pastoral Response*, is divided into eight chapters dealing with the personal, relational, cultural, sociological, and religious realities of Hispanic young people, and the response of the Catholic church to the pastoral needs of Hispanic young people.

- **Volume 2,** *Evangelization of Hispanic Young People,* is divided into eight chapters dealing with the evangelization of Hispanic young people, the evangelization process, a model of evangelization for small communities, and the role of Mary in these evangelizing efforts.

13 These two volumes are intended as *guides* for pastoral work and the formation of pastoral agents and young leaders. Volume 1's presentation of the reality of Hispanic young people and young adults is only a beginning and will continue to develop as this reality is further studied and analyzed. The pastoral-theological vision is evolving and crystallizing through praxis and will be renewed as young Hispanics and those who minister to them put it into practice and reflect on that practice. Thus, to take full advantage of these books, readers must use their own creativity, experience, and reflection in adapting the material to their concrete reality. They must also avoid using the books as if they were textbooks or how-to manuals of techniques.

14 In using this volume, it is important to remember that the English concepts of *youth* and *young people* do not correspond to the Spanish concepts of *juventud* and *jóvenes,* although these are the correct equivalents in translation. References in this book to Hispanic youth or young people include Hispanic single young adults as well as Hispanic adolescents.

15 Special terms like **animation** and **conscientization** are boldfaced at their first appearance in the book beginning with the initial reflection. A definition for all the boldfaced terms can be found in the glossary at the end of the book. Before beginning to read the chapters, we suggest that you scan the glossary to acquaint yourself with any terms that may be unfamiliar to you. Also note that the paragraphs in the book are numbered in the margin to make it easier for leaders to use both the English and Spanish volumes together in a bilingual setting.

16 We wrote this book for youth ministers, young leaders, pastoral agents, and adult advisers of young people. Prophets of Hope can also be useful to anyone who wants to understand more deeply the reality of Latino young people and young adults and improve

their human and Christian formation. We share our hope that these books will stimulate dialog, reflection, and *pastoral de conjunto,* not only among Latinos but within the entire church.

17 We especially ask Mary to bless our young people and all those who minister to them. We pray that the Holy Spirit may fill us with enthusiasm and hope, so that our work will continue the work begun by Jesus, our brother and prophet of the Reign of God. In that way, we will fulfill with him his dream and his mission: to inaugurate the Reign of God among us.

Initial Reflection

Mary, Pilgrim in Faith and Prophet of Hope

Initial Reflection

Mary, Pilgrim in Faith and Prophet of Hope

1 In the first volume of Prophets of Hope, we reflected on the **reality** of young **Hispanics** in the United States and on the church's pastoral response to that reality. This second volume is dedicated to the **evangelization** of Hispanic young people and young adults. But before presenting theories, methods, and models of evangelization, we want to offer Mary as an example of the interior attitude of faith that every evangelizer should have in order to discover in Mary's life the living and active presence of God.

Mary's Yes Response

2 Mary was a young woman from a small, poor town in the region of Galilee. She was only sixteen or seventeen years old when she became engaged to marry a young worker named Joseph. Painters frequently portray Joseph as an old man, but the Gospels never say this. Therefore, we may assume that he was a typical bridegroom-to-be, a young man. Surely both Joseph and Mary joyfully awaited their wedding day, but God had bigger plans for them, which God communicated through the messenger angel Gabriel. In an atmosphere of mystery and joy, Gabriel praised Mary and told her of God's plan for her. The Gospel of Luke tells the story:

> In the sixth month, the angel Gabriel was sent by God to a town in Galilee called Nazareth, to a virgin engaged to a man whose name was Joseph, of the house of David. The virgin's name was Mary. And he came to her and said, "Greetings, favored one! The Lord is with you." But she was much perplexed by his words and pondered what sort of greeting this might be. The angel said to her, "Do not be afraid, Mary, for you have found favor with God. And now, you will conceive in your womb and bear a son, and you will name him Jesus. . . ." Mary said to the angel, "How can this be, since I am a virgin?" The angel said to her, "The Holy Spirit will come upon you, and the power of the Most High will overshadow you;

> therefore the child to be born will be holy; he will be called Son of God. And now, your relative Elizabeth in her old age has also conceived a son; and this is the sixth month for her who was said to be barren. For nothing will be impossible with God." Then Mary said, "Here am I, the servant of the Lord; let it be with me according to your word." Then the angel departed from her. (Luke 1:26–38)

3 Naturally, young Mary did not understand how she could become pregnant without ever having had intimate relations with a man. So Mary spoke her doubts to the angel, even in the midst of such strange and disconcerting events. In the angel's response, Mary understood that although she could not fully comprehend what God was asking of her, it was important for her to answer yes to the grace God was giving her. So she told the angel: "'Here am I, the servant of the Lord. Let it be with me according to your word.'"

4 In reality, even after hearing the angel, Mary did not really know what God was planning for her. Yet she abandoned herself confidently to God, responding with a total and absolute yes. From then on, Mary's life direction would be given over to God's plan for her, even if she did not understand it. Mary's yes was not an easy one; rather, it was a yes spoken from the darkness and mystery that must have been the most important secret in her life.

Mary Shares Her Experience and Her Faith

5 God's plan for Mary and her son was linked in important ways to God's plan for Mary's cousin Elizabeth and her son. Elizabeth was a sterile, older woman who, through God's special intervention, awaited a son. In the culture of Mary and Elizabeth's time, women who could not have children were held in scorn; people even believed that sterile women were being punished by God for their sins or the sins of their ancestors. So sterile women carried in their hearts both shame and psychological oppression resulting from others' scorn and their own feelings of guilt.

6 Luke tells us that as soon as Mary knew that her cousin Elizabeth was to have a child, she went to visit Elizabeth. Many reasons moved Mary to travel to Elizabeth's house. Surely she wanted to share with Elizabeth her mysterious experience with the angel and

her bewilderment at what had happened. Mary also needed to share her faith and hope, her joy and uncertainty. At the same time, Mary must have wanted to hear of her cousin's encounter and to seek understanding from a **person** who had experienced a similar event; together they could wonder at the power of God in their lives and find mutual support.

7 Luke's story holds another important message: Elizabeth's coming son was to be John the Baptist, the last prophet of the Hebrew Scriptures, whose mission was to prepare the way for Jesus. Mary's visit to Elizabeth emphasizes the relationship between the period of expectation and the period of fulfillment of the promise. Mary carries in her womb the One sent by God to fulfill the divine promise of **salvation** that God had made to the people of Israel. Luke describes Mary's encounter with Elizabeth this way:

> In those days Mary set out and went with haste to a Judean town in the hill country, where she entered the house of Zechariah and greeted Elizabeth. When Elizabeth heard Mary's greeting, the child leaped in her womb. And Elizabeth was filled with the Holy Spirit and exclaimed with a loud cry, "Blessed are you among women, and blessed is the fruit of your womb. And why has this happened to me, that the mother of my Lord comes to me? For as soon as I heard the sound of your greeting, the child in my womb leaped for joy. And blessed is she who believed that there would be a fulfillment of what was spoken to her by the Lord." (Luke 1:39–45)

8 This scene of joy and tenderness shows us two generations of women who love, embrace, and understand each other. Both women recognize within themselves and in each other the mystery of God's action in their lives. Elizabeth's recognition of the greatness of God's work in Mary and the depth of her cousin's faith fills her with joy and assures her that through Mary's faith, the Lord's promises will be fulfilled.

Mary as Prophet: The Canticle of Hope

9 Mary could not contain her happiness. Full of strength and peace, and perhaps with streaming tears of joy and thanksgiving, she broke out into a song of hope, the Magnificat:

"My soul magnifies the Lord,
and my spirit rejoices in God my Savior.
for he has looked with favor on the lowliness of his servant.
Surely, from now on all generations will call me blessed;
for the Mighty One has done great things for me,
and holy is his name.
His mercy is for those who fear him
from generation to generation.
He has shown strength with his arm;
he has scattered the proud in the thoughts of their hearts.
He has brought down the powerful from their thrones,
and lifted up the lowly;
he has filled the hungry with good things,
and sent the rich away empty.
He has helped his servant Israel,
in remembrance of his mercy,
according to the promise he made to our ancestors,
to Abraham and to his descendants forever."

(Luke 1:46–55)

10 In this song, we see once again Mary's strength and creativity. Here her heart overflows, and she expresses her faith in a great God who wills that through her all future generations might live joyfully. She praises God because she recognizes that God's favor extends to all those who follow the Holy Spirit, especially to those who are poor. She confesses her faith in a God who is committed to her people forever.

11 Mary is just beginning her great adventure of faith. Full of the power of the Spirit, she is ready to start walking the path on which God leads her. How many times did Mary pray the Magnificat? Surely it was through frequent prayer that this young woman from Nazareth acquired the strength to abandon herself to God's hands, to trust God, to continue believing in and accepting the mystery of God's action within her, and to embrace her double maternity—mother to Jesus and, later, mother to us all.

Mother of the Savior

12 Months went by and the time approached for Mary to give birth, but a difficult journey lay ahead. She had to leave the security of her home to fulfill her civic duties, for Caesar in Rome was demanding that all citizens go to their city of origin to register themselves. Mary and Joseph set out on the long journey to Bethlehem; Mary faced all the discomforts of traveling in the final month of pregnancy. She felt the weight of her son in her womb. They walked slowly, resting from time to time. This was the second time that Jesus traveled the roads and byways of Israel with his mother; the first time had been when they went to visit Elizabeth to share with her Mary's faith experience. Now Mary went to fulfill her responsibility as a citizen.

13 Mary walked contentedly; she was walking with God. At her side, the young man to whom she was betrothed accompanied and supported her. Within her womb, she carried Jesus.

14 "Will we find a place to stay?" they may have wondered. Because so many people were traveling in order to register themselves, all faced the difficult task of finding a place to stay the night. When they arrived in Bethlehem, Mary and Joseph had to walk the streets, asking for lodging. This was a shorter but more humbling journey, knocking on doors and asking for an empty room. Doors opened and closed; people said no, each in his or her own way.

15 Undoubtedly, before knocking on each door, Mary and Joseph prayed to God for help, but it appeared that God was not listening or appreciating the gravity of their situation. We do not know if Mary and Joseph spent hours or days this way. Mary began to feel her time of labor drawing near; their prayers and requests for housing must have become more urgent, more anguished. Finally, they had to seek refuge in a stable, for there was not even room for them in the poorest of lodgings.

16 Mary and Joseph themselves were poor, and poor people then, as today, do not easily find a place to stay. Some of the people of Bethlehem probably decided they could gain nothing from this young, bedraggled couple. Because Mary and Joseph were poor, perhaps others thought they were sinners and troublemakers, rightfully abandoned by God. Still others, perhaps the majority, simply thought of their own needs and were incapable of feeling compassion for a poor mother about to give birth.

17 At this moment of desperation, Mary must have looked tired and worried, seeing no way out of her difficulty. But at the same time, Mary might have shown signs of peace and hope in her look and bearing, for she always placed her trust in God.

God in the Lap of a Young Woman

18 We now watch one of the most profound moments in Mary's life: the birth of her son. Luke tells the story:

> While they were there [in Bethlehem], the time came for her to deliver her child. And she gave birth to her firstborn son and wrapped him in bands of cloth, and laid him in a manger, because there was no place for them in the inn. (Luke 2:6–7)

19 It was nighttime, and Mary gave birth in a manger, attended only by Joseph. God-become-human emerged from her womb and cried on this earth for the first time. Mary took him in her arms, wrapped him, and soon nursed him at her breast.

20 This piece of Mary's story symbolizes our own history. Mary carried Jesus inside of her, but she had to wait for his birth in order to recognize him in the mystery of a defenseless child. We, too, carry Christ within us; from the time of our baptism, by the power of the Holy Spirit, Jesus becomes incarnate in our life. But many Christians have not discovered this, nor have they recognized Jesus in themselves or in the faces of the many strangers whose lives touch theirs. Like Mary's, our journey with Jesus has to be enlightened by faith. We discover God's loving presence and designs for us only as we gradually deepen our yes to God's action in our life.

Piercing Her Heart

21 Jesus appeared to be a typical child to his mother and to other people who saw him. Mary had to discover God's plans gradually throughout her life, in the darkness of an unfolding mystery. Luke recounts an experience that must have made a strong impression on this young woman, for even as it revealed God's plans, it wrapped those plans in an even more dense and difficult mystery.

22 On the day that Mary and Joseph took the child to Jerusalem to present him at the Temple, as the Law required, two holy people

named Simeon and Anna were there. These two people symbolize all those who anxiously awaited the coming of the Messiah. Simeon, recognizing in Jesus the promised Messiah, took him in his arms and blessed him with a song that expressed his joy at seeing the promise fulfilled. Mary and Joseph must have marveled to see and hear Simeon's response to their child; Mary's heart must have been filled with peace and joy, until Simeon's final words left her feeling insecure and dismayed:

> "This child is destined for the falling and the rising of many in Israel, and to be a sign that will be opposed so that the inner thoughts of many will be revealed—and a sword will pierce your own soul too." (Luke 2:34–35)

23 Surely these words left a mark on Mary's heart: the mystery kept getting more difficult to understand, and more challenging. Mary must have returned to Nazareth darkly moved by this experience and full of questions: When would the cruel moment of "piercing" come? What did it mean? Why would this piercing occur? Mary's yes to God kept getting more difficult, but she moved forward, trusting in her decision: "May it be done to me according to your Word, even if I do not understand it and am hurt by it, because I am sure there is a good reason for this."

24 Later, Mary, Joseph, and Jesus had to flee to Egypt because King Herod wanted to kill Jesus. This must have been another painful journey; they had to enter the strange and distant country where their people had been enslaved years before. Once again they faced mystery and uncertainty, as well as the need to deepen their trust in God. Later, when Herod died, Mary and Joseph returned to Nazareth with Jesus. There Mary continued serving God through the quiet life of a village woman. Joseph went on working as a carpenter.

25 Nothing else unusual happened until Jesus was an adolescent. At that time, Mary, Joseph, and Jesus went to the Temple for a festival. During their journey home, Mary and Joseph realized that Jesus was not with them. They looked everywhere. Mary must have felt Simeon's words resonate tragically in her heart: "a sword will pierce your own soul." In the confusion, amidst terrible conjectures about her lost son, Mary must have asked herself, "Is this the moment?" But the time of piercing had not yet arrived; this was only a painful episode in which Mary did not understand her son. The mystery kept intensifying and penetrating her soul more deeply. Mary "treasured all these things in her heart" (Luke 2:51).

26 Sometimes we think that it is enough to respond to God's first call to us, and then everything will become clear and straightforward. But it was not like that for Mary, nor will it be like that for us. When God calls us, it is not to open a door for us to enter and remain there, paralyzed. God always calls us anew, either to begin walking a fresh road or to continue walking, day by day, on the path God has shown us.

Mary Hastens Jesus' Public Ministry

27 While Luke shows us Mary's attitude during Jesus' childhood, John tells us about her at the beginning and end of Jesus' public **ministry.** Much time has gone by: Jesus is a young man of thirty; Mary is about forty-seven years old. At the end of the week during which Jesus called his first disciples, three days after calling Philip and Nathanael, Jesus attends a wedding, accompanied by his mother and his disciples. John's narrative says:

> On the third day there was a wedding in Cana of Galilee, and the mother of Jesus was there. Jesus and his disciples had also been invited to the wedding. When the wine gave out, the mother of Jesus said to him, "They have no wine." And Jesus said to her, "Woman, what concern is that to you and to me? My hour has not yet come." His mother said to the servants, "Do whatever he tells you." Now standing there were six stone water jars for the Jewish rites of purification, each holding twenty or thirty gallons. Jesus said to them, "Fill the jars with water." And they filled them up to the brim. He said to them, "Now draw some out, and take it to the chief steward." So they took it. When the steward tasted the water that had become wine, and did not know where it came from (though the servants who had drawn the water knew), the steward called the bridegroom and said to him, "Everyone serves the good wine first, and then the inferior wine after the guests have become drunk. But you have kept the good wine until now." Jesus did this, the first of his signs, in Cana of Galilee, and revealed his glory; and the disciples believed in him. (John 2:1–11)

28 In this passage, John tells the story of Jesus' first miracle, which carries deep symbolism regarding the arrival of the **Reign of God** and Mary's role in it. The key symbol here is the marriage banquet. Both marriage and the banquet itself symbolize the Reign of God: the wedding symbolizes the intimate union between God and the people, and the banquet celebrates that union.

29 John's whole Gospel is an invitation to participate in the coming of the Reign of God. In the following passage, Mary's role shows us *how* we are to participate. John begins the story by saying, "on the third day," meaning three days after Jesus chose his disciples. Shortly after the Cana banquet, Jesus uses this same expression to proclaim his own Resurrection:

> "Destroy this temple, and in three days I will raise it up." . . . But he was speaking of the temple of his body. After he was raised from the dead, his disciples remembered that he had said this; and they believed the scripture and the word that Jesus had spoken. (John 2:19–22)

30 With the miraculous sign at Cana, John's Gospel frames the story of Jesus' ministry with reference to the three days at the end when, through the Easter mystery, a new era of human history begins. And here in Cana, in these key moments at the beginning of the coming of the Reign of God, stands Mary—not just as another guest, but as an active participant in the events at the wedding banquet—promoting through her intercession with Jesus the coming of the Reign.

31 According to John's story, the banquet hosts have run out of wine. Mary realizes this and worries that the new couple will be embarrassed by the shortage. She brings her generous concern for her hosts to Jesus' attention, confident that he will do something for them. However, Jesus responds, "Woman, how does your concern affect me? My hour has not yet come." Mary nevertheless says to the servants, "Do whatever he tells you." Jesus' apparent refusal to help leads Mary from a simple attitude of service to an attitude of unconditional faith in Jesus. Although she did not know what would happen, Mary knew that Jesus would respond to the situation. As on the day of the Annunciation and as today, Mary's act of faith had marvelous results: although Jesus said his time had not yet come, the water was changed into wine.

32 In these passages from John's Gospel, four symbols—the water, the wine, the "hour," and the "glory"—help us to understand Jesus' mission. Mary's life was closely tied to this mission in her vocation as servant of the Reign, woman of faith, and loyal disciple. Through Mary's intercession and Jesus' action, the water with which the Jews ritualized purification from sin was changed into wine, which later became the symbol of the blood spilled by Jesus for the forgiveness of sin. This miracle testifies that although the "hour" of salvation had not yet arrived in its fullness, the glorious coming of the Reign of God had already begun.

33 The message is clear: Mary's absolute faith motivates Jesus to act. Her faith in Jesus and his service to others leads the disciples, just chosen the previous week, to grow in their faith in Jesus and to become his faithful followers.

34 Mary does not become the heroine of the Cana story. Her mission as mother of Christ is to collaborate actively with Jesus to bring the Reign and to strengthen the faith of the disciples. Every evangelizer should be like Mary: one who trusts in Jesus and his word, discerns people's needs, and takes the initiative to lead them to encounter Jesus so that he can show them the way of salvation.

Mary, Model of Discipleship and Mother of the Disciples

35 After the Cana story, John does not mention Mary again until the nineteenth chapter, where she reappears accompanying Jesus as he gives his life for the **redemption** of humanity. The Gospel says:

> Standing near the cross of Jesus were his mother, and his mother's sister, Mary the wife of Clopas, and Mary Magdalene. When Jesus saw his mother and the disciple whom he loved standing beside her, he said to his mother, "Woman, here is your son." Then he said to the disciple, "Here is your mother." And from that hour the disciple took her into his own home. (John 19:25–27)

36 Mary is shown to be a heroic and unconditional follower of Jesus. On that Good Friday afternoon, so full of denials, absences, and betrayals, Mary is where she must be—at Jesus' side, a strong woman accompanying her son and the other disciples. At that moment, as Jesus was finishing his earthly mission and preparing him-

self to return to God to fulfill his promise to give living water to all who believed in him, Jesus gave Mary a new role—to be a mother to his followers, to walk with them, and to accompany them in the mission he had given them.

37 Mary is the ideal model for every evangelizer. The attitude that led her to put her whole life in God's hands also allowed God to become human through her, to become incarnate in human history. By following Jesus all the way to the cross and by accompanying the disciples there, Mary collaborated actively in Jesus' mission. So those of us who desire to follow Jesus and accept our own missions in history follow Mary as a model and ask her to accompany us in our efforts to lead young people to Jesus. Mary's faith allowed the Incarnation of God to take place. The faith of committed Hispanic young people and young adults today is also key for the Incarnation of Jesus in the life of other young people and in the course of history.

1

Personal Development and Evangelization

1

Personal Development and Evangelization

Human beings, by virtue of their dignity as the image of God, merit a commitment from us in favor of their liberation and their total fulfillment in Christ Jesus. Only in Christ is the true grandeur of human beings revealed. Only in Christ is their more intimate reality fully known.

—Consejo Episcopal Latinoamericano (CELAM), *Puebla and Beyond*

1 This chapter focuses on young people's **holistic** development. It begins by examining young people's **integral** development: the development of their personal center, their personality formation, and their growth toward wholeness. The second section reflects on the process of discovering, encountering, and establishing a personal identity as the path to personal fulfillment. The third section examines the importance of formation for young people; the fourth reflects on freedom as the road to full humanity; and the fifth presents the integrative power of ideals. In addition to reflecting on these processes of integral development of young people, this chapter also examines the role of evangelization in each process.

2 Evangelization involves helping people fulfill themselves as persons through an encounter with Jesus, who opens them to the action of God's grace in the emotional, intellectual, **volitional,** and sociopolitical dimensions of their lives. Therefore, the need exists for an integral evangelization that centers on and collaborates with Jesus in transforming and orienting young people from within.

Young People's Holistic Development

3 Before identifying young people as Hispanics, Christians, Catholics, adolescents, or young adults, we must remember that every one of them is a *person.* Persons are spiritual and physical beings who are unique, free, and dynamic individuals, capable of thinking, developing, and being true to themselves. Persons are also interdependent

members of creation and of the human family, capable of knowing and loving one another, of helping one another to develop to fullness as persons and to seek together the common good.

4 All human beings are called to live in union with God, to love one another, and to collaborate with God in perfecting all of creation and in being agents of positive change in history. Hearing this call and responding to it depend on God's grace, which heals and perfects human nature, and on the action of the ecclesial community that proclaims and lives the Gospel.

The Personal Center of Young People

5 Human history takes place almost entirely in the context of interpersonal relations. Young people, like all persons, are beings-in-relation. They have an essential relationship with the divine as daughters and sons of God, who is their creator and final destiny. Young people have a relationship as sisters and brothers to other persons, a relationship as stewards to all of creation, and a relationship with themselves as free human beings searching for fulfillment. These relationships give rise to the many varied experiences that together constitute the personal experience of each young person.

6 In this book, the place where each person's relationships are rooted and where the emotional, intellectual, volitional, and sociopolitical dimensions of a person's life converge is defined as the "personal center." There, in the depths of their own self, young people become aware of their personal and social world. There, in the personal center, young people respond to their **existential** questions, receive and give love, become reconciled with themselves, heal the bitter experiences of their past, build their life on fundamental principles, determine their values and commitments, and find their motives for acting. There, too, young people experience God and identify with Jesus. The Bible uses images such as "seeing," "hearing," and "feeling" to refer to a personal center that has been enlightened by faith and transformed by God's love. Using these and similar images, the Scriptures refer to the need to find and touch the transcendent nature of each person.

7 Young people grow as they gradually integrate the different relationships and dimensions of their life and go through the dynamic process of individualization (or acquisition of personality).

To creatively participate in history and grow as Christian persons, young people must become fully conscious of their experiences, interpret them in the light of faith, and convert them into actions and ideals that further the Reign of God. Just as creative tension usually exists between the emotional and the intellectual, the personal and the **communitarian,** and the church and the world, so will tension occasionally exist between young people's growth as persons and their growth as Christians. This tension is a necessary part of an integrating Christian formation, because such tension is creative and tends to spark new ways of Christian expression in a constantly changing world.

Formation of Personality

8 Personality can be thought of as the way one composes and shows his or her unique self, and how one relates with other people and the world that surrounds him or her. Personality, the combined whole of a person's attitudes, behaviors, and characteristics, is the fruit of an intentional process governed from within the person, a process that involves intellectual activity, attention to the feelings and reactions of oneself and others, and a constant use of one's ***voluntad.*** Personality formation is a process of self-education that gradually shapes a person's attitudes and values and orients them toward a conscious goal.

9 The elements that most influence personality formation are the following:

- *the already-established, natural constitution of the person,* which includes the person's gender, inherited physical characteristics, and age
- *the temperament of the person*—the person's tendency toward certain emotional states and reactions, which despite being mostly conscious, is highly influenced by genetic factors
- *the personal history of the person,* which is largely formed by concrete experiences and is therefore influenced by the social environment

10 Although these factors strongly influence personality formation, they do *not* necessarily determine it. Young people can modify their temperament, reinterpret their experiences from different perspectives, and to some extent manage the influences to which they are exposed—physical, emotional, intellectual, and spiritual.

11 The formation of personality begins in childhood, when the process of integrating all the dimensions of human life starts, and when behavior patterns that will affect later conduct are initiated. Parents have a strong influence on their young children's personality formation. Beginning with adolescence, however, young people gradually develop the potential to take into their own hands the integration of their life, the development of their personality, and the formation of their character.

12 A person's character develops in response to the person's life experience, especially her or his education. Though firmly linked to personality, character can be defined as the mental processes, ethics, and values that give shape to a person's life and manage the various elements of her or his personality. As young people gradually form their personality and character, they simultaneously acquire a philosophy of life that serves as a frame of reference for determining how they will influence and be influenced by their environment.

13 Today, psychology plays a very important role in shaping our ideas about human formation. Although various psychological perspectives are useful for recognizing the mechanisms that facilitate learning and motivate human behavior, adopting a psychological perspective can also generate some problems. Psychology's analytical focus as well as its focus on isolated processes sometimes discourages attention to character formation and its ethical emphasis.

14 Worse still, the morals and **moral relativism** of **modern culture** shift almost as constantly as sand, leaving little or no firm base on which people can build their character or identity. Without an ethical vision and a philosophy of life rooted in God as an absolute value, people are led into a moral void, or relativism, in which they lack the strong frame of reference needed to confront the manipulative influences surrounding them. When all people, but particularly young people, have the chance to root their life values and philosophy in God, they have both a solid base for establishing their character and identity and a strong frame of reference for decision making. As Jesus proclaimed:

> "Everyone then who hears these words of mine and acts on them will be like a wise man who built his house on rock. The rain fell, the floods came, and the winds blew and beat on that house, but it did not fall, because it had been founded on rock." (Matt. 7:24–25)

Growth Toward Fullness as Persons

15 Like most people, young people are typically in a dynamic process of development; they are beings in constant flux. They both *are* persons and are *becoming* persons at the same time. Young people are what they are as a result of their genetic endowment; the influences of their family, society, and environment; and the decisions they have made and continue to make. Many factors contribute to the formation of young people as persons, but in the end, each young person must choose his or her life path and responsibly move toward maturity. Young people mature to the extent that they come to know themselves and center their attention and energy on discovering healthy means for growing and changing, as well as for transforming the world in which they live.

16 Growing in personal maturity is a complex process, one that involves several specific processes, of which five stand out:

- the process of identity formation
- the process of communication, intimacy, and communion
- the process of physical and emotional maturation
- the process of sexual development
- the process of **conscientization** and **liberation**

The rhythm, direction, and intensity of each of these processes vary from person to person and manifest themselves in different elements and characteristics throughout adolescence and young adulthood.

17 As these processes develop in relation to one another, a philosophy and a worldview take shape in young people's lives. Also, a characteristic spirit, or ***mística,*** begins to orient young people's values, allowing young people to act more freely, maturely, and responsibly. Growing in personal maturity always involves interaction with oneself, with others, and with the surrounding world. Growing in Christian maturity involves the same interaction, but with Jesus—the model of human perfection and fullness—as the example to be followed. Thus, as young people grow in Christian maturity, they advance toward fullness as persons—toward loving God with their whole heart, their whole strength, and their whole mind, and toward loving their neighbors as themselves.

Human Formation and Evangelization

18 The growth of young people as persons and as Christians occurs in human history and through human experience. To evangelize means to help young people encounter and recognize the presence of God in their personal and social history. Spiritual and religious values that are located outside of young people's life experience may create an alienating spirituality that impedes young people from taking responsibility for their freedom. Therefore, any effective human formation with young people must focus squarely on their life, consider their experiences, and see the relationships with the culture in which they live.

19 The *effectiveness* of an integrating human formation and an integral evangelization with young people depends on several other factors as well. Young people need to do the following:

- become aware that they were created *by* God and *for* God, and that therefore they possess a value and a dignity that no one should take from them. By nature, all human beings are inclined toward wholeness and life, called to become integrated, "complete" persons.
- see that they were created in freedom, are ***dueños de sí mismos,*** and are capable of personal development. It is important for young people to realize that God acts in their life and that whether they move toward maturity, moral paralysis, or self-destruction depends on how they live their life.
- know, from experience, that they are the fruit of God's love and that their fulfillment as persons can only occur in love.
- relate with Jesus alive in the other members of their church community. By hearing and responding to Jesus' call with compassion and solidarity, young people can undergo a continuous **conversion** as disciples who try to know and love Jesus better by serving and loving other people.
- participate actively in the life of the church community, finding there the help necessary for their faith journey and Christian life.

20 Broadly speaking, integral evangelization with young people can be achieved in the following ways:

- through the testimony of adults or other young people who have discovered God in their life
- through dialog about how God has been revealed in the history of each young person, how God has touched each young person's

life, and how God has been present and active in the history of different peoples and nations
- through helping young people enter into solitude intentionally so that they can find God in the silence of their own heart
- through communitarian experiences in which young people encounter a living and acting Christ in the community of disciples

Evangelizers can use various steps and techniques to facilitate the action of God's grace in young people. Chapters 5 through 8 describe the evangelization process from different perspectives and assist evangelizers in their mission.

21 The U.S. bishops offer this insightful summary on what evangelization should encompass:

> The evangelizer must share the earthly needs of the ones called, needs that often must be addressed before the message can be heard. Evangelization sounds a call to leave a sinful way of life, by showing Jesus as the one in whom the power of God can be encountered. The encounter with Jesus is also an encounter with his community. . . . The most profound needs of the human person are fulfilled by the privileged worship ("in Spirit and in truth") of the community of Jesus.[1]

Young People's Discovery and Establishment of Personal Identity

22 Searching for and establishing one's identity constitutes one of the most exciting and difficult tasks of being human. Identity consists of knowing and encountering oneself. The search for one's identity is a lifetime endeavor, though this search is generally most intense during adolescence and young adulthood. Commitment to the search for personal identity springs from the key existential questions confronting all human beings: Who am I? How am I? What is my situation in life? Where do I come from? Where am I going? What must I do? What is the meaning of my life? What happens after I die?

23 Responding to these questions is necessary to discovering ourselves as beings created by God who are called to a special mission during our lifetime. The search for self-identity should occur in the framework of a Christian worldview and be aimed at discovering

God's plan for oneself—the way each of us is called to live, to project our own self in the world, and to help build the Reign of God through love and service.

24 Because the search for self-identity does not occur in a vacuum but within each person's sociocultural setting, young people who embark on this search while immersed in a bicultural or multicultural society need to clarify their own cultural identity. They require special support and direction to advance in their process of personal identification.

Discovering Aloneness and Uniqueness

25 People broaden their acquisition of a personal identity upon becoming aware that although they are part of an extensive community, they are also unique and alone in the world: *unique* because each person is individual, original, and unrepeatable; *alone* because each person is created and called to be personally complete and **autonomous**—free in being himself or herself, and free in determining his or her values and beliefs.

26 To find an identity, we must accept the aloneness of being. We are born alone. We are going to die alone. And in the end, we have to confront life as individuals; no one can live life for another person. Self-reflection and solitude are necessary to knowing oneself and facing encounters with other people and God. These realities should not be interpreted as detractions from human value, however. In fact, these realities are extremely enriching because they show our value as human beings—we cannot be replaced by anybody or anything else. Likewise, this solitude should not be confused with self-marginalization from society. A fertile solitude encourages the growth of personal freedom and responsibility, while an unhealthy self-removal from society in order to avoid conflict and evade one's responsibility to a productive participation in society marginalizes people and hinders their personal development.

Facilitating Young People's Self-identity

27 An individual's personal identity cannot be given by another person or be imposed from outside the individual. Every young person has to find her or his own identity and live her or his own life. Parents,

educators, and **pastoral agents** sometimes try to project their own identity onto young people, hoping to make the young people into copies of what the parents, educators, or pastoral agents are—or wish they were. Such identity substitution is not healthy for either adults or young people.

28 Many psychological problems besetting young people—and contributing to suicide among them, especially among young men—are rooted in parents' expectations of who and what their children should be. Adults' formative and educational roles with young people are not opportunities to "shape" them or "mold" them by following a pre-established model. Rather, these roles give adults the chance to accompany young people and facilitate their process of self-formation. Adults in formative and educational roles with young people often serve better through quiet personal example, opportune advice, and support than through any obvious teaching.

29 To find and form their personal identity, young people need to reflect on their own life, confront past experiences and integrate them with their present knowledge and perspective, and become conscious of their freedom and responsibility. Only by accomplishing these feats can young people be authentic, grow as persons, and project the best of themselves—their personal best—into history. All these processes require opening up to others. If young people close themselves off from others, they can easily form an inaccurate vision of themselves or substitute a mask for their real self. Adults—especially educators, **youth ministers,** and pastoral agents—can help young people open up to others by supporting them in creating environments in which they feel at home (physically, emotionally, and socially) and free to be themselves with other young people.

Self-knowledge as a Means for Fulfillment

30 Young people fulfill themselves as persons in relationships with other persons. Knowledge of oneself is attained to the extent that one communicates with others and establishes a relationship between "I" (self) and "you" (other). This encounter with another person or persons must be direct—without intermediaries—and must occur in a setting of spontaneity and freedom. Young people become "available" to other persons by an act of communication

and self-bestowal. In a relationship of self-bestowal and exchange, young people come to know themselves through their own reflections and through the sincere opinions of the people who love them. Knowing oneself and developing one's own identity can only occur in an environment that encourages good communication and one in which love, respect, and mutual understanding prevail.

31 In discovering themselves, young people become aware of their personal dignity and individual value, as well as the gifts they have received from God. With this awareness, young people gain greater self-respect and security, acquiring a basis for hope and a foundation for their life projects. Recognizing their own faults, limitations, and weaknesses also realistically orients young people toward the possibility of developing and improving themselves as persons. As they come to know themselves, young people begin to explore their vocation, decide what they want to do with their lives, and become agents of transformation in history; these explorations, in turn, help shape their self-identity.

32 This process of searching for identity is complemented by a process of conscientization that allows young people to see more clearly their own lives in relation to the people around them and to the world in which they live. Through conscientization, young people come to accept themselves, increase their self-confidence, and assume responsibility for their past, their present, and their future.

Evangelization and the Search for Identity

33 The evangelization of young people who are searching for self-identity involves facilitating their discovery that God dwells in them. In this context, evangelization is meant to help young people realize that God has chosen them in Christ Jesus to fulfill themselves as unique persons created in God's image.

34 To proclaim the Good News is to show that God respects young people's identity and accepts them as they are. God asks them to continue being who they are, but in a new way—strengthened by God's grace to grow toward perfection. For some young people, this growth will mean a gradual increase in their trust in God and in their own basic goodness and love for other people. For others, it will mean a profound transformation of their lives as they turn away from evil and fall into God's embrace. Although people have physical and other external limitations, they also have interior

lives in which they can always grow. The interior life transcends material things. It puts people in contact with God and sees life on earth from a perspective of hope for eternal life.

35 When, thanks to evangelization, young people appropriate and assume the realities of the Incarnation and of redemption in Jesus, they gain in self-understanding and self-esteem. The discovery that through baptism they are living temples of the Holy Spirit, chosen children of God, and human beings who have "put on Christ," leads young people to respect themselves and to see their lives in less superficial ways.

36 It is difficult for youth ministry to compete with sports, homework, employment, and entertainment for young people's time and attention. However, the church can offer young people the possibility of becoming truly integrated persons and followers of a powerful and moving Jesus. To evangelize is to show Jesus as a person embodying ideals worth living for, as the teacher who constantly urges us to personal development and a deeper life—and toward transformation of the world.

Formation for Personal Development

37 As children, we experience time as a series of disconnected moments, each one infinite. We enjoy or mourn each moment with all possible intensity, so that we lack virtually any awareness of history, the passing of days, and the irreversibility of the past. For the child, space consists exclusively of the place he or she happens to be at a given moment. Children are unaware of any wider reality, either in the sense of geographical space or of the social environment in which they live. This concrete conception of time and space means that children's happiness at any given moment depends on what they are then experiencing and on the concrete stimuli they are receiving from the persons and setting around them.

Adolescence and Young Adulthood as Crucial Stages for Education

38 With adolescence comes the ability to understand the passage of time, remember and reflect on events of the past, analyze the present, and begin to think in terms of the future. Adolescents can

compare and contrast diverse geographical places and social settings, think in the abstract, and form concepts. These abilities, as well as the possibility of seeing life from a personal perspective and not through the eyes of their parents or other adults, make adolescence a key stage of life. At this point, the soul flourishes for itself and for others. Young people can begin to discover the meaning of life, to give direction to their own lives, to transcend themselves, and to initiate relationships of communion with other persons.

39 In addition, by consciously integrating their past and present, analyzing their lives and the environment around them, identifying their desires and ideals, and deciding what they want to be and do, adolescents search for their identity and discover who they are. Because of this, adolescence is a vital stage in young people's development and in their journey toward love and happiness.

40 This awakening to life is gradual and uneven. Adolescents are half adults and half children—and at times they can be either totally childish or completely adult. They ask and demand vehemently that adults respect them and take them seriously, yet they are still not entirely sure of themselves. Thus they are vulnerable to situations in which they feel ignored or attacked by adults, and to pressure from peers with whom they identify and feel secure.

41 These adolescent traits place young men and women in a crucial stage of their educational process. To educate is to work with young people so that *they* find direction for their lives. To educate is to facilitate in them an internal process of self-knowledge that leads them to discover and accept themselves as unique and irreplaceable persons made in the image and likeness of God and destined for love and happiness. Educating young people requires taking them seriously, entering into dialog with them to promote self-discovery, loving them so they feel secure, and guiding them so they discover the meaning of their lives.

42 Education that facilitates reflection on one's life and that respects the normal vulnerabilities of youth helps young people develop as persons, forge strong personalities, and prepare themselves for love and happiness. The drive for independence, so common among adolescents, is a clear sign that in the depths of their soul an *I*, an ego, is taking shape—far more intensely than during childhood. The characteristic striving for emancipation during adolescence, and for autonomy during young adulthood, are natural

phenomena. To educate adolescents and to facilitate the education of young adults means to offer them orientation in their process of emancipation, support in their search for autonomy, accompaniment in their daily experiences, guidance in their efforts to give direction to their lives, help in elaborating their plans, and a comforting presence in their successes and failures.

43 These natural processes of adolescence and young adulthood must always be taken into account in working with youth so as not to defeat their tendencies toward independence and autonomy. Adolescents develop goals for themselves as ways of discovering how far they are capable of moving forward. They demand to be treated as adults in order to demonstrate their capacity for decision making and responsibility. For example, they may begin a long journey in bad weather in order to test their strength and assure themselves that in something they are as strong or stronger than others. Or they may challenge the rules imposed on them by their parents in order to measure their degree of independence and test how close they are to the adult world. These actions demand understanding and guidance so that they can contribute to young people's growth into maturity.

44 The passions of adolescents and young adults are as great and powerful as those of adults; at times these passions exert a decisive influence over the future direction of young people's lives. Many incidents in which young people lose their faith, hate their parents, or systematically rebel against authority are caused by a lack of understanding from their elders. Frequently, parental lack of awareness and untrained leaders' manipulative tactics lead to injustices against young people that destroy their internal peace and generate violent emotions within them. Thus, young people need to be able to count on the support of well-prepared adults, and to find noble and powerful ideals toward which to guide their lives and channel their passions and energy.

Evangelization and Knowing the Truth

45 Truth leads us to freedom, freedom to love, and love to happiness and fullness of life. All young people yearn for these values and seek them passionately. But not all young people move toward them or find them. To evangelize young people is to share truth, freedom, love, and the life of God with them so that they aspire to live

according to the Gospel. To evangelize young people is to help them discover the truth about themselves and about God, become aware of the radical freedom God gave them at the moment they were created, experience the love of the trinitarian God that gave them life through their parents, and develop their capacity to love others and be a source of life for them. In accepting the Gospel and making Jesus the center of their lives, young people awaken to truth, freedom, and love with all the intensity and splendor possible.

46 During youth, the human person gradually awakens to the truth and penetrates more fully into it. Young people thus gradually advance in understanding and in exercising their freedom. The more these two things occur, the more likely it becomes for young people to achieve personal integration and to develop a spirituality deeply incarnated in their reality. To be awake is to be aware of who one is, where one is, where one comes from, and where one is going. This awareness is crucial for discovering the truth that makes us free and for liberating ourselves from the ties that hold our freedom in bondage.

47 As the saying goes, "What you see depends on the color of the glasses you're wearing." A person's happiness or suffering depends on her or his vision of life. It is often said that young people are a problem or that their lives are full of problems. But problems arise from the way people approach life and from the attitudes with which they confront the situations they encounter. People are the ones who create and solve problems, hold attitudes of joy and hope in the midst of life's vicissitudes and pain, or become depressed, confused, violent, rebellious, or destructive in the face of the large or small challenges that confront them.

48 In this way, problems become chains—chains that come not from outside, but from within ourselves—and attack our freedom and prevent us from loving and living joyfully. When young people refuse to see the reality of their lives and allow themselves to be manipulated by peer pressure, they lose their freedom to love and to live beyond the norms dictated by the group. When they submerge themselves in music and television in order to escape family relationships, they lose opportunities for dialog, understanding, mutual support, and enriching expressions of warmth among the family. When they become intoxicated with alcohol or other drugs to escape reality, they lose their capacity for reason and for guiding their behavior and feelings freely and consciously. In general, young people gradually embrace these chains almost without realizing it, which leaves them unaware that they are losing their freedom and, with that freedom, the possibility to love and to be happy.

49 To live in bondage is a sign of ignorance to the truth and of being mistaken about the value of the human person. It thus means holding a mistaken or limited understanding of one's own value and abilities. To evangelize is to discover the truth by awakening awareness of the chains that inhibit freedom and allow escape from reality. To evangelize is to help break those chains, guided by Jesus and supported by the strength of his Spirit. To discover truth it is essential to have humility, avoid prejudice, and exhibit love toward others. These are virtues acquired through God's grace; promoting them therefore demands the constant work of evangelization.

50 The greatest support in this journey toward truth and freedom lies in illuminating one's life with the light of the Gospel. The light Jesus gives us with his life and message challenges us in the very depths of our being. In knowing Jesus we know ourselves better, because he fully revealed what it means to be human and what kind of relationship we ought to have with God and with one another.

51 Only through sincere and profound self-knowledge can we open ourselves to others and relate to them in a context of freedom and love. So every effort at evangelization must encourage a double growth in knowledge: knowledge of Jesus and knowledge of oneself. In this double dynamic, in which both parts move forward simultaneously, young people experience themselves as both the source and the fruit of God's love and, through this awareness, become evangelizers of other young people. The importance of this dual process of discovery lies in young people allowing themselves to be called by Jesus in such a way that it is he who leads them to change their lives. The fundamental basis for achieving an integral Christian and human development lies in seeing life as Jesus sees it.

To Die in Order to Be Reborn

52 Jesus said clearly: "'Very truly, I tell you, unless a grain of wheat falls into the earth and dies, it remains just a single grain; but if it dies, it bears much fruit'" (John 12:24). Through his death and Resurrection, Jesus demonstrated the truth of this saying. Dying in

order to be reborn to a new life is a normal process leading to human development and happiness. Awakening to truth and freedom presupposes the following:

- *dying* to a limited or deformed vision of life in order to be *reborn* to the truth of the mystery of life
- *dying* to the bonds that we impose on ourselves through ideologies, emotional manipulation, and social conventions in order to be *reborn* to the freedom to think, feel, and act as persons made in God's image and likeness
- *dying* to a limited vision of the *I* in order to be *reborn* to a complete life of being in communion with God and with other persons
- *dying* to a passive and boring life in order to be *reborn* to an active life guided by heroic and noble ideals
- *dying* to self-pity in order to be *reborn* to a new life of placing our God-given gifts at the service of those who need them
- *dying* to a distorted understanding of human reality in order to be *reborn* to a life of faith in ourselves as daughters and sons of God
- *dying* to the bondage of our own egoism in order to be *reborn* to a life of love for our sisters and brothers

53 This process of death for rebirth helps young people forge a sense of themselves as integrated beings incarnated in the world in which they live. Young people grow as integrated persons when they are born again after a period of depression or an experience of hatred; when they re-establish a friendship after a fight; when they recover their faith in others after having been betrayed; when they restore honor to another person after having disrespected him or her; when they revalue their life after having been tempted to commit suicide; or when they recognize the need to ask forgiveness after having offended someone. Only by interrelating within the depth of their soul the affective, intellectual, spiritual, psychological, and social dimensions of life can people die to old ideas and acquire a new vision—die to feelings of anger, dislike, and vengeance, and open themselves to love.

54 For the process of death and rebirth to be an enduring reality and not just a passing event, young people need to have a realistic chance of acquiring the promised new life. This means that they must have viable alternatives within their reach and be able to count on the guidance and support necessary in their new journey.

The way to help young people achieve a new life is not, as is sometimes thought, through prohibitions and punishments related to their old lives.

55 To resist the seductive power of dangerous friendships, young people need an environment that teaches them to love what is great and beautiful, encourages heroic and generous hearts, and helps them forge good friendships. It is not enough to constantly insist on the dangers of bad friendships; at times it is even counterproductive due to the rebelliousness common at this age. For high ideals to be awakened in them, young people must have noble goals that draw them in and crystallize the exuberant passions of their soul, so that to extinguish those ideals would require destroying the whole personality. To form a personality that is strong, healthy, and well integrated, young people need to invest themselves totally in commitment to great ideals and not allow themselves to be carried away by cold reasoning or psychological manipulation.

Evangelization to Energize the Lives of Young People

56 In comparison with other stages of life, adolescence and young adulthood are times of extraordinary energy and open-mindedness. So young people are at an ideal age for finding the Christian meaning of their life and for living the Gospel intensely. Anyone who knows the human soul knows that everyone needs powerful and profound inspiration in order to acquire strength and joy that will endure for the rest of their life. However, one frequently encounters people who consider themselves evangelizers, educators, or formation directors, but who only know how to present the demands of "dying" to their followers; they have no idea how to offer them a new way of being. These persons commonly present the Christian life as a series of prohibitions, negations, rules to follow, and sacrifices to make, forgetting that none of these are meaningful unless they lead to a life of love and happiness.

57 Jesus' command is to love. To encourage and persevere in love, people need heroic works and strong sacrifices. Self-denial and sacrifice that do not lead to love, service, peace, joy, freedom, or justice are meaningless from the perspective of the Gospel of Jesus, which is a constant invitation to love and to action. Therefore, Christianity holds an irreplaceable teaching power, the most powerful that has ever existed.

58 For Christians, Easter means dying to sin, being forgiven by God, and being born to a new life that is liberated from sin's bonds; dying to the desires of the ego and rising to the love of others; dying to self-centeredness and being reborn to Jesus' mission to extend the Reign of God among all people. Being reborn is one of the greatest experiences that a young person can ever have. God becomes present in the lives of young people when they discover him in their processes of death and life, trust in his mercy, realize that he lives in the depths of their soul, hear his call to conversion, and answer his call to live ever more intimately with him.

59 To evangelize is to instill in young people confidence and love for the God who gave them life. This God lives in and among them, giving life to their heart, sight to their eyes, and intelligence to their mind. To evangelize is to make Jesus the center of young people's lives in such a way that he guides their thoughts, feelings, and actions. It is to facilitate the external flowering of the power of the Spirit that resides within every young person, so that they become evangelizers of other youth. Further, to evangelize is to lead young people to prefer life in communion with God over momentary pleasures that quickly pass away.

The Freedom of the Way to Wholeness

60 Freedom involves the capacity to direct one's own life at both the personal and social levels. Freedom, even at the personal level, is not an individual achievement; it always occurs through interpersonal relationships.

61 Although this chapter focuses on the personal freedom of young people, it is important to clarify that the concept of freedom presented here, and the principles associated with it, can also be applied to social groups and to society as a whole. For example, we could speak of the freedom of Hispanic youth in the United States, the freedom of U.S. youth in general, or the freedom of U.S. society as a whole.

Freedom and Responsibility

62 Education in freedom and for freedom occurs primarily in the family and should take place from the earliest years of life. As children

grow, they gradually sever their dependent ties to their parents or guardians and to the adult world. This occurs as they develop physically, emotionally, and mentally, and as their new abilities are integrated into their personality. In this way, human beings intensify their process of individuation and acquire a broader space in which to search for their freedom. Due to the power of the physical, emotional, and mental changes that occur during preadolescence and adolescence, education in freedom should intensify during these stages. Then it should continue in a subtle way during the early years of adulthood, when young people have acquired the rights of adulthood and begin to acquire adult responsibilities.

63 Parents or guardians (hereafter referred to simply as parents) bear primary responsibility for education in freedom. Parents in turn need the support of the community in order to carry out this task. In addition, education in freedom is one of the most vital areas for a truly evangelizing youth ministry, for it is closely tied to the formation of critical awareness and moral conscience, which, according to our faith, have their roots in the Gospel.

64 Freedom is the premise or essential base on which all personal development and fulfillment must be founded. People grow and mature as they consciously choose to develop their abilities and place them at the service of their neighbors and their own growth as persons.

Education of Freedom

65 Although freedom represents the basis of all human development, human sinfulness often leads people to abuse this very freedom. So young people's sense of freedom must be educated and formed under the influence of the Spirit. This education of human freedom should focus on four key aspects:

- *freedom to accept themselves and others,* respecting others autonomy while still motivating them to respond fully to God's call to conversion
- *freedom to choose the good* consciously and intentionally, both in themselves and in others
- *freedom to take creative initiative* in favor of an ideal, to resolve a conflict, or to confront a challenge
- *freedom to assume responsibility and commitment* to a concrete ideal, a certain set of values, a specific way of life, a specific goal, or a particular activity

66 Through a solid education and proper use of freedom, young people can mature ever more fully in developing their intellectual life and critical judgment; in managing their affective life and controlling the emotional impulses that can injure other persons; and in furthering their moral life, their capacity for transcendence, and their spiritual life. Freedom is a personal triumph that prepares young people to judge, value, decide, and act with wisdom, ultimately transforming their potential into creative actions that generate fuller life around them.

67 People always exercise freedom within their own sociocultural context. Freedom moves dynamically between one's rational decision to act in a certain way and whatever possibilities for the chosen action exist within the social structures and cultural norms in which the person lives. Thus freedom has two basic foundations: the interior freedom of the person and the exterior freedom provided by the sociocultural system.

68 In general, **Latino** youth in the United States have both kinds of freedom within their reach, but they need an education of their freedom and adequate support for using that freedom for their own growth and for improving society. Only two things can deny young people their freedom: *(a)* complete deprivation of physical freedom or *(b)* a severe neurotic illness that prevents them from seeing reality objectively and from making rational decisions. Thus, youth ministry and evangelization efforts that liberate young people from the bonds of personal and social sin are vital elements in the process of educating young people's sense of freedom.

Qualities of a Solid Education of Freedom

69 To be free and to act in freedom imply being authentically in command of one's own thoughts and personal will. Therefore, freedom implies that a person is capable of the following:

- making rational decisions that give intentional direction to one's life, which was previously dominated by traditionalism, custom, the search for prestige, or the power of an external authority
- activating the way of life chosen freely and consciously through a process of rational decision making
- achieving full personal development through the development of one's own personality, always connected through mutual collaboration with other persons who also seek to exercise their own freedom and achieve personal development

- always keeping sight of the goal of personal self-fulfillment within a horizon that always seeks the common good

70 Educating in freedom and for freedom, whether it is done by parents, in school, or through pastoral ministry, means:

- *using moral authority* to help young people channel their energies and abilities toward their fulfillment as persons and for the good of society
- *respecting the independence and autonomy* of young people in such a way that the young people will be able to develop and use their rational ability to analyze reality critically and make wise decisions about how to act in keeping with their own personality and the context in which they live
- *encouraging creative initiatives* so that young people can carry out projects that let them freely, consciously, and voluntarily express their intellectual capacities, personal dynamism, and affectivity
- *encouraging interior discipline* that responds to the deep needs of human nature and the personality of each young person. This discipline will allow young people to move forward in a continuous process of integral fulfillment and to strengthen their desire to journey steadily toward personal maturity.
- *offering guidance to young people when they face confusing situations and crossroads* so that they can make decisions, resolve problems, solve conflicts, and confront challenges through a process of conscious analysis based on the values of the Gospel
- *helping young people form habits of life they have freely and consciously chosen,* and that serve as points of reference and support for promoting the ideals they have freely and intentionally chosen
- *encouraging self-control* by helping young people coordinate the various dimensions of their lives. In this way, young people will be able to manage the physical, intellectual, affective, spiritual, sexual, social, and cultural dimensions of life by intentionally choosing values and attitudes to guide them.
- *offering ideals for which it is worth struggling, and placing these ideals within the reach of young people* so that they can discover and follow their vocations in all their dimensions: as human beings in a specific state of life, in a particular profession, in a certain kind of service to society, and so on

71 Those working in the education of freedom should have in mind various challenges and threats to freedom in order to

confront them intentionally so that they do not undermine young people's freedom. Among these threats, the following stand out:

- *individualism,* which promotes personal interests and viewpoints—whether rational, irrational, or subconscious—as the measure of all behavior. This leads to a kind of self-centeredness that fails to recognize the right of other persons to enjoy their freedom, and that not only fails to consider the good of others but actively tramples on them if it is necessary for achieving one's own goals.
- *authoritarianism,* especially that of parents who, in a belief that only they are right, impose their will on their children and thus impede their children's development of critical thought, creative initiative, strong will, and responsible freedom
- *liberalism*—both on the part of parents and of society—that allows young people to develop without intervening to educate their freedom with care and intentionality. Liberalism leaves young people without direction in life, with arbitrary and short-lived motivations, subject to being controlled by their natural impulses, vulnerable to manipulation by others, and with a tendency to manipulate others to get what they want.
- *formality and social conventionalism,* which focus on maintaining certain formalities or social behaviors. Social conventionalism is concerned more with exactly how behaviors are carried out rather than their spirit or the reasons for which they developed. Thus certain behavioral norms remain out of sheer custom, regardless of whether they are meaningful or whether they further important human values.
- *manipulation,* allowing oneself to be controlled by other people or by the surrounding culture, so that one's actions become automatic reactions to stimuli imposed by others
- *dictatorial leadership,* which strips followers of their freedom of thought or action. This type of leadership may originate in the manipulative behavior of the leader or in the irresponsible behavior of the followers, who do not embrace their own freedom or use their capacity to act responsibly and to give direction to their lives.

The Integrative Power of Ideals

72 Some young people have grand ideals and goals for their lives; they embrace specific causes and struggle for them with great intensity and tenacity. The majority of them are young people with dreams and ideals rooted deep within their beings, which they allow to flower into concrete action to give life to their ideals. Some young people struggle mightily for personal ideals regarding professionalism, art, or service. Others meet in groups who share similar ideals, or join social-action groups or political organizations that struggle for social transformation. The majority hold love as their central ideal and seek to form a family.

73 The personal formation of young people and the level of Christian **praxis** in which they will engage depend largely on the ideals they hold and on the means they use to achieve those ideals. Having an *ideal* is an invitation to personal improvement. Having an ideal is always a source of life, hope, and joy. From the perspective of our faith, the greatest and most empowering and liberating ideal a young person can have is to love the way Jesus loved.

74 In contrast to ideals, which are by nature free and give rise to freely and consciously chosen activities, *desires* can easily become chains that lead to dependency, because they usually involve attachment to fame, power, a person, or an object. To desire something is to depend on something and to make happiness dependent on having it. Therefore, when one desires something and cannot possess it, disillusionment results that may in time lead to insecurity, frustration, and desperation.

75 Our commercialized culture artificially creates needs that cause young people to desire things that easily lead them into dependency. Many young people lead lives centered on their desires to own more and to have more pleasure. Furthermore, the dominant culture is not content with encouraging people (especially young people) to follow their desires and seek happiness outside the human person. Instead, it promotes newly stimulated, frequently unobtainable desires, and manipulates people into wanting immediate satisfaction of these desires. The need for immediate gratification makes young people even more dependent on the chains they have imposed on themselves through their desires and attachments.

76 The ability of young people to develop their freedom is one of the principal objectives of every evangelizing effort. A Christian life can only be achieved through heroism, renunciation, and sacrifice. These demand the formation of the will. The first step in forming a strong will lies in holding generosity and heroism as concrete ideals.

The Will Allows Achievement of Ideals

77 People can strengthen their will by following the examples of virtue offered by generous persons. The greatest power leading toward Christian praxis lies not so much in intellectual justification of the moral life as in the living Incarnation of the Gospel and of the spiritual life shown in the heroic lives of individual Christians. In this context, faith in the spiritual destiny of the human person becomes not a dream, but a reality witnessed to and sealed by persons who have loved it and lived it intensely and with dedication. The examples offered by these persons move young people to form their moral conscience, so that the Gospel takes deeper root in them.

78 The formation of the will requires daily effort. As the saying goes, "The only people who achieve freedom are those who are forced to achieve it every day." Young people are very open to this calling and hear it enthusiastically. The challenge lies in living with noble ideals. The will is forged in the process of dying to an old way of life in order to be born to a new life in Jesus. Thus it is vital that young people recognize the power of their own will and become conscious that good intentions are not enough. It is too easy to succumb to the manipulation of our culture or to allow themselves to be guided by bad friendships instead of overcoming the temptations that arise from their environment and from their own passions.

79 To forge an ideal and make it a reality from day to day, it is necessary that young people's every act be directed toward this ideal. In this way, they shape their will. The will is not the same thing as willfulness. The will is the source and fruit of freedom and is related to ideals. Its prize lies in being what one aspires to be and in loving as one aspires to love. Through their will, people reconcile their mind and their heart, and thus become capable of sustaining their ideals and moving toward them as they overcome the obstacles and temptations of the journey. Happiness is the prize won by those who form their will, for the will generates attitudes of confi-

dence in oneself, trust in God, and hope for life. Stated simply, the will helps achieve the ideal.

80 In contrast, willfulness consists of allowing oneself to be guided by desires and external bonds, or by the fruit of emotional impulses or ideologies that dominate the person. In U.S. **popular culture**—frequently referred to as "pop" culture and marked by people's desire to be in the limelight rather than to simply be, to profit rather than to love—people easily confuse their desire to stand out and achieve fame and power with more authentic human ideals. So the important thing becomes running faster, being thin, dressing fashionably, scoring more goals, fighting better, making more money, or being popular with others. Many young people make competence and outdoing others their life goals, thus confusing the ideal with the simple desire to stand out. This generates a willfulness that implies moving toward the goal even if it means destroying the integrity of one's own personality or attacking anyone who stands in the way of the road to triumph. Thus, willfulness destroys freedom and causes fear, tension, anxiety, and suffering.

Religious Ideals

81 Only God can satisfy the infinite thirst for love that lives within every person. Therefore, the firm foundation that sustains and gives meaning to all aspects of life should be a spirituality that is deeply incarnated in reality. In a life of communion with God, young people will find the intellectual foundation and emotional support they need for the love born in their soul to flourish. Because many young people do not know God and have not discovered God's love, they wallow in sadness and desperation, and experience hatred and deep suffering. Through the process of evangelization, young people can gradually express these feelings and become capable of acknowledging them as their own. With God's help, they can die to be reborn to a different life, and new ideals can guide their life, aspirations, and will.

82 God, for love of all men and women, became human like us. Jesus' utter identification with his Father led him to embrace his Father's plan for humanity as his own mission, and to embrace this mission as the ideal that would guide his life until the moment of his death and Resurrection. In this way Jesus liberated us from our sins—through forgiveness during our life and through eternal life when we rise with him to live with God forever.

83 In evangelizing young people, we must infuse them with the power of the spiritual life so that they identify their lives with Christ's; aspire always to say truly that "Christ lives in me and I in Christ"; live to the last consequences their role as the Mystical Body of Christ, in solidarity with all people; are aware that good works serve all humanity and that sin is not just an individual evil but also a social evil. The certainty of all being members of one body and of carrying within us the life of Christ is the greatest motivation imaginable for respecting and serving others, for overcoming and renouncing egoism so as to love as Jesus taught us to love, and for dedicating our lives to serving the good of all. The sacrifices required by the Gospel will then find their proper motivation, stimulus, and reason for being. In this way we will see the things of this world and the next with the eyes of Christ, and thus become Christ for others by radiating his love to those around us.

Human Solidarity as an Ideal for Young People

84 Social action and the social sciences should be incorporated into every process of evangelization and every effort to shape the affective and intellectual lives of young people, for the social sciences contribute powerfully to shaping a spirit of understanding and social cooperation, which nourishes love for needy sisters and brothers. Human solidarity is a powerful dimension of love. It leads toward the shaping of profoundly Christian personalities. Further, solidarity helps prevent young people from remaining content with having vague feelings of compassion for those who suffer. Human solidarity inspired by the Gospel places the mind and heart of young people at the service of the sublime ideal of love for all persons, especially the most needy.

85 Sharing human suffering through visits to hospitals, jails, and poor people's homes can be a highly effective way of helping young people understand the many situations that demand their generous collaboration and the various possibilities available to them for taking action to address these situations. Young people might offer friendly visits, emotional support, aid with legal or administrative procedures, financial contributions, or many other kinds of specific aid, but all these must be wrapped in their total gift of love for poor people.

86 Self-bestowal to the poor and needy moves young people to study and to form themselves as Christian persons in order to work toward social justice by raising the material and moral levels of people. The love that surges in the souls of young people will thus find a goal that is worthy and appropriate for their age; this is the best imaginable stimulus for fulfilling their duties as students, citizens, and employees. In contrast, it is a bad tactic to guide young people toward "anti-" causes, in which the focus lies in rising up against evil and pursuing the politics of opposition. Instead of offering young people terrain for creative action, following such tactics kills the love within them and raises barriers to taking authentic Christian action.

> Discovering the face of the Lord in the suffering faces of the poor . . . challenges all Christians to a deep personal and ecclesial conversion. Through faith, we find faces emaciated by hunger as a result of inflation, foreign debt, and social injustice; faces disillusioned by politicians who make promises they do not keep; faces humiliated because of their culture, which is not shown respect and is sometimes treated with contempt; faces terrorized by daily and indiscriminate violence; anguished faces of the abandoned children who wander our streets and sleep under our bridges; suffering faces of women who are humiliated and disregarded; weary faces of migrants, who do not receive a decent welcome; faces aged by time and labor of people who lack even the minimum needed to survive decently. . . . Merciful love also means turning toward those who are in spiritual, moral, social, and cultural need.[2]

2

The Path to Interpersonal Communion

2

The Path to Interpersonal Communion

God's inner life is a life of radical sharing and communication among the Father, Son, and Holy Spirit. It is in, through, and out of that mysterious love within God that all life and love come. Created in God's own image, we find inscribed in our hearts one core universal vocation, that is, to love and to be loved.
—United States Catholic Conference, *Human Sexuality*

1 Chapter 1 focused on the individual dimension of the person, although it also asserted that people develop in relationship to others. This chapter centers on interpersonal relationships as the way to the communion that God calls us to from the moment of our creation.

2 The chapter begins by reflecting on love as the place where young people exist. It then presents the call to live in communion and discusses the integration of sexuality and love. Finally, the chapter focuses on ***noviazgo*** as a preparation for Christian marriage.

I Exist in Love

3 Throughout life, all human beings search for love. Children are eager to be loved by their parents; adolescents hope for the love of friends; young adults yearn to love and be loved by a partner to fill their life. These aspirations originate in people's search for communion and in their personal awareness of their individuality and solitude as human beings.

Created to Love

4 All people possess a deep need to overcome loneliness through love. As sons and daughters of God, we are born of love and thus possess the capacity to live in intimacy with God and with other persons.

Authentic intimacy is always characterized by love, which consists of opening oneself to others and accepting them as they are. Love involves giving oneself wholly and establishing a relationship of profound mutuality that constantly strengthens itself.

5 To love is to actively concern oneself with the life and growth of the beloved person. Love involves a set of feelings that influence one's entire life. Love's form and intensity vary according to whether the relationship is between parents and children, between friends or ***compañeros,*** or between spouses.

6 We are all born with the capacity to love. At first, the love of our parents awakens the joy of living among others. In the family environment, children learn to move beyond themselves, to find ways of making other people happy, to deny themselves some pleasures in order to enjoy acceptance from and friendship with others. When love is lacking in the home, or when formation in a context of love fails, children and young people tend to focus on themselves and fail to perceive the reality, needs, and rights of others. In other words, they do not learn to give themselves to others.

7 To love is to awaken to the reality of the other person, not simply to consider him or her an extension of oneself, but rather a unique person with his or her own experiences, ideas, freedom, and mystery. A person cannot love someone he or she does not know, for love is based on knowledge. At the same time, true love carries a person to deeper knowledge and complete acceptance of the other person, including the other's likes and dislikes, thoughts and ideals, strengths and weaknesses. People achieve this knowledge of each other through profound dialog founded on truth and proven through sincerity and action in favor of each other.

8 Authentic love is easy to recognize because it always seeks the good of the beloved. Whoever truly loves strives to enrich the other person's qualities, to avoid hurting her or him, to forgive her or his limitations, and to seek **reconciliation** with her or him. Life takes on new meaning through loving, including giving oneself to another person and offering one's time, talents, and help.

Clarification of Some Concepts About Love

9 Many young people believe that love consists of being loved, rather than of loving. They think that if they manage to succeed and become powerful, they will receive love from more people. Other

young people try to become objects of love through their style of dress or by following examples promoted by the media. Still other young people desperately seek love because they have never received real love or have never developed their own capacity to love. These young people are often seduced by illusions of love.

10 To love is not just a matter of feeling attracted to others, admiring them, experiencing a positive affection for them, tearfully sentimentalizing their suffering, or feeling one's heart race when speaking with them. These emotions may be manifestations of love, but they may also represent simple sentimentality. To love and to desire a person are not the same. A person who loves someone puts his or her own heart in search of the good of the other person. The person who desires someone, on the other hand, wants that person for himself or herself and for his or her own benefit. Someone who desires another as an object of pleasure does not really love the other at all, but rather demonstrates his or her own selfishness.

11 Many people believe that loving another person is easy, but that finding the right person to love is difficult. Therefore, they try hard to find the appropriate person to love and be loved by, instead of looking at people in their family, school, workplace, and neighborhood, and learning how to love them. Christian love is not limited to one "appropriate" person. It is for *all* people, especially for those with whom we live and relate in daily life.

12 Some people think that "to fall in love" and to love are the same. Loving is a more profound experience than simply falling in love. Love requires constant effort, learning, and self-giving. Love matures through a continuing intimate relationship with another person.

13 Love presupposes a permanent bond. To love is a conscious act, part of a free decision that includes the whole beloved person and focuses on helping her or him to grow. Therefore, love is lasting; it finds the patience and creativity to overcome crises and confronts the difficulties that exist in every human relationship. In contrast, falling in love is more spontaneous, transitory, and shortsighted. It results in being attracted to *some* qualities of the other person, and unless the relationship deepens, it is destined to die when the initial enthusiasm passes and one comes to know the other more fully.

14 "Making love" and "loving" are also not the same. Apart from the committed and mutually responsible love between spouses,

referring to sexual intercourse as "making love" leads to a serious devaluation of the meaning of love and a manipulative attitude toward sexuality. When two people have sexual intercourse without truly loving each other, both of them are reduced to being objects.

15 Love is free and mutually respectful of each other's individuality and dignity. It generates interdependence and coresponsibility. Love does not seek to possess, dominate, or manipulate. It does not consist of letting oneself fall under the power or enchantment of another person; it does not mean abandoning oneself to another and giving up a sense of *I*. Dependence on another person diminishes one's self-awareness and freedom, makes personal development more difficult, and stands in the way of Christian growth. Dependence converts the person into an object, thus sacrificing his or her capacity to love.

Loving Like Jesus

16 Recognizing the dynamic relationship between love and the breaking of human relationships is a central theme in salvation history. Genesis speaks of harmony between people and their Creator, and of the tragedy that results when people separate themselves from God through sin. The covenants of God with Noah, Abraham, and Moses show a first effort to re-establish union with God and harmony with neighbors. However, these covenants were not enough; we needed the Incarnation of the Son of God in human history and the presence of the Holy Spirit in and among us to definitively restore the possibility of human love.

17 To evangelize means to facilitate young people's discovery of God's love in their call to life and in the love and blessings they have received in their relationships with God and with other persons. Many young people have been surrounded by love but are unaware of it. Others think that they are loved because they deserve it; they do not see love as a free gift. Young people who are learning to love must first become aware of the love that surrounds them. Those who have lived without love or are passing through difficult times need to be loved in a special way.

18 Jesus is the most excellent teacher for those learning to love. His love is born of the intimate love of the Father, Son, and Holy Spirit. Jesus' love is free and gracious; it values the beloved person and does not wait for this love to be returned. It is a merciful and

redemptive love that recognizes the weaknesses of the other person. These weaknesses awaken in Jesus a still greater love. Jesus loves sinners in a special way and tries to give them new life by liberating them from their sins, thus restoring their freedom to love.

19 Even amidst the pain and bleakness of life, loving the way Jesus loves produces happiness, joy, and peace, because it gives meaning to suffering, sickness, sacrifice, and all the difficulties that people encounter. Because of the limitations of human nature, it is truly difficult for people to give themselves to others, to seek the common good instead of their own good, and to undergo personal sufferings for the sake of others. However, humanity's attraction to wholeness leads people to attempt loving as God loves. This love frees people from their personal problems, pulls them away from egoism, makes them abandon destructive competitiveness, and helps them move beyond mediocrity. Jesus loved to the point of giving his life for the people he loved. He renounced his own comfort, personal success in the world, and all other pretexts for not loving. The person who loves loyally and passionately as Jesus did is happy.

20 **Pastoral action** must be based on this kind of love. Young people who participate in groups, communities, and apostolic movements grow in love through service to their neighbors. Young people in the church become an effective sign of the love of God—a sign that overcomes all egoism, inspires decisiveness, and moves others to become sources of love in the world.

Searching for Interpersonal Communion

21 When young people focus on discovering or "finding" themselves and do not see themselves objectively, they acquire an exaggerated self-importance, or in the other extreme, they become mired in depression. Either extreme leads to self-doubt and anxiety, which many young people evade through alcohol or other drugs, or by reacting violently toward other persons or toward social groups.

Created to Live in Communion

22 As human beings, we are created in God's image with the ability to know and love our Creator and to know and love one another. Each person is called to live in a community of love with God, with other persons, and with nature. God did not create people to live in solitude. From the beginning, God created human beings as man and woman, thus making the human couple the first expression of interpersonal communion. In addition, God gave couples the increased ability to live in communion with other persons by giving them the gift of procreation. By nature, we are called to be persons-in-communion.

23 In the beginning, God also gave us the freedom to maintain or destroy this communion with God, other persons, and nature. The greatness of our human nature is rooted in this freedom. God made us autonomous and responsible for ourselves. We decide how to use our freedom.

24 The abuse of freedom weakens or destroys our communion with God, other people, and nature. We call this reality *sin*. By sinning we further abandon our tendency toward the good and allow ourselves to be guided by selfish interests. In contrast, as long as we live in communion with God we are in harmony with ourselves, other persons, and the rest of creation.

25 Evangelization emphasizes human nature's tendency toward the absolute good, who is God, because when God's Creation was finished, "God saw everything that he had made, and indeed, it was very good" (Gen. 1:31). In addition, all evangelization processes facilitate the encounter with the *you* and re-establish the communion broken by the abuse of freedom. Evangelization helps young people to be responsible for themselves so that they can consciously and courageously seek ways to live in communion. When young people take responsibility for the search for communion, they become increasingly disposed to reconciliation with God and with others.

Communication and Interpersonal Intimacy

26 Mature intimacy consists of an encounter between an *I* and a *you*, each of whom carries his or her own identity. Knowing and defining oneself is a necessary condition for entering into true intimacy. Communication creates the *I* and *you* relationship. The *I* cannot emerge without the *you*. The *I-you* personal relationship presupposes a calling and a response. It demands intercommunication, leads to mutual self-giving, and results in something new and unique, the *we*.

Forming a *We* Through Intimacy

27 The *we* is always a new and renewing reality that requires a mutual presence. Being present for the other person implies mutual communication—perceiving or understanding who the other is, what her or his desires, feelings, and thoughts are. It also means sharing oneself—what one desires, feels, and thinks. This mutual presence ties one person to the other, making each a person-in-communion with the other.

28 Intimacy demands communication and sharing of what is going on in life and in the personal center, where the root of all that is truly meaningful lies. Remaining at a superficial level, speaking only of events, films, fiestas, and news about other people, does not lead to intimacy. Interpersonal communication should comprehend the complexity of inner feelings, thoughts, ideals, fears, confusions, and so on. This communication must be based on mutual empathy, which is the capacity to put oneself in the place of the other, to feel what he or she feels, and to see life from his or her perspective. But intimacy includes more than sharing personal experiences and empathy; it requires a reciprocal giving of oneself and a mutual solidarity founded on and guided by love.

29 Intimacy implies a profound intercommunication. Its characteristic mark is love mutually expressed. Intimacy generates a dynamic in which each person draws the other toward giving herself or himself as each helps the other to mature as a person. Communication, intimacy, and mutuality are three facets of the prism of interpersonal communion.

30 Intimacy can exist between friends, between parent and child, between boyfriend and girlfriend, and between spouses. All young people can and should have various intimate relationships at the same time. Intimacy between two people should be open, allowing each person to enter into new relationships of interpersonal communion. This multiplying dynamic allows the formation of human communities in which all members sustain a communication and intimacy that constantly nourishes unity, solidarity, and love.

31 To achieve intimacy, a person must have acquired a certain level of identity, self-confidence, and freedom from threat. Intimacy demands that people show sincerely what they are, think, and feel. In addition, intimacy requires that persons develop the arts of dialog, listening, and reflection as they share their interior life.

These arts require the ability to use language in a way that communicates what one wants to express.

Intimacy Overcomes Individualism

32 Contemporary culture, with its emphasis on egoism, superficial expressions, and **consumerism,** makes it difficult for young people to give themselves in love to other people. As a result, relationships emphasize appearances, and young people try to define themselves through what they possess and do, rather than who they are. In this context, young people ignore their value and freedom as persons and develop profound existential problems. Some young people avoid the search for communion by isolating themselves—watching television or listening to music all day. They need to learn how to befriend the kind of solitude that leads to communion with God and other people.

33 Young people need to find ways of communicating with one another, of projecting their *I* toward the *you* of other people, so that together they form a *we* and establish authentic intimacy and human community. The lack of love and intimacy in young people's lives impedes their integration as persons, alienates them from themselves, and isolates them from others. As a result, possessions and consumption predominate over personal generosity; greed and power defeat spiritual values; money and prestige become more important than justice. In all these cases, the *I* becomes more important than the *you,* and the *we* does not exist. As a result, friendships die, families disintegrate, and marriages fail.

Evangelization of Young People Through Interpersonal Communion

34 As Christians, we are called to be images of the Holy Trinity, this means a God who is community. Evangelization supposes an *I-you-we* relationship with Jesus, similar to the relationship of Jesus with the Father and the Holy Spirit, and the relationship he had with his disciples. Jesus was not closed within himself or in his relationship to the Father. Jesus went beyond himself to encounter other persons. He saw life from others' perspectives and, with profound empathy and love, felt what they felt. This experience gave birth to Jesus' compassion, mercy, and solidarity with people, especially sinners, sick people, and needy people. Jesus opened himself to other

people so that they could participate in his intimacy with God. In this way, Jesus helped people understand God's intentions and become collaborators in God's redemptive mission.

35 Young people in search of intimacy and communion are evangelized as they learn to communicate and establish an *I-you-we* relationship with God and with other persons. God has communicated with people since the beginning of human life. God communicated with the Israelites in a special way and communicates with us still through historical events, prayer, the Scriptures, sacramental life, nature, people, the community, and our efforts to extend the Reign of God.

36 Jesus' intimacy with God and with the disciples formed the foundation for a radical *we,* a new reality that became the ecclesial community. To evangelize young people is to help them form a church community in which they can develop their capacity for intimacy and for authentic human relationships. Evangelizing also means helping them go beyond themselves to encounter people who are signs of Jesus alive and active today, as well as of Jesus suffering among us.

37 Intimacy with God and with other persons is a continuous source of deepening interpersonal communion, and it is the only way to overcome human egoism. The trinitarian God is the perfect image of intimacy, because the Trinity is a communion of three persons who project themselves outward, giving life to human beings and attracting them to communion. The great devotion of Hispanic people to the **Divine Providence,** who takes care of everyone, especially in times of need, is a constant sign of the love between God and Hispanic people.

38 Evangelizing means offering young people and young adults the marvelous gift of the love of God, a love that gives new life, keeps them strong in the midst of difficulties, and is the source of all their love for others. Evangelization means offering Hispanic young people the gift of reconciliation by giving them the opportunity to re-establish and strengthen communion with God, with themselves, and with other persons.

39 In God everyone exists, lives, and breathes. God sustains life and makes humanity into one family. With Jesus, all are sisters, brothers, and disciples struggling for justice, love, and peace. The relationship with the Holy Spirit, who lives in and among us, gives

us the strength and the light needed to follow Jesus and to live in communion with God and our brothers and sisters.

Integration of Human Sexuality in Love

40 Sexuality has always been a fascinating mystery. Its power provides the possibility of the most profound relationship between people. Chapter 1 of volume 1 discussed physiological sexual development, and chapter 2 of volume 1 explored the relations between men and women. This section emphasizes the need for young people to integrate their sexuality into their personal life, and gives a Christian meaning to this integration.

Human Sexuality from the Christian Perspective

41 Human sexuality is rooted in biology—especially in the reproductive system—which, as in all sexual animals, is made up of organs, glands, and hormones directly oriented to procreation. However, human sexuality transcends the physiological function of genital sexuality. In humans, sexual intercourse is not linked exclusively to the reproductive phases, as it is in most animals.

42 In addition to the procreative function, human sexuality incorporates the psychological dimension of the person. Through our sexuality we experience and share our similarities and differences, as well as our complementarity as men and women. We feel a mutual attraction and find interpersonal enrichment in the encounter between the two sexes.

43 Human sexual attraction and sexual activity depend primarily on the psychological and emotional excitation that consciously or unconsciously activates the reproductive system. This psychological dimension of sexuality makes it a human experience, gives sexual activity a personal meaning, and opens human sexuality to interpersonal relationships.

44 In contrast to animals, whose sexuality is guided only by instinct, human sexuality involves conscience, freedom of choice, will, and responsibility. In human beings, the psychological, physiological, sexual, and spiritual realities are intertwined; they affect the process of maturation and significantly influence personal behavior. Throughout life, people's gender influences their thoughts,

feelings, behaviors, and relationships. Their gender affects their relationship with God, other people, and the universe.

45 The possibility of being co-creators with God ties sexuality to the mystery of God and of human life. The foundational principle of Christian **anthropology** (Christian perspective on the person) lies in our conviction that we were created in the image and likeness of God.

46 Christian faith is based on God's revelation as a community of persons, the Trinity. The internal life of God involves a profound communication of love among the Father, the Son, and the Holy Spirit. Through and from this mysterious love, all kinds of life exist. Human love finds its source here. The Trinity is the starting point for our belief that all people have ingrained in their heart the mystery of God's communion in love. All people yearn for this communion and are called to generate life from it.

47 We can visualize this mystery as a way of life that has its origin in the communion of God's love (the Trinity), and has as its goal the full enjoyment of communion in the Reign of God. Everyone has to journey through this path to achieve the final goal for which they were created. In walking this path, sometimes we approach this ideal; other times, we remove ourselves from it. Evangelization illuminates and gives strength to young people in their faith journey. They establish a relationship with Jesus and through him, go to the Father through the action of the Holy Spirit. In this way, they approach the Reign of God.

Toward a Christian Spirituality of Sexuality

48 For many young people, speaking about sexuality from a religious perspective always has the moral connotation of prohibition. As a consequence, feelings of sinfulness and guilt abound. Although it is possible to discover in history the reasons why these erroneous impressions about sexuality were taught, it is more important to facilitate the development of a Christian spirituality of sexuality.

49 Human sexuality is sacred because it comes directly from God's love. It is oriented toward the total communion of a couple in the sacrament of marriage and has the capacity to generate life. To be sexual human beings is a blessing, a gift that allows us to enjoy the beauty of conjugal love and the presence of children as a fruit of

that love. As a result, we should be grateful to God and show our gratitude by honoring the sacredness of our sexuality.

50 God not only created men and women as sexual beings but also assumed life as a human being. John's Gospel tells us, "And the Word became flesh" (1:14). God became one of us, taking a human body, with its functions, sensuality, and sexuality. As a human person, Jesus accomplished his mission on earth. In that human body, Jesus walked the length and breadth of Palestine, courageously proclaiming his message, relating to people, touching sinners with mercy, and healing sick people.

51 In our Christian tradition, we have the beautiful image of the human body as the temple of the Holy Spirit. Our body is the instrument we use to learn, reflect, form our attitudes, and act. It is in our body (male or female) that God's love moves us to carry the message of salvation to people—to touch and comfort the suffering, to heal the wounded, and to feed the hungry. Every young person needs to feel comfortable in her or his body and to learn to guide it in a way that leads her or him to service and communion in love.

52 Evangelization tries to help young people become aware of their sexuality as a gift from God. Judean tradition did not support or approve of the possibility of friendship between men and women. Jesus brought a new perspective regarding human sexuality. He proclaimed the Reign of God among men and women. Jesus' friendships with Mary and Martha, his relationship with Mary Magdalene and the Samaritan woman, and the inclusion of many women among his disciples are clear signs that his mission included both men and women.

53 Evangelization encourages young people to value their sexuality as a gift that allows them to have interpersonal relationships with people of the same and other sex, providing them with rich experiences. Also, evangelization helps to get rid of prejudices against the body, to heal moral wounds due to misunderstandings of sexuality, and to discern the appropriate place and dimension of remorse and guilt feelings in Christian life. Above all, evangelization tries to facilitate young people's integration of their sexuality into the totality of their life, and encourages the virtue of chastity. In this way, young people prepare themselves to live the marriage commitment faithfully and to form a family responsibly.

Chastity as a Christian Ideal

54 All human beings have the capacity to live in the communion of God's love. In this search for intimacy with God, people find their maturity, discover their personal vocation, and design their life project. People also base their interpersonal relationships and their search for meaning in this intimacy with God.

55 Only in this context of intimacy with God is it possible to understand and value the meaning of the virtue of chastity in all different lifestyles: as a single person, in marriage, and in religious life.

> *Chastity* consists in self-control, in the capacity of guiding the sexual instinct to the service of love and of integrating it in the development of the person. Chastity is often misunderstood as simply a suppression or deliberate inhibition of sexual thoughts, feelings, and actions. However, chastity truly consists in the long-term integration of one's thoughts, feelings, and actions in a way that values, esteems, and respects the dignity of oneself and others. Chastity frees us from the tendency to act in a manipulative or exploitive manner in our relationships and enables us to show true love and kindness always.[1]

56 When evangelizing young people, it is necessary to present this ideal of chastity to them, relating it to the Christian vision of the human person, to their vocation of full communion in God, and to the meaning of Christian matrimony. It is hoped that young people will freely decide to keep their virginity and have a chaste life. This decision is not easy. Adolescents and young adults are physiologically capable of sexual intercourse. Their natural curiosity about sex and their desire for intimacy are both strong forces that drive them to have sexually active relationships. The moral liberalism that pervades our society, as well as the peer pressure, the impact of the media, and the influence of a culture that romanticizes and trivializes sexuality makes this challenge even stronger.

57 Parents and pastoral agents must try to witness to the value of chastity and provide young people with a sound formation about sexuality. In doing this they will help to form the moral conscience of each young person and create a positive attitude toward the human body, an attitude of healthy modesty that avoids the kind of guilt and shame that hinders relationships with people of the other

gender. In addition, parents and pastoral ministers must nurture a Christian spirituality that sees sexuality as a gift of God, not as an obstacle or distraction that leads young people away from God.

58 An inappropriate sexual formation may cause young people to experience strong but unfounded guilt feelings. Because of these feelings, young people may abandon the practice of their faith and stop participating in church life. Pastoral action supposes an open attitude that seeks to understand the anxieties of young people and to talk with them about the sacredness of sexuality, and of natural processes of human sexuality.

59 Young people who try to cultivate the virtue of chastity as a way to personal maturity and authentic love, should do the following:

- be aware of the sacredness of the human body and of sexual relationships in such a way that they value their own body and the body of others as God's gifts that demand care and respect
- talk about sexuality with openness and respect, help to create social groups that behave with modesty and prudence, and have an attitude of honesty and modesty in interpersonal relationships
- integrate their sexuality in love by overcoming egoism through giving attention and love to others, eliminating sexist family customs, keeping fidelity and exclusiveness in loving as a couple, and preparing for marriage
- analyze the causes of difficulties in remaining chaste and reflect about the consequences of the misuse of sexual activity
- promote noble, generous, and heroic ideals as motivations to form the will and as a help to maintain the ideal of chastity by developing an attitude of service, sacrifice, and self-denial, as well as a practice of charity and social responsibility
- have a life of prayer that allows them to deepen the sense of chastity and gives them strength to live it
- cultivate physical work, art, and sports as areas in which creativity is developed and young people can invest their physical energy

Christian *Noviazgo* and Marriage

60 *Noviazgo* is a period of preparation leading to marriage and has an important function in the growth of a couple's interpersonal com-

munion. During this time, the partners' relationship as ***novios*** leads them to integrate themselves as a couple. In this context, the intimacy that characterizes friendship takes on an exclusive dimension and is geared toward achieving full psychological, spiritual, and physical intimacy.

Christian *Noviazgo*

61 A Christian *noviazgo* is the best preparation for the sacrament of marriage. In it, the *I* is reshaped in relationship with the *you*, in order to build a *we*. As *novios* relate to each other, they acquire a better knowledge of themselves and their partner—a gradual understanding of one another's ways of life, thinking, desires, and activities. They travel together toward and with God as they learn to share their feelings, common ideals, and love.

62 This love means more than getting along well and sharing activities. It also involves physical attraction, spiritual identification, human enrichment, contemplation of the new reality that is being created between the *novios*, and a desire of the *novios* to make their love a sign and instrument of God's love in the sacrament of marriage.

63 The Christian *noviazgo* should facilitate a deeper knowledge of oneself and of one's partner. This knowledge should include facets of each other's life that if not disclosed may later destroy their love. In other words, it is important that all *novios* be honest about themselves and about their past, their way of seeing life, and their expectations for the future.

64 In general, a *noviazgo* should be neither very brief nor very long. Enough time should be allowed for the *novios* to know and accept each other and to complement and adapt to each other with love and understanding. If the *noviazgo* is too brief, the couple may commit themselves in marriage without really knowing each other or without possessing the maturity needed to be a Christian couple. If the *noviazgo* is too long, the couple may fall into routines without advancing together toward an intimate union, or may have sexual intercourse before marriage and before they have established a complete commitment to each other.

65 A man and a woman who love each other seek immediate and mutual companionship and help. The couple's relationship and reciprocal gift of themselves bring the richness of each person's values,

a new interest and excitement for life, and a desire to unite more fully in marriage. Christian *noviazgo,* like marriage, must be a relationship between equals and not a relationship of domination and submission. Only by recognizing the dignity and identity of the other is it possible to achieve the *we* that is so essential to a relationship in which neither person dominates.

Commitment and the Sacrament of Marriage

66 The majority of young people dream about marriage. Many seek romance, affection, or economic support. However, Christian marriage is more than all of these. It is the appropriate setting for a couple to give themselves to each other mutually, completely, and forever, and to live together in communion with God.

67 Mutual self-giving of spouses leads to their free, total, and definitive commitment to each other. This commitment is based on love; it is formalized in an exchange of vows; it implies sexual intimacy; and it strives for the unity and indissolubility that marriage implies. Through solemn vows, husband and wife offer their heart, soul, and body to the beloved and promise fidelity and exclusiveness for life. It is a commitment made before God and others. The husband and wife are the ministers of the sacrament. They are the means by which God's love is communicated to each other and to their children, the fruit of their love.

68 The Rite of Marriage is the unveiling to others of a couple's inner promise to share life together—with all of its hopes and disappointments, its pleasures and pains, its joys and sorrows, its successes and failures. It is not an external action that simply makes marriage legal in the church and society.

69 In this spirit of communion in God's love, husband and wife join their bodies physically to express their total union, make their lifelong promise more definitive, and deepen their commitment to each other. Thus, the union in one flesh acquires a sacred meaning and becomes a source of life for the couple and their children, when and if they are blessed with them.

70 Conjugal love includes the sexual expression of love between married persons but is also much broader than this. It incorporates all the dimensions in which spouses are united with one another, reinforcing their communion of ideas and attitudes. This love is a participation in and a reflection of God's gracious love, which con-

tains the energy of the Holy Spirit. It respects the autonomy and freedom between the partners, and it is unlimited, open, liberating, sincere, and never self-serving. Conjugal love constantly nurtures the mutuality and exclusiveness of the marriage and demands permanence and total commitment. Marital chastity guides and disciplines sexual pleasure, making sex a sign of total and exclusive self-giving. Marital chastity also encourages a harmony that nourishes acceptance and tenderness in the couple.

71 In a Christian marriage, a couple is united by many factors that serve to strengthen their relationship and to overcome the weaknesses of each spouse. Their love facilitates mutual tolerance of those things that are not pleasing to each other. This kind of love is able to survive and be reinforced in spite of the difficulties of the couple and of the family, thus making the couple able to confront the annoyances, crises, and problems of married life.

72 Spouses who truly love one another are united by a profound friendship that leads them to communicate their experiences, thoughts, feelings, ideals, and worries. They also like to collaborate on projects, to share activities they both enjoy, and to accompany each other in activities that only one of them enjoys. Their shared faith helps them mutually support each other in their journey toward God and in fulfilling their personal vocations.

73 Couples who do not fully understand the sacrament of marriage may consider the exchange of vows merely a contract that requires or delineates obligations and responsibilities for both people. This interpretation of marriage prevents the couple from seeing the sacramentality of marriage and from keeping their love alive. It is an effective sign and instrument of God's love. To live marriage as a sacrament requires continual effort, a joint search for the best path, a permanent disposition toward reconciliation, and unity in prayer. When these attitudes and practices do not exist, the Rite of Marriage is reduced to a religious ceremony from the past and thus loses its sacramental meaning.

74 As a sacrament, Christian marriage is an expression of the love that Jesus holds for the church, a faithful love that remains constant, especially in difficult moments. It is easy to love when everything is going well, but love is especially necessary when one's partner fails and needs the support of the other in order to regain self-confidence. For conjugal love to mature and resist withering

over time, it needs to move toward perfection and fulfill the qualities described by Saint Paul:

> Love is patient, love is kind; love is not envious or boastful or arrogant or rude. It does not insist on its own way; it is not irritable or resentful; it does not rejoice in wrongdoing, but rejoices in the truth. It bears all things, believes all things, hopes all things, endures all things. (1 Cor. 13:4–7)

The Family as a Domestic Church

75 Through conjugal love, a couple opens itself to fecundity and to the service of life. The spouses collaborate with God in the gift of life by creating a new human person "who [is] a living reflection of their love, a permanent sign of conjugal unity and a living and inseparable synthesis of their being a father and a mother."[2]

76 A Christian marriage is a pillar of the "domestic church," which is the smallest cell of the great ecclesial community. Parents have the mission of facilitating the presence of the Reign of God in their home in such a way that the whole family lives in love, justice, and peace, and becomes an instrument and a sign of the Reign of God.

77 When several families join together, they form a small ecclesial community. There they live out their faith, provide education for their children, and become effective signs of God's presence in the world. Youth ministry should share with young people and young adults the vision of the family as a domestic church so that with full hearts, they can plan to shape their own homes with the elements of a communitarian church that helps build the Reign of God.

78 Ministry with young people and young adults should include preparing them to build Christian families. In this regard, young people do not need to wait until marriage to form their own family. They also have a role in their family of origin, with their parents, brothers, and sisters.

> The family, like the Church, ought to be a place where the Gospel is transmitted and from which the Gospel radiates.
>
> In a family which is conscious of this mission, all members evangelize and are evangelized. The parents not only communicate the Gospel to the children, but from their chil-

dren they can themselves receive the same Gospel as deeply lived by them.

And such a family becomes the evangelizer of many other families, and of the neighborhood of which it forms part.[3]

3

Toward Human Maturity

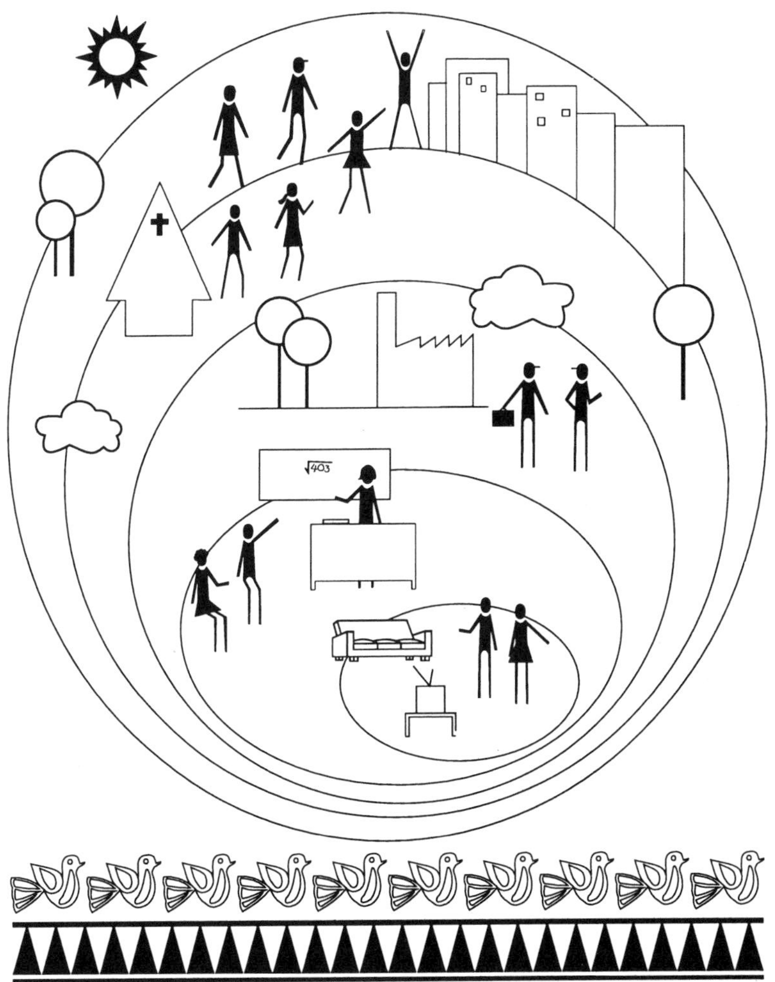

3

Toward Human Maturity

Youth is a time of an especially intensive *discovery* of a "self" and a "choice of life." It is a time for *growth* which ought to progress "in wisdom, age and grace before God and people" (Luke 2:52).

—John Paul II, *Christifideles Laici*

1 Chapter 1 focused on personal development and evangelization, and chapter 2 dealt with interpersonal communion. This chapter expands those horizons and reflects on the broader life perspectives and relationships involved in the maturation process of young people.

2 First, this chapter presents a holistic perspective on young people's Christian growth based on their affective, cognitive, moral, behavioral, and spiritual development. Second, this chapter emphasizes the need to engage young people in a process of conscientization and liberation. Third, this chapter explores the importance of a personal life project as a means of helping Hispanic young people become prophets of hope.

A Holistic Perspective on Young People's Christian Growth

3 Everyone seeks to relate to others—to support, accept, and understand them and, in turn, to feel understood, accepted, and supported by them. When this dynamic characterizes interpersonal relationships, people have achieved personal maturity. Mature people establish complementary relationships in which the interests of the *I* are balanced with the interests of the *you.* They respect the autonomy of the people with whom they relate and accept the counsel and help of others without losing their personal freedom.

4 Evangelization facilitates young people's growth into maturity by orienting their interpersonal relationships toward the feelings, attitudes, motivations, and values of Jesus. The following explores

the affective capacity, the ability for learning, and the intellectual and effective processes that direct human life.

The Affective Life

5 All human relations are influenced by the affective lives of the persons involved. The affective life is a dynamic experience that happens in the interior dimension of a person, the personal center. The affective life shades and tones relationships with the external world.

6 The affective life consists of a variety of phenomena with significant differences due to intensity, durability, and physiological and cognitive implications. Everyone organizes their affective life in a particular way, according to their physiological nature and to their lived experiences. Among the variety of affective phenomena, we can distinguish four different types:

1. *Mood:* Mood is the interior environment of the person, which can be provoked by external agents and may cause permanent or temporary changes linked to biological factors and rhythms. In general, every person has a tendency to one of the two basic conscious states of mind—joy or sadness—which are often interpreted as the optimism or pessimism of a person.
2. *Emotions:* Emotions are intense, temporary, sudden, and acute experiences with a strong physiological component. Emotions are the ways through which an individual is affected by the external world. They are related to motivations, because both are a source of movement representing a psychological energy that determines a particular kind of behavior. Emotions are related to personal experiences, interpersonal relationships, and the experience of life in general.
3. *Feelings:* Feelings are affective states that are more structured, profound, complex, and stable than emotions, but less intense and less physiologically rooted than emotions. Feelings are a way to express externally the permanent personal affectivity. They have a global nature and are formed by a set of subjective experiences. The depth and stability of feelings allow a person to express a permanent willingness to seek the well-being of another person, for example, despite a temporary emotional state of rage as an emotional response to a harm received.
4. *Passions:* Passions are affective phenomena with the stability of feelings and the intensity of emotions. In general, they are

marked by a strong presence of cognitive elements, and they are able to express vehemently the special meaning that a person or object has. Because of their intensity, passions can be the source of great ideals, motivate great enterprises, and lead toward heroism. At the same time, they can be sources of severe frustration.

7 In English usage, emotional and affective are usually synonymous. However, in Spanish usage, the two terms are distinct: the emotional life refers to only one of the dimensions of the affective life.

8 The maturity of young people's affective life largely depends on their ability to channel and express their emotions in accordance with their own scale of values. For young people to become mature emotionally and affectively, they must do the following:

- learn to express their emotions and feelings appropriately, taking care not to suppress them and not to hurt the people around them by the way they express them
- become aware of the nature, direction, and intensity of their emotions and feelings
- learn to value their affective life
- avoid manipulation by other people at the affective level
- be conscious of the influence of powerful experiences on their personality
- accept and be reconciled with themselves and with other people whenever they have hurt others or others have hurt them
- channel their affective life in ways that encourage their integral development as persons and facilitate harmony with other people

9 Evangelization is concerned with young people's affective life. Evangelization should awaken in young people the same kind of feelings that Jesus shared with his friends, acquaintances, and enemies, and should move young people to embrace a passion for fulfilling their mission as Jesus did. Then they will be deeply convinced of and engaged in a process of conversion that will lead them to be permanent sowers of the seeds of the Gospel and untiring promoters of the Reign of God.

The Cognitive Life

10 Human beings acquire knowledge and personal qualities through learning, which is a complex process. We all have the following learning abilities, which must be developed and used if we are to grow toward maturity:

11 **1. The abilities to know and to think:** The abilities to know and to think permit us to absorb, store, and remember information. These skills provide the basis for acquiring new knowledge, shaping concepts, and organizing abstract ideas, as well as for expressing one's own ideas and feelings. They also allow us to perceive, identify, classify, relate, interpret, and analyze the messages we receive from our environment through verbal symbols, such as words and songs; visual symbols, such as writing and graphic art; and physical symbols, such as gestures.

12 Only by using our abilities to know and to think can we recognize the truth about ourselves, God, and the world around us. These abilities allow us to see the problems and challenges in our life and then think through those problems to find creative solutions to them.

13 In the process of evangelization, both the evangelizer and those being evangelized use their abilities to know and to think in order to do the following:

- acquire the basic concepts that help them understand human nature and behavior
- deepen their knowledge of God revealed in Jesus Christ, and then share this knowledge with others
- know the doctrine that helps them understand the faith, and acquire a vocabulary for expressing their knowledge and religious experience
- see human life from Jesus' perspective, thus allowing them to understand Jesus' teachings
- analyze reality from a faith perspective before making important life decisions

In other words, a close relationship exists between the gift of knowledge and the gift of faith. Young people need to learn and understand the substance of the faith to the best of their ability.

14 **2. The ability to discern and to choose:** The ability to discern and to choose allows us to elect one path or another as we confront the challenges of life. It requires the following:

- adequate analysis of the situation within which the choice is being made, so that one recognizes the various elements that enter into the choice
- identification of the alternative actions possible, taking into account the possible consequences of each

- some process to discern the best alternative based on the person's intentions and values
- the interior freedom to choose the best alternative, so that the choice will not be determined by external pressure
- the freedom to act according to the choice made

15 We use our ability to discern and to choose both for the simple affairs of daily life and for occasional situations of vital importance, such as facing life choices, making moral decisions, choosing a lay or religious vocation, selecting a profession, planning our future, and resolving conflicts. It is important in childhood to begin developing these abilities with regard to simple aspects of life, so that later, young people can confront the challenges of adolescence with mature and thoughtful processes of **discernment** and election that incorporate the characteristics mentioned above.

16 We use this ability to order our life in keeping with the values of the Reign of God. In this way, we can respond to the needs of people with the feelings and attitudes that Jesus embodied, seek perfection by living according to the Beatitudes, and live with the joy of disciples who follow the footprints of the Teacher.

17 **3. The ability to learn from personal experiences and exemplary figures:** We are able to learn by seeing how other Christians live and by imitating their behavior. We can also learn by embracing and experimenting with the creative ideas with which we are born. In both cases, it is important to undergo a process of analysis, discernment, and reflection on the experiences so that we do not fall into mere imitation of others or into constant experimentation that does not lead to personal development.

18 We use this ability to learn from other persons and to bear witness to how to live out Jesus' values. We also use it to pursue discipleship with an orientation to Christian practice, and to promote pastoral work that is both evangelizing and missionary. Evangelizing through example and experience is frequently more powerful than trying to evangelize strictly through cognitive teaching.

Values and Attitudes

19 *Values* can help give direction to the lives of persons, social groups, and whole societies. Values are objective realities that exist independently and refer to the social, cultural, ethical, aesthetic, and

religious dimensions of life. They are transmitted to future generations as absolute and permanent goods. For example, the Gospel teaches people to be honest always and totally, not to be a little bit honest or to be honest only occasionally.

20 Values are complex, permanent, and ratified by the conviction that they constitute a personal or social good. Values have three dimensions:

- *the cognitive dimension,* which refers to knowledge of the value
- *the affective dimension,* which is expressed as a feeling in favor of the value, a tendency to seek it enthusiastically, and a willingness to defend it passionately
- *the behavioral dimension,* which indicates that the value has been embraced by the person or group and is therefore reflected in the resulting behavior

21 Acquiring values and ordering them into a scale or hierarchy occurs through a process of valorization. This process has two phases:

1. *Internalization,* which involves knowing the value, considering it good, choosing it consciously and freely, experiencing it positively, and committing oneself to making it a reality in one's personal life and in the life of the social group. Values are appropriated in distinct ways by different people according to their personalities, and by different cultures according to their respective characteristics.
2. *Ordering,* which is a process of discernment of the closeness or distance of a given value with respect to those values considered absolute. This places values in a hierarchy or scale as seen from a personal or social perspective.

22 A person, event, or object is valuable when it favors the dignity of human persons and helps them develop themselves. When the dignity of human persons is denied or not recognized, or when human development is impeded, **antivalues** or **disvalues** are present. When values are seen subjectively as affirming that what is valuable depends on the likes or preferences of each individual, people may be falling into subjectivism or relativism. In these situations, young people are left to find the meaning of life, give direction to their lives, and evaluate their personal and social experiences without any frame of reference.

23 Values play several important roles in the lives of people, social groups, and society:

- They give direction to life by helping people select from various alternative actions and by encouraging people to behave in certain ways.
- They guide the way people relate socially and provide criteria for evaluating and judging one's own behavior and that of others.
- They provide a basis for critically judging reality and for resolving conflicts.
- They help anchor one's reasoning in making decisions.
- They predispose people toward specific religious beliefs.
- They allow one to take a position regarding social questions and political ideology.

24 *Attitudes* are patterns of personal behavior based on one's scale of values in the social, moral, and religious spheres. Attitudes generate consistent and habitual dispositions in a person's conduct that come to characterize the way he or she relates to other persons, confronts life experiences, and manages things in the wider world.

25 Other people's examples play an important role in how we learn our attitudes. If values, moral principles, and rational arguments are ratified by the living testimony of the person proclaiming them, they are capable of shaping attitudes and motivating behavior in others. For a given attitude to become an integral part of a young person's personality, she or he must apply it consistently in all the many circumstances that demand it.

26 Every sociocultural system is founded on a worldview that provides a frame of reference for seeing the world and for relating to God, oneself, other persons, and society in a particular way. Our loving, thinking, and living are guided by this worldview and by the system of values contained in it.

27 The religious values that Jesus revealed, which form part of the Christian tradition, provide a frame of reference for selecting and ordering the values that give meaning and direction to believers' lives. These values are transmitted into our daily lives through learned attitudes regarding how Jesus related to his Father, other persons, and the world.

28 The values and attitudes revealed by Jesus should be embraced by all his disciples. Values constitute the criteria for making real the Reign of God here and now. Attitudes incarnate those values in daily life. Young people give their lives a Christian orientation by making Jesus' values and attitudes their own. Evangelization helps young people embrace these values as the fundamental criteria through which they decide to commit themselves to promoting the common good, and to a discipleship that leads to their self-realization as persons.

Moral Conscience

29 To be a disciple of Jesus is to make his life's norm one's own—the commandment to love, which is carried to perfection in the Beatitudes. Fulfilling this commandment requires the formation of a Christian moral conscience, constant motivation, and a serious commitment to live in accordance with the Gospel.

30 To be responsible Christians, young people must make a **fundamental option** to follow the teachings of Jesus and to strengthen their faith-life. This fundamental option is a decision made from within the personal center, where one freely and consciously chooses the ideals, values, and attitudes that will guide one's life. Upon taking root in the most intimate level of one's life, this option

- *guides and motivates* one in following the ideals put forward by Jesus
- *orients and gives meaning* to all of life
- *acquires a normative character* that conditions all of one's actions

31 As young people mature and come to know Jesus more deeply, they can reaffirm their basic attitudes, purify their intentions, and order their values based on their decision to follow Jesus. The formation process of a young person's moral conscience encourages a clear presentation of Christian ideals according to the stage of human and faith development the young person has achieved. It presents, in a positive and enthusiastic way, the meaning of being a Christian young person in the modern world. It respects the freedom of young people and avoids imposing norms, manipulating them with a false piety, or undermining them with fear and guilt. It leads to the search for greater commitment to love as Jesus loves and avoids converting the Christian life into a routine.

32 To live according to the fundamental option of following Jesus, one needs to be responsible and to count on God's help. Therefore, young people need to develop a profound spirituality.

Following Jesus as Teacher

33 Jesus was an excellent teacher and should be followed by every Christian and in particular by every evangelizer. His teachings respond to human yearnings because Jesus, assuming our full humanity, comes to us within the circumstances of our life. He takes us as we are, accepts our desires and frustrations, and establishes with us a personal relationship of love and forgiveness. In addition, Jesus shares his very life with those disciples who, accepting the action of the Holy Spirit in their life, accept him as teacher.

34 Jesus used diverse teaching methods to communicate his message and to motivate his followers. First of all, his attitudes and behaviors provided a clear example of how to live if one wanted to extend the Reign of God among one's brothers and sisters. Second, he extended radical invitations and harsh warnings to move people to conversion. Jesus also used a variety of teaching techniques. Sometimes he used silence to facilitate discernment. Other times he argued with people to challenge them. He questioned his listeners to encourage them to think and to reflect, and he spoke directly and provocatively to clarify his ideas.

35 Jesus told parables to teach difficult lessons and to illustrate his moral teachings. He taught with sayings and proverbs to stimulate popular wisdom, and cited scriptural passages as foundations for his teaching. He pointed out contradictions and made comparisons in order to spread his teachings. He used exaggeration to emphasize important concepts. He asked the disciples to take concrete action in their lives so that they might learn to fulfill their mission. He let them ask questions to clarify their doubts. In all these ways, Jesus facilitated dialog with the disciples to provide them with greater enlightenment when they did not see clearly and to correct them when they were wrong.

36 Jesus evangelized by taking the disciples and their concrete reality as his point of departure and focusing on what they needed in order to receive the Good News and re-establish their covenant with God. He spoke clearly and radically so that his truth would effectively guide people's personal, social, and religious lives. He held his disciples responsible for their actions. In this way, Jesus called them beyond their personal needs and pulled them out of their egoism so that they could become promoters of the love, justice, and peace that are born of communion with God.

The Power of Christian Spirituality

37 *Spirituality* is the way a person's life reflects the relationship he or she has with God, people, and the world. Young people and adults acquire a spirituality and express it in a way that is consistent with their gender, personality, abilities, and limitations. Spirituality reflects the values and attitudes of people, as well as their historical and sociocultural contexts.

38 Christian spirituality springs from our discipleship of Jesus and our attempt to have a Christian praxis. It is characterized by being the following:

- *communitarian, Christocentric, and trinitarian,* centered in being a member of Jesus' church and in a life of communion with God
- *a source of life* oriented toward love and service to others, and focused on living out the values of the Reign of God in society
- *integral and human,* including our ideals, values, attitudes, and behaviors; it involves our complete person and everything that God has created and redeemed
- *pluralistic in its expressions,* which correspond to different personal and cultural ***idiosincrasias*** and lifestyles

39 Everyone should seek a spirituality appropriate to their calling and way of living out their faith. Various schools or expressions of Christian spirituality have been created by persons who have lived their relationship to God in diverse ways.

40 Francis of Assisi was an emotional and artistic young man. He was born to a rich family of merchants during feudal times, when society was sharply divided between lords and serfs. Francis realized that to follow Jesus, he had to abandon his rich lifestyle. Responding to his calling, Francis began to develop a spirituality marked by a relationship with the God he encountered through nature and expressed with a simple lifestyle. Francis's life was filled with love, compassion, poetry, and song. Francis's relationship with God led him to a life of extraordinary charity toward needy people and to the lifestyle of a beggar, dependent on the charity of others. His radical life inspired many people who followed his way by becoming itinerant preachers and beggars.

41 Ignatius of Loyola began his faith journey as a vigorous man and an experienced soldier. After becoming injured on the battlefield, he had to remain hospitalized for a long time. During this period, Ignatius had an opportunity to reflect on his life and on the Protestant Reformation that was dividing the church. Ignatius saw

that following Jesus in that historic moment demanded a special loyalty to the pope and a spirit of struggle to call the Roman Catholic church to purification, reform, and interior renewal so that a more authentic Christianity might be possible.

42 Ignatius developed a spirituality based on action and reflection, on discernment of the **signs of the times** and each person's intentions, and on the effort to form independent, loyal, and strong-willed leaders to help fulfill Jesus' mission. Ignatius's relationship with God led him and his followers to struggle for their faith and for their church in universities, centers of power, and social environments that influenced the development of ideas.

43 Teresa of Ávila was a strong woman in a body full of pain. She possessed a rich understanding of life and a great self-awareness. She had an indomitable spirit as a result of her family background, which—characteristic of an old aristocratic, traditional Castilian family—did not allow for mediocrity. Teresa heard God's call at a time when people who had consecrated their lives to God through religious vows were extremely lax. They resisted returning to a spiritually disciplined life based on Christian values and virtues.

44 The contrast between Teresa's strong spiritual life and weak physical life led her to create a spirituality of profound humility and self-abandonment through contemplative prayer. In her spirituality, the historic Jesus—his preaching, life, and death on the cross—had a dominant place. From her prayer, the central focus of Teresa's spirituality emerged: passionate and profound love of God. However, this love was not based on sentimentalism and emotion, for Teresa had spent many years of affective dryness in her relationship with God. Teresa saw love as the only source of energy capable of reforming religious life and keeping people firm in fulfilling God's will. From this insight, she built an intense apostolic and charitable life that compelled her to tirelessly undertake journeys through the cities and the countryside, where she gave testimony and promoted authentic discipleship, particularly in Carmelite convents—the religious community to which she belonged.

45 Was Teresa's spirituality better than Francis's, or Francis's better than Ignatius's, or Ignatius's better than Teresa's? No one spirituality was better than the other. Spirituality synthesizes people's way of being, their intimate relationship with God, and their particular way of living out their faith in the historic context in which they live.

46 For evangelization to be effective among Hispanic young people, it must generate a variety of appropriate spiritualities that serve as models or paths for them to follow in their attempt to develop a more profound faith-life. Hispanic youth ministry cannot be content with providing young people with superficial approaches to Christian spirituality or with isolated spiritual experiences. Rather, Hispanic youth ministry must make serious efforts to facilitate the development of profound spiritualities. Only in this way can the Gospel deeply penetrate young people's lives, giving them the elements they need to discern wisely and to forge an authentic Christian spirituality that corresponds to their personal vocation, history, and lifestyle.

Conscientization, Liberation, and Praxis

47 Like all human beings, young people not only exist in the world but also relate to it and must be responsible for it. To become aware of this reality, young people need to see objectively the dynamic relationship among nature, persons, and things. Gaining this awareness is a gradual process that should begin in childhood and take on greater importance as young people enter adolescence, the stage at which they are capable of critically analyzing a situation and engaging in transformative action to build a more humane world.

48 The process that leads to this kind of consciousness and responsibility is called conscientization and begins with questions like these: Where am I? Why am I here? Why do I live the way I do? Who else shares the same kind of life that I have, and who has a very distinct type of life? Why do things happen the way they do? Is this the way God intended things to happen? Responding to these questions leads individuals and communities to develop a perspective of themselves as subjects of history, people inserted in the world to be coprotagonists with God and with other people for the history of salvation. Without conscientization, young people are left outside the vital communion for which they were created.

49 A successful conscientization process helps young people identify the relationship they have with themselves and with other people, the circumstances in which they live, and the reasons that they live as they do. In addition, conscientization helps young people see

themselves as agents of action in the world, both at the personal and communal levels. This way of facing life implies four dynamics:

50 **1. Assuming one's personal history:** Young people see themselves as the subjects, or protaganists, of their life, who have in their hands their past—in order to discover their family and sociocultural roots and be enriched by past positive experiences and reconciled with past negative experiences. Also, they take in their hands their present, in which to make decisions and act on them, and their future, which they must craft with care and hope.

51 **2. Assuming one's collective history:** Assuming their collective history implies first acknowledging the cultural and historical roots of the Latino–North American people of which they are a part, as well as their religious roots as Catholic Christians. Second, it implies considering Hispanic youth as a collective unit, with a concrete mission and responsibility in the church in the United States and in society today and in the future. Third, it implies being aware of their role in union with all other people, helping to form part of U.S. society.

52 **3. Assuming responsibility for the present and the future:** Young people need to become active agents of their personal history and the history of the society in which they live. To accomplish this, they must acquire a critical vision of their situation and a realistic vision of the possibility of guiding their lives in ways that favor their personal development and promotion of the common good.

53 **4. Assuming the history of salvation:** Young people need to become aware of their own history of salvation and to be agents of salvation to others. This means recognizing the presence of God in their life and in the lives of others, committing themselves to the mission of Jesus, putting in the hands of Christ their hurts to be healed, trusting in God's mercy and obtaining forgiveness, and joining others in their efforts to create a better world.

54 Young people need to be aware that these four life dynamics should be evaluated in terms of fidelity to their relationship with God and the authenticity of their Christian praxis. Christians do not secure lives free of problems, frustrations, or failures, but with confidence in God, they can find the meaning of human limitations and struggle with faith and hope to overcome them.

55 The process of conscientization occurs through the continuous interaction of four phases, or moments: internalizing the **Christian utopia;** acquiring a critical consciousness of reality; converting one's heart, mind, and life; and engaging in historic praxis.

Internalizing the Christian Utopia

56 A utopia is an ideal toward which one strives. The Christian utopia is the full accomplishment of the Reign of God on earth. Jesus, in taking on our human nature and fulfilling the mission entrusted to him by God, clearly revealed the Christian utopia: The Reign of God is already partially present; it is realized through the works of the Spirit and the collaboration of the People of God. The Reign bears fruits of love, justice, and peace in human history—the seeds and beginnings, the firstfruits of the plenitude of the Reign of God.

57 The search for the ideal of the Reign of God generates a creative tension between denouncing situations that are inhuman and therefore contrary to the Reign, and announcing and creating a new reality in which love, justice, and peace reign. In this context, a utopia is not an abstract ideal, a dream, or an ideology, but a historic commitment that young people can make.

Acquiring a Critical Consciousness of Reality

58 Young people acquire a critical consciousness when they see their personal and collective experience realistically, understand the causes that generated it, and judge it with the criteria of the Gospel. In analyzing their reality in this way, young people can identify those aspects of their life that keep them from loving and acting freely. They thus encounter a challenge to personal and communal conversion and to transformation of the situations and structures that oppress, manipulate, or enslave them.

59 People frequently have a naive or magical consciousness rather than a critical one. People with a naive consciousness refuse to analyze concrete realities. Some people feel free to understand reality according to their own internal experience alone and to interpret it in a way convenient or pleasing to them. Others may have a magical consciousness and understand a particular reality well, but they believe it is caused by superior forces to which they willingly and docilely submit. Both attitudes impede young people from taking responsibility for their life and for their society.

Converting One's Heart, Mind, and Life

60 Conversion can occur as a result of a person's relationship with Jesus, by the impact of particular aspects of Jesus' life and message, and as a consequence of relationships with other people. Conversion may happen in an individual person as well as in a group of people. "Then Jesus said to the Jews who had believed in him, 'If you continue in my word, you are truly my disciples; and you will know the truth, and the truth will make you free'" (John 8:31–32). Conversion consists of letting Jesus' truth about God and human beings convince the person or the group, influence their heart, and bring about new attitudes and behaviors toward God, oneself, and others. Conversion always has an impact on people, changing their deepest personal center.

61 The first two phases of conscientization—internalizing the Christian utopia and acquiring a critical consciousness—lead young people to confront the truth about themselves, their situation in the world, and their goal as human beings. Conversion calls young people to put themselves in God's hands, to surrender to God their personal and collective weaknesses, to ask God for forgiveness of their sinfulness, and to offer their desires so that God can lead their life.

62 At this point in the process, young people arrive at the moment of prayer, of individual and communal encounter with God. Here they ask for God's grace, light, and help so that the truth they have seen may set them free. This is precisely the time when young people abandon themselves into God's hands and say, "Your kingdom come, your will be done, on earth as it is in heaven." This is the encounter with the Lord who, in liberating young people from their personal and communal sin, restores their capacity to love and gives them the freedom to develop and act, guided by love. These moments of profound reflection carry them to a stronger and more intimate communion with God.

Engaging in Historic Praxis

63 Jesus' praxis happened in history. Through that praxis, he brought hope to all people who believed in him. Today, through concrete actions, young people must continue the struggle to extend the Reign of God. Young people's work in history keeps alive their Christian hope and gives hope to others around them. The term

praxis describes this continuous fulfillment of Jesus' project, of people taking on the role as God's coprotagonists in history and converting their individual and communal histories into salvation history.

64 Praxis describes a dynamic of repeated action and reflection. Preparation for praxis begins when people identify and denounce realities that must be changed, and announce a project or plan to transform those realities. But praxis also consists of putting this project or plan into practice—making it one's life project. Praxis means acting to transform history intentionally and through the guidance of the Gospel. To analyze and plan without engaging in action is to fall into a new kind of magical consciousness. Young people in this situation may see the complexity and the difficulty of changing reality and fail to become agents of history. If this happens, the world will continue exercising its oppressive power over young people, who will become even more depressed and frustrated.

65 Using the gifts we have received from God, we must make history, not just plans. Putting plans into practice is what converts young people into light that illuminates the world, yeast that transforms their interpersonal relationships, and salt that gives their life new flavor.

66 In taking responsibility for the world by engaging in action, young people recognize that they can make some changes on their own. But in order to effect significant changes, they must work in union with others who share their ideals. Young people also become aware that every process of transformation is slow and demands training, knowledge, conversion of personal attitudes, and availability of resources. That is, transformation requires planning and constant action. Engaging in this process of transformation leads young people to a new critical analysis made in dialog with other persons committed to the same actions.

Young Hispanics, Prophets of Hope

67 Young people do not exist just to develop themselves and become integrated as persons. They have a more transcendental calling. All young people have a concrete mission within history that they are called to, moved by the Gospel and led by a Christian worldview.

The Personal Life Project

68 The Christian worldview becomes a reality when young people have a life project that energizes them. The noun *project* means "forward orientation." As a verb, *to project* means "to give forward orientation to." To project one's life means to thrust one's energy toward the world in an intentional way, and to make a commitment to forging one's own destiny. A young person's life project is intimately related to his or her personal center, which gives birth to creativity and the personal will to continue forward. Having a personal life project implies knowing oneself, being convinced of one's self-worth, and being aware that personal fulfillment depends on living a productive life.

69 Each human being becomes more fully a person to the extent that she or he makes a personal contribution to the world through work, service to others, and sociopolitical participation in society. When young people have personal projects, their energy and vitality cannot be contained. Their lives overflow into the world, as they live the present passionately and prepare for the future with realistic optimism. They meet the unknown future with confidence and face the struggles of life with hope.

70 Life without a personal project cannot truly be called life. The void kills hope. This happens in several ways: when people do not have concrete goals, no energy exists; when only short-term goals are made and achieved, motivation to grow further halts; when efforts to attain concrete goals fail, frustration and bitterness appear. Young people who do not project their life beyond themselves simply move themselves through time and are distracted by daily occurrences, leaving themselves open to life's whims and vulnerable to whatever influences them. Their lives lack direction and meaning; therefore, they take no risks. They see history passing by them, rather than challenging them to become creators of history.

71 In contrast, those who have a project in life continue forward wherever they are and in whatever circumstances they find themselves, for their project always accompanies them. It is part of their very being. A life project leads young people to make choices, to decide in favor of their own authenticity, to stand up for their convictions, to confront difficulties with a courageous and optimistic spirit, and to engage in society productively.

72 By definition, life projects have the following characteristics:

- They are *dynamic,* because they grow, adjust, and become clearer as young people develop and mature, and as the reality where they live changes.
- They are *original,* because each young person has unique and irreplaceable gifts, circumstances, ideals, and vocations.
- They are *coherent,* because they are part of the self-definition of young people, and are oriented to what young people can and want to become.
- They are *permanent,* because they are based on fundamental and nonnegotiable principles rooted in the Christian vision of the world.
- They are *born of a radical freedom,* because they arise from a voluntary commitment to an ideal.
- They are *authentic,* because they originate and partake of the truth about oneself and the world in which one lives, and they always demand fidelity.

73 Intentionality, spontaneity, and commitment are intermingled in a life project. These three components generate a spirit or *mística* that nourishes the project. This *mística* helps a person live more passionately, because it promotes continuous personal development and a personal contribution to history. This *mística* helps one live more optimistically, because failures become opportunities for improvement, and new contexts challenge creativity. Finally, this *mística* helps one live more transcendently, because it is oriented toward an ideal that transcends personal interests and the limitations of the present moment. In this context, even the tedious aspects of life have meaning. Weariness helps young people identify and accept their physical and psychological limitations. Monotony and struggle can be seen as inevitable elements of continuing with their project.

74 In order to assure fulfillment of a life project, young people must enter into dialog with other people who can help them discern their projects' authenticity and viability, reorient them during moments of confusion, and support them in moments of weakness. Young people need to join forces with people who share their values and ideals, and who have similar projects. They also need periods of silence and solitude that facilitate greater self-knowledge and help them to reflect about the world and to evaluate their life project.

Agents of Change in History

75 Young Latinos will be ***agentes de cambio*** in their historic moment and will offer real hope for a better future to the extent that they take possession of their own history, take on their heritage from their parents and others who came before them, and acquire an awareness of their historic role in the society in which they live. History is like a chain of epochs (time periods), each characterized by new needs, aspirations, and values. For Latino young people to be creators of a culture of sharing and peace, they must collaborate with others to construct history intentionally rather than allow themselves to be dragged along by events and circumstances.

76 Although the political, economic, cultural, and religious situations of Latino people in the United States vary from place to place, the broad outlines are similar. Critical social analysis by Latino youth awakens questions, challenges, and hopes that are valid for the majority of young Latinos and that can generate solidarity and common projects.

77 For conscientization to occur and for young people to commit themselves to transforming the situations that dehumanize them, they need an educational process that makes them free and responsible human beings. Evangelization and Christian formation of young people should help them to critically analyze their reality and to commit themselves to expressing the truth—as they see it after the analysis—through concrete actions that show consistency between what they say and do and what Jesus said and did.

78 To engage successfully in this process, Hispanic youth ministry should do the following:

- strive to help Hispanic youth become integrated in society. Hispanic young people alone, without clear connections to the rest of society, cannot build a better world or a culture of sharing and peace.
- support Hispanic young people in fulfilling their evangelization mission in the world
- seek the ways and means required to develop a Hispanic youth and young adult ministry capable of implementing the National Pastoral Plan for Hispanic Ministry

A Christian's Life Project: To Be a Young Prophet of Hope

79 Christians find in Jesus the model for making their greatest personal contribution to a culture of sharing and peace. Jesus internalized God's plan and made it his personal life project. Although he carried out his project throughout his life, he spent his last three years focusing on the utopia of the Reign, engaging daily in action to make the Reign a reality. Convinced that his personal project was in accord with God's plan for all humanity, Jesus did not strive to fulfill it alone, but formed disciples to continue his mission.

80 Every process of evangelization should help young people shape and carry out their life project. This project should synthesize all the processes that integrate them as persons and launch them into the world, animated by the spirit of the Gospel. The integral evangelization of young people should do the following:

1. take young people as they are, in their concrete reality and in their search for *identity;* help them encounter themselves as children of God and disciples of Jesus
2. transmit God's *love* to young people and help them open up to God so that they, in turn, will be capable of loving others
3. facilitate young people's discovery of God's presence on the path to *intimacy* with other persons
4. help young people incorporate and responsibly integrate their *affective life*, guiding this dimension of their life with Jesus' sentiments, attitudes, and motivations
5. help young people understand and integrate their *sexuality* in ways that let them fulfill themselves as persons according to the teachings of the church
6. facilitate young people's *conscientization*, helping them embrace their vocation, personal mission, and call to be cocreators of history with God
7. encourage young people to personally integrate a *Christian vision of life* that gives them coherence as persons and a basis for making the fundamental options that guide their life
8. help young people as they shape a *life project* that affirms Jesus' project
9. form communities of young people that, inspired by the *utopia* of the Reign of God, will be evangelical and missionary

81 Through integral evangelization, Latino young people may fulfill their role in society, as it was clearly stated in the Third General Conference of the Latin American Bishops in Puebla, Mexico:

> Young people who share the attitudes of Christ promote and defend the dignity of the human person. . . . More and more they come to regard themselves as "citizens of the world," as instruments for building up the Latin American and world communities.[1]

4

Jesus, Prophet of the Reign of God

4

Jesus, Prophet of the Reign of God

> We believe in Jesus Christ, our Lord and Savior, revealed in our history through his loving and transforming presence, which invites us as a people to the building of the Kingdom.
>
> —Secretariat for Hispanic Affairs, *Prophetic Voices*

1 The previous chapters of this book focused on young people's personal development, integral evangelization, journey to interpersonal communion, and process of maturation. Later chapters focus on various aspects of the evangelization process. In this chapter, we pause on this road of evangelization to center ourselves on the person, life, and mission of Jesus. In this way we express our recognition that Jesus is the foundation of our **pastoral-theological vision** and the beginning and end of all evangelization.

2 The chapter begins by reflecting on the key questions that youth ministry confronts when it presents Jesus to young people. Later it speaks of some aspects of the person, life, and mission of Jesus. It then addresses the encounter with the Risen Jesus and concludes with a reflection on the Emmaus event (Luke 24:13–35).

Jesus and Young People Today

3 Every effort to evangelize Hispanic young people confronts the reality of rapid cultural change and religious pluralism in their lives. This environment requires all evangelizing youth ministry to respond to two key questions—one regarding *identity* and the other regarding *meaning*.

- The question of *identity* leads evangelizers to ask: Who is Jesus? What is the identity of young Christians?
- The question of *meaning* leads evangelizers to ask: What place does Jesus have in young people's lives today? What does it mean to be a young Christian?

Presenting Jesus to Young People

4 To respond to these questions about the identity and relevance of being a young Christian today, young people need to encounter Jesus, come to know him well, and relate to him as authentic disciples. In other words, what to *be* and what to *do* as Christians can only be defined in relation to Jesus. Presenting an accurate picture of Jesus to young people requires three perspectives: a historical perspective, a universal perspective, and a salvation perspective. Evangelization from these three perspectives will initiate a living faith within youth, a faith that will be capable of bearing witness to Christian love and of generating authentic hope.

5 The *historical perspective* is the fundamental path that any person wishing to know Jesus should choose. Christians' basic task is to come closer to Jesus through the Scriptures, which present the historical figure of Jesus as a person who acts strongly and decisively before the social, cultural, and religious challenges of his people. The four Gospels are particularly crucial here; it is in the Gospels that young people discover who Jesus of Galilee was, what he meant to the people who knew him, and how he influenced the history of his time.

6 An evangelization based on a historical perspective of Jesus leads young people to carry out the following actions:

- read and savor the Gospels, in order to encounter Jesus and learn to relate to him as did his mother, friends, and disciples
- know the setting in which Jesus lived, in order to understand his culture, way of being, and way of acting
- tell Jesus' story, in order to deepen their insight into his way of thinking and the reasons for his actions
- analyze the meaning of God-made-human in Jesus, who was incarnated in a human body subject to the same limitations as their bodies and entered the history of his people to create a new human reality
- discover what it means to be a disciple of Jesus, and understand the different ways that the first Christian communities continued recreating the new reality that Jesus inaugurated

7 The *universal perspective* allows us to locate Jesus in every historical epoch, culture, and circumstance. Jesus is "the same yesterday and today and forever" (Heb. 13:8). Through his church, Jesus questions every culture, ideology, and social system created by

humanity throughout history. The community of Jesus constantly re-encounters the experience of Jesus of Galilee, who lived, died, and rose again to remain among us and invite us to accept the new life that he offers.

8 Taking on this universal perspective implies discovering Jesus within the culture of the United States of America and among *all* young Hispanics. It also implies discovering what it means to acquire the new life brought by Jesus, both at the level of young people's interpersonal relationships and at the level of social systems that shape their lives. In order to preserve faithfully the memory of Jesus and to be able to interpret Jesus' meaning for their own lives, youth of every epoch need to come close to the Jesus to whom the first Christian bore witness, as well as to embrace the Christological tradition of succeeding generations.

9 The historical and universal perspectives converge in the *perspective of salvation.* God became human in Jesus in order to reconcile humanity with God. God thus defeated sin and overcame the limitations of human nature through the fullness of divine life. Here lies the core of the Christian faith: In Jesus is fulfilled the promise of salvation offered by God to the people of Israel. The essence of our faith consists in professing in word and deed that Jesus is the Christ, the One sent by God to give us new life.

10 To evangelize is to reveal the mystery of salvation in Jesus in such a way that young people experience liberation from personal and social sin as the first fruits of eternal life with God. This will generate in young people a living and integral faith that will bear the fruit of love and make them prophets of hope.

The Faith of Young People in Jesus Christ

11 Every evangelization effort strives to inspire faith in Jesus, with his mystery and offer of new life. This faith, the only one capable of giving Christian meaning to life, has four essential characteristics:

1. *It is a personal and communitarian faith.* This means that all young persons should encounter Jesus and relate to him in the context of the ecclesial community. There the Spirit's presence can promote authenticity in the faith through relationships with others and with God. Thus, evangelization should not encourage a purely subjective faith in keeping with individual preferences, nor should it encourage young people to focus on their

individual needs and consider their personal vision the measure of what Jesus is.

2. *It is a faith that accepts and confesses christological dogma.* Acceptance and confession is how the church enters into, lives, and expresses the great mystery of Jesus. Therefore, evangelizers must present these teachings in ways that help express the mystery of Jesus' Incarnation and the salvation he offers, not as empty formulas that must be accepted without understanding, nor as rational philosophical or theological concepts learned by memory.
3. *It is a faith that expresses a living and current creed.* In every moment of history, young people faithfully recover the creed of the early church and update it according to their life's context through continuous dialog between both their faith perspectives and their own Christian practice. In this way, the creed becomes a deep experience of what it means to live the mystery of the saving Christ rather than a repetition of what the Christian faith has already proclaimed.
4. *It is a faith translated into Christian practice.* Faith must find expression beyond the interior worlds of individuals and the ecclesial community. An authentic and dynamic faith projects itself into the world through practices that reflect God's love and justice, as Jesus did. This generates a Christian way of daily living and acting that confronts the challenges of modern culture and society. This faith is lived out day to day and celebrated in community, especially in the Eucharist. It thus prevents Christianity from falling into ritualistic custom and from being reduced to moralizing.

The Church, a Vital Setting for Faith in Jesus Christ

12 In order for the three Christological perspectives to generate a living faith in young people, rather than simply becoming intellectual exercises or leading only to momentary religious experiences or isolated instances of service, young people need to *be church, experience themselves as church, and live as church.* The early Christian communities encountered Jesus in the context of their personal and communal lives. That is also where young people today will encounter the Risen Jesus. Like the early church, today's Christian community encounters Jesus

- in the mysteries that it believes, proclaims, and announces—that is, in its ***kerygma***
- in what it knows, understands, and teaches about Jesus and his project—that is, in its ***catechesis***
- in the moments when it gathers to deepen in the faith, mutually support one another, or strengthen the members' identity as Jesus' disciples—that is, in the formation of a *community*
- on the occasions when it receives new members into its midst, commemorates in the Eucharist Jesus' death and Resurrection, reconciles with God and the community, and recommits itself to the Christian life—that is, in its *liturgy*
- in the way it expresses God's love to others by serving and forgiving, accepting the marginalized, reconciling with one another, and loving truth—that is, in *Christian praxis*

13 In being church, experiencing themselves as church, and living as church, youth acquire, live, and strengthen their faith even as they conserve and revitalize the faith that was passed on to them. The role of each generation and, therefore, especially of the youthful church in each moment of history, is to *regenerate* the faith of its ancestors. This church is the living body of the Risen Jesus that constantly makes present once again the salvation offered by Jesus. So it is vital that young people become an evangelizing and missionary church, and not close themselves off to the wider world. To regenerate the faith, it is not enough to gather together to have a good time or to use interesting pastoral methods; young people need to discover Jesus by living as a community of disciples. The only path that Jesus left among us was the faith of his disciples; he influences history only through his disciples' living faith. So young people should ask themselves what kind of footprints they are leaving for others to follow, aware of the paths they are creating for future generations.

Jesus Present and Active Within the History of Hispanic Young People

14 Jesus was incarnated in history within a specific culture and people, sent by God to bring salvation to humanity. In this context he developed his mission and changed the course of history.

15 History is more than the accumulation of isolated events, a process of evolution, or the flow of days and years. It is the

relationship between what no longer exists and what does not yet exist, between received tradition and what is yet to come. History is the horizon within which all human activity occurs and in which God acts. Salvation history is something deeper and more meaningful than just acquiring personal well-being. It involves opening oneself to the action of God, recognizing and accepting the reconciliation that God offers us.

16 We Christians hold history in our hands, just as Jesus held it in his hands. Christian youth become agents of history when they build their life projects from within current reality, based upon the faith inherited from past generations and with a vision of the future informed by faith. Creating a life project should begin with each human being's freedom to love and embrace the mission of Jesus.

17 Authentic faith always leads to personal conversion and the transformation of society through the use of freedom. The goal of Christian faith lies not in satisfying personal, psychological, social, or religious needs, but in creating a new reality. Its newness lies in creating a world in which love, justice, and peace reign and in which people embrace the hope of eternal salvation.

Jesus, a Person Who Impacts

18 The previous section asserted that the most important thing to all Christians is finding Jesus and establishing a relationship with him—personally and as a member of the faith community, which is the church. Thus, it is vital to know that Jesus was a person like us in all except sin. To know the human nature of Jesus brings us near to him and helps us to relate to him as brothers and sisters, and to follow him as disciples.

19 We do not have pictures, biographies or writings by Jesus; nor do we have his carpentry tools, his worn sandals, or his fingerprints. But we can discover Jesus in the Christian Testament, which contains the personal witness and narratives of his disciples, who knew Jesus through encounters with him, mysterious experiences, times of joy and sorrow, crises and growth situations, frustrations and hopes, rejections and communion.

20 Although the natural environment and cultural setting of the first disciples were very different from those in which we live today,

their emotional lives, human relations, and processes of growth and development still have much to teach us today, two thousand years later. If we wish to be authentic disciples of Jesus, it is crucial that we encounter, know, and follow him with the enthusiasm of the first Christians.

The Hidden Life of Jesus

21 Jesus of Nazareth lived in Palestine during the first three decades of what we now call the **common era,** probably between 6 or 7 B.C.E. and 30 C.E. He was born during the reign of Roman Emperor Augustus and carried out his ministry during the reign of Emperor Tiberius, when Herod was the local tetrarch (governor) under the Roman procurator (treasury officer) Pontius Pilate. The biblical sources on which we must rely make it impossible to construct a biography of Jesus, because the Christian Testament mentions historical data only occasionally and indirectly, and the other available sources are inadequate.

22 Only the Gospels of Matthew and Luke tell of Jesus' birth and infancy. They follow narrative models of the Hebrew Scriptures. In writing these Gospels, the Evangelists were striving to record **theology,** not to write a biography of Jesus. We know very little of Jesus' physical appearance or psychology. The central goal of the Gospels is to express the Christian community's faith in Jesus and to show that God's promises to the people of Israel are fulfilled in Jesus.

23 Although the Gospels say almost nothing about Jesus' childhood, we know that he was a Jewish child who, like all children, learned to walk, eat, play, interact with friends and neighbors, and acquire certain other basic skills. His parents taught him to pray, and little by little he came to know God better by discovering God in nature, other people, prayer, and the Scriptures. The story of Jesus as a twelve-year-old boy questioning the teachers in the Temple (in the Gospel of Luke) reveals the concerns and wisdom he had acquired through his relationship with God and through his reflection on the world around him.

24 Then, after Luke's brief description of the twelve-year-old Jesus—nothing. We have no other knowledge about the next eighteen years of Jesus' life. In spite of this, we deduce from his lifestyle, his keen observations, and his dedication to his ministry, that during his youth and young adulthood Jesus must have spent much

time coming to know his people and deepening his experience of God. In praying, meditating, and analyzing the reality in which he lived, Jesus gradually discovered aspects of God that had not previously been revealed to God's people or that had been misinterpreted or manipulated over the course of history.

Jesus of Galilee

25 To come to know Jesus is a passionate adventure. Jesus was born in a poor and underprivileged region, lived in a period when his nation was divided and dominated by the Romans, when its culture had lost its splendor. The religious situation was no better. His people's fidelity to God left much to be desired, and only a small faithful remnant followed the teachings of the prophets. Jesus' life itself was not easy: like every human being, he had to confront many conflicts and suffer sadness, frustration, betrayal, and disillusionment.

26 In this setting devoid of hope, Jesus carried out his ministry. Incarnated among his people and profoundly human, Jesus shaped a personality that allowed him to fulfill God's will. Jesus was a warm, compassionate, and merciful person and, at the same time, a powerful and audacious prophet. He lived in solidarity with the poor, marginalized, and unfortunate, and he promoted justice and peace. Jesus gradually forged these personal qualities through his struggle to fulfill the mission that his Father had given him, a mission that demanded courage and tenderness, confidence in himself and in others, strength to challenge others, and loyalty to support them in their struggles for liberation, a willingness to heal and to forgive, and the valor to demand and to question.

27 Jesus was a Jew who lived within the culture and society of his time; his intellectual and religious roots lie in the Hebrew Scriptures. However, Jesus does not fit any category of his time. All the titles given to him—Teacher, Messiah, Lord, Prophet, Liberator, the Risen One, and others—capture important aspects of him, but they do not capture Jesus in his totality.

28 According to the three synoptic Gospels, Jesus' public life occurred principally in Galilee and the cities located around Lake Gennesaret. But we do not know for sure how long his public ministry lasted. On one hand, the synoptic Gospels record only one visit by Jesus to Jerusalem, during which he was taken prisoner and

sentenced to death. On the other hand, the Gospel of John tells us that Jesus spent three Passover feasts in Jerusalem and provoked the hostility of the Jewish hierarchy during confrontations with them in several visits to the city. The lack of agreement between these Gospel narratives makes it difficult to know with certainty many details of Jesus' life. In general, the Gospels provide very little historical material through which to follow Jesus' footprints. The intention of the Gospel writers was to express their faith in Jesus, to share their experience of him, and to emphasize the newness and validity of his message.

29 We know that Jesus' ministry began when he was baptized by John in the Jordan River, and that it ended with his death on a cross outside of Jerusalem. The baptism and death of Jesus, told in each of the four Gospels, puts us on firmer historical ground regarding when Jesus' public ministry began and ended. The Gospels also make it clear that from the beginning of his ministry, Jesus' activities and message awoke admiration, fascination, and enthusiasm, even though they also provoked rumors, rejection, rage, and hate.

30 To speak of a God who loved all people, especially sinners, challenged the Jewish conception of holiness and divine salvation. This led people to perceive Jesus as a false prophet. Furthermore, although it is not likely that Jesus described himself as the Messiah, his **eschatological** preaching, concerning the fulfillment of the promise of salvation, clearly led to messianic hope and a messianic movement. The inscription on the cross, "King of the Jews," noted by all four Gospel writers, indicates the reason he was condemned to die: for claiming to be the promised Messiah. According to Jewish Law, the appropriate punishment for false prophets was death; thus, the violent end to Jesus' life was a consequence of his ministry.

31 Then who was this Jesus of Galilee: a blasphemous, false, and rebellious prophet? Or the carrier of messianic salvation? Herod thought he was crazy, and even Jesus' closest relatives considered him insane. Some of his followers said that he was John the Baptist resurrected, while others thought he was Elijah, the prophet they awaited at the end of the world.

A Profile of Jesus

32 The unique, most characteristic, and most surprising thing about Jesus appears especially in his *way of acting.* Because he wanted

to show God to us as the Father of all persons, and to teach us to live as brothers and sisters, Jesus projected toward others the love of God that completely filled him. Jesus did not want anything for himself, but everything for others. This is why his behavior was so disconcerting for the Jews.

33 Among the most well established characteristics of Jesus' life, which led to admiration from his followers and discomfort and persecution from those who opposed his teachings, are the following:

- his humble origins, his invitation to persons from lower social classes to accompany him and eat with him, and his concern for the daily difficulties of poor people (while at the same time not rejecting rich people or expressing hatred toward them)
- his service to others and commitment to work
- his association with sinners and people considered ritually impure, to the extreme of seeking them out, offering them God's forgiveness and a new life, and becoming their friend
- his break with the rules of purity and the Jewish commandment to observe the Sabbath
- his respect for women: Jesus had female friends and accepted women as his disciples, which was uncommon during his time
- his special love for poor people and sick people, and his refusal to see poverty and illness as punishments from God

34 Jesus' way of acting can only be understood in connection with his message of God's Reign—that is, with his mission of extending the Reign of God and of trying to fulfill God's will for all to love one another as sisters and brothers. Jesus struggled to defeat the demonic powers of evil in people as well as in social institutions.

The Jesus of the Beatitudes

35 All the Gospels disclose a great deal about Jesus' personality, but the Sermon on the Mount in particular reveals the spirit that gave Jesus consistency as a person. Because he intensively lived out the Beatitudes, Jesus could speak of the happiness of those who embody them. Being a friend and a follower of Jesus means knowing him and identifying with him.

36 **Jesus chose to be economically poor and poor in spirit.** Jesus was an itinerant preacher who did not seek possessions that would tie him down and prevent him from fulfilling his mission. He was profoundly humble in recognizing that he existed through God's

love and that the fruit of his work depended on God. He was not possessive in his love, but loved other people to give them life and to make them participants in his mission.

37 **Jesus was sensitive to pain.** Jesus suffered loneliness, misunderstandings, and frustration. He cried at the tomb of Lazarus, was saddened by the impending destruction of Jerusalem, and felt the pain of betrayal by one of his disciples. In the midst of these struggles, Jesus found consolation in God, who provides meaning in the face of pain, offers tranquillity in confronting tragedy, and allows hope to prevail.

38 **Jesus was patient.** Jesus projected God's gentleness through his attitude of respect, service, and mercy toward human weakness and conflict. His patience was rooted in his recognition that he was penetrating people's hearts, in his strength in confronting adversity, and in his confidence that—in spite of all signs to the contrary—the Reign of God was being born amidst the many people who accepted his call to conversion.

39 **Jesus was a man with infinite love and a hunger for justice.** Throughout his travels, Jesus acted according to God's plan—forgiving those who repented, denouncing oppression, seeking the conversion of people, and trying to put resources, power, and the Law at the service of people, especially poor and marginalized people. Jesus' greatest desire was for his people to appreciate the gifts they had been given and not to allow their own egoism or the wisdom of the world to prevent them from realizing the Reign of God.

40 **Jesus was compassionate.** Jesus shared other people's pain because he made himself vulnerable to their problems, failures, sufferings, and sins. His compassion was active and creative, he did not simply lament people's pain or resign himself to accepting human misery. He tried to defeat evil with good: he helped people rebuild their personalities and their lives, he gave life to those who had lost it, and he healed the ill and forgave sinners.

41 **Jesus was pure-hearted.** Jesus encountered God in himself, in creation, and in people, without making idols of any of them. This pure-heartedness led him to fully identify with and share his Father's glory after having defeated, through his Resurrection, the evil and sin of humanity.

42 **Jesus was a person of peace.** Jesus possessed a complete and profound interior peace flowing from his communion with his Father and from the tranquillity that accompanies fulfilling God's will. Furthermore, Jesus actively promoted peace by struggling for justice, knowing how essential justice is in creating a reign of harmony and love among all people.

43 **Jesus was an authentic and committed person.** Jesus gave testimony of God through his daily life and his unyielding struggle for the Reign of God. With faith and hope, he accepted the consequences of his struggle. Instead of choosing to rule people, he chose to live in solidarity with all people, to serve people. Thus, Jesus made enemies among the authorities who marginalized, scorned, and exploited those under them. Jesus responded to his calling not only by confronting evil and injustice but by dying at the hands of others for the sake of God's cause.

44 Jesus lived so intensely and meaningfully during the last three years of his life that with his praxis he managed to change the direction of history. A handful of people—energized by Jesus, his message, and his project—extended his work so successfully that day by day, through two thousand years, millions of people have taken Jesus as the foundation and goal of their life.

Jesus' Mission and Praxis

45 Jesus took interest in one thing only: the arrival of God's Reign in love, the convergence of God's action and the history of humanity. *This was his mission.* Jesus had no program; he had nothing planned or organized about his ministry. Jesus discovered his mission in and through daily events, as he went along discerning God's will within the diverse situations and circumstances of his personal life and the lives of others.

46 Jesus did God's will as soon as he recognized it, in the here and now of his life, with a trust similar to that of a child. His praxis consisted precisely in doing God's will. This was beautifully expressed in his prayer to his Father, which nourished his deepest roots. Jesus is not simply a man who lived for others, but a man *of* God and *for* God. So in order to see the mystery of Jesus, we must look at his mission and his praxis. To do this, we need to take a

theological perspective that allows us to discover God's design for Jesus' life. Without this perspective, it is easy to fall into a narrow, distorted, or false understanding of Jesus' personality and ministry.

Jesus and the Dynamic of Love in Salvation History

47 We can assume that Jesus was a member of John the Baptist's movement, and that he accepted John's eschatological message. But clearly, Jesus' life and message were significantly different from John's. In contrast to John, who lived a life of self-denial apart from the world, Jesus approached people and lived among them. For Jesus, the world is God's creation and the things of the world are good gifts for humanity.

48 Jesus preached in terms similar to those of John the Baptist, but he began his own very different ministry. While John preached that the arrival of God's Reign would be characterized by the final judgment, Jesus proclaimed and emphasized God's love and compassion for sinners. Jesus' central theme is not final judgment, but the Beatitudes. His message is one of joy and hope: He offers God's compassion and mercy in the midst of pain and sinfulness here on earth. He offers as well the definitive grace of eternal life with God.

49 From the beginning of salvation history, God revealed Sacred Mystery to the people for the benefit of all. God's commandments, especially the love commandments, are given within this general framework. The essence of God's will, expressed initially in the covenant with Moses and more fully through Jesus, is that we love God and other persons. In Jesus, the love commandment becomes total and absolute; it responds to the abundance of compassion and mercy in God's love, a love that makes the sun rise on the good and the evil. The love commandment is so demanding that Jesus asks us to love all people, including our enemies. The revolution that Jesus brought is the implantation of love without boundaries throughout a world that yearns to love and be loved, but that is easily carried away by egoism and power.

50 Jesus, like all who love, wants to heal his loved ones' wounds of suffering. In order to revolutionize the world, he chose the way of love, service, and reconciliation. Jesus' miracles and exorcisms also belong in this context of love: they illustrate the arrival of God's Reign in Jesus and are signs of God's unconditional offer of salvation to all persons who repent and believe. Love conquers evil and,

in doing so, overcomes it and creates the possibility of a new beginning.

51 Doing God's will fills Jesus totally. Many of his sayings disclose a radical demand and a fundamental commitment to fulfill his mission of offering to humanity the redemptive love of God. This concern leads him to "abandon everything," to leave his family and his home. Yet Jesus was no religious fanatic. Unlike the Pharisees who thought they could satisfy their religious obligations by maintaining orthodox purity regarding ritual practices, Jesus centered his understanding of God's law on *love;* he freed people from the heavy weight of ritual laws. In contrast to the Sadducees, who represented the "liberal" tendency of the time, Jesus remained faithful to the fundamental beliefs of the Jewish faith. In contrast to the Zealots, who promoted armed revolution, Jesus promoted peace and used nonviolent means to achieve it.

Jesus Relates to God as His Father

52 Jesus was a young man of prayer who nourished his faith through the Scriptures, through an abiding hope in the fulfillment of God's promises, and through his love for his neighbors. In prayer, Jesus learned to relate to God as Father. The concept of God as Father was not common among the Jews, who ordinarily treated God as Creator, Judge, Liberator, and Protector, but not as Father. Calling God "Father" expresses a close personal relationship of love that liberates people from all anxieties.

53 As Jesus matured in his relationship with his Father, he gradually recognized that the relationships around him did not reflect the mind and heart of his Father. Thus, Jesus discovered his own vocation of leading others to accept God as Father and to treat one another as brothers and sisters.

54 Luke, in narrating Jesus' baptism, indicates that the Holy Spirit descended on Jesus and marked him as the beloved Son of God, the One chosen by God. Following Jesus' baptism and return from the Jordan, the Spirit led Jesus into the desert. During his time in the desert, Jesus gained a clearer awareness of his mission. Prayer, fasting, and the severity of desert life helped him defeat the temptations that confronted him: using power for his own benefit; reducing his interest only to the materialistic aspects of life, without seeking to be nurtured by God; and renouncing God's plan by seeking worldly fame and fortune.

55 The Gospels show Jesus frequently at prayer, especially at crucial moments and before and after important actions. On some occasions, Jesus prayed alone and in silence. At other times, he prayed with his disciples. Jesus clearly taught that prayer should occur in intimacy with God, who sees the secrets of our heart. Jesus' prayer was a prayer of silence, of surrender and trust in the will of God, and of identification with God.

56 Jesus' life of prayer must have impressed his disciples, because they asked him to teach them to pray. Jesus taught them the prayer we now know as the Lord's Prayer, which is not only a concrete prayer but also an expression of the attitude that should dominate our life. That attitude is one of striving to live continuously in God's presence and of dedicating time for prayer, for being with and listening to God and sharing with God our worries and yearnings. This prayerful commitment lies at the heart of evangelization, because prayer facilitates God's action in us and moves us to greater faithfulness to God's loving plan for all humanity.

Jesus, Prophet of the Reign of God

57 Long before Jesus' appearance, the majority of the Jewish people awaited a Messiah sent by God who would liberate them from the power of the Roman Empire and make them a powerful and prosperous nation. Only a small group, the "faithful remnant," knew that the promised Messiah would renew God's people by writing the law in their hearts, as the prophet Ezekiel had said.

58 In Jesus' day, teaching was in the hands of priests, scribes, and rabbis, who were considered experts in the Law and who taught their own interpretations and applications, forming different schools of thought. Jesus carried out many activities similar to those of the scribes: he taught a circle of disciples and argued over interpretations of the Law, and people came to him for consultation regarding legal questions. Undoubtedly, Jesus had not studied theology and was not ordained, which were prerequisites for being a scribe. Jesus was not a theologian; he spoke in simple terms, dynamically and directly. When his disciples addressed him as "Rabbi," they were not giving him the title of theologian or professor. Rather, they were using this word as a common expression referring to wise people who passed their wisdom on to others.

59 The common people immediately saw the difference between Jesus and the theological and legal experts around them. Jesus taught with his own authority, while the experts drew their teachings from the traditions of their schools. Jesus' authority was prophetic authority. The newness of his message about the Reign of God and about norms for living surprised everyone. His emphasis was not on maintaining the tradition of the schools, but on communicating the authentic message of God and inducing people to accept it.

60 Prophets also taught, but the word of God they passed on was not based exclusively on tradition; rather, they received their teachings directly from God within the historical context in which they lived. In contrast to other teachers, prophets emphasized God's covenant with his people, exhorted them to conversion, promised a better life if they truly converted, and did not focus on law and ritual.

61 The best description of Jesus is that he was a prophet: His disciples considered him a prophet, he put himself in the role of prophet, and he was accused and condemned to death for being a false prophet. However, because Jesus said that John the Baptist himself was more than a prophet, and that the least important in the kingdom of heaven is greater than John the Baptist (Matt. 11:9–11), it is clear that not even the category of prophet can adequately describe Jesus of Galilee.

62 When Jesus began to announce the coming of the Reign of God, he spoke first and foremost to the common people, who yearned for a just king who would defend and protect the weak, the oppressed, the abandoned, and the poor. In the beginning of his ministry, Jesus proclaimed that the covenant and the new life promised by the prophets were now being fulfilled in him and in his message, as Luke describes in his Gospel:

> He unrolled the scroll and found the place where it was written:
>
> "The Spirit of the Lord is upon me,
> because he has anointed me
> to bring good news to the poor.
> He has sent me to proclaim release to the captives
> and recovery of sight to the blind,
> to let the oppressed go free,
> to proclaim the year of the Lord's favor."

> And he rolled up the scroll, gave it back to the attendant, and sat down. The eyes of all in the synagogue were fixed on him. Then he began to say to them, "Today this scripture has been fulfilled in your hearing." (4:16–21)

63 For three years, Jesus traveled tirelessly throughout his land, proclaiming the Good News and calling people to reconciliation with God. Like other prophets before him, Jesus denounced injustices and abuses of the Law and urged people to share their possessions with those who had none. Jesus invited people to leave everything they had and follow him. And he asked his disciples to love their enemies, share their goods, seek peace, and respond to evil with goodness.

64 Jesus knew that his Father's cause was humanity's cause, so Jesus gave primacy to persons rather than to the Law or the Temple. Also, in confronting the abusive and unjust religious and political structures of his time, Jesus was inviting people to transform themselves and their world in building the Reign of God on earth. Jesus clearly stated how people reach the Reign of God in his discourse on the last judgment:

> Then the king will say to those at his right hand, "Come, you that are blessed by my Father, inherit the kingdom prepared for you from the foundation of the world; for I was hungry and you gave me food, I was thirsty and you gave me something to drink, I was a stranger and you welcomed me, I was naked and you gave me clothing, I was sick and you took care of me, I was in prison and you visited me." Then the righteous will answer him, "Lord, when was it that we saw you hungry and gave you food, or thirsty and gave you something to drink? And when was it that we saw you a stranger and welcomed you, or naked and gave you clothing? And when was it that we saw you sick or in prison and visited you?" And the king will answer them, "Truly I tell you, just as you did it to one of the least of these who are members of my family, you did it to me." (Matt. 25:34–40)

65 Matthew tries to express more fully the nature of Jesus by using intensified comparisons to others, saying that Jesus was greater than Jonah and greater than Solomon (Matt. 12:41–42). This "greater than" carries an eschatological connotation. Jesus is not

just another prophet in the long line of prophets. Rather, he is the eschatological prophet, the one who brings the ultimate word of God—God's definitive will. Jesus is full of God's Spirit. In Jesus, we finally encounter God face-to-face. The life of Jesus, and therefore our encounter with Jesus, is the only way that we can answer the question, Who is God?

Jesus Proclaimed the Reign of God

66 We know that Jesus' central message, as well as the goal of all his actions, was the arrival of the Reign of God on earth and the promise of enjoying eternal life with God. Through his message and his way of living, Jesus showed that to make the Reign of God possible, we must act toward one another as God acts toward us—by loving without measure and behaving justly to all.

67 When Jesus proclaimed the Reign of God, he announced the establishment of a new covenant between God and the people. This new covenant implies being led by the mind and heart of God and recognizing God as the Lord of history. That is, the Reign of God begins in freely accepting Jesus, his message, and his mission; in repenting from evil and changing sinful attitudes; and in following Jesus' teachings. Jesus also made it clear that the Reign of God was already present in people and that it would arrive in fullness at the end of time.

68 In the Gospels, Jesus often explains different aspects of the Reign of God through parables—that is, through stories that have a message or a key moral. He describes the Reign of God as a mustard seed that grows until it becomes a leafy tree in which birds can nest. In portraying the Reign of God as a seed that develops through God's action, Jesus notes that the growth of the seed depends on the quality of the land and must not be suffocated by weeds or killed by a lack of roots. Jesus also compares the Reign of God with a treasure hidden in a field; when the treasure is discovered, the discoverer sells everything in order to have it.

69 Through all these parables, Jesus clearly shows that God expects and needs our cooperation to make the Reign of God a reality. Jesus, in the parable of the great feast (Luke 14:15–24), likens his proclamation of the Reign of God to an invitation to a great feast: people have a choice; they must choose whether they will accept the invitation (that is, be part of the Reign of God). Reconciling

people to God will not be achieved by simply asking that justice, peace, and love reign. We have to work so that God reigns in people's hearts and in society's goals.

70 The Reign of God is manifest today in persons, communities, and societies that share their goods with those who experience misery and vulnerability. Jesus often spoke about having and using money, power, and prestige. He asked his followers to choose God over money. And through discourses and parables (like the parable about the rich man and Lazarus the beggar), Jesus emphasized the consequences of ignoring poor people.

71 The Reign of God also becomes present today in service to others. Jesus denounced all those who wanted to gain status or stand out at the cost of others, and he asked his disciples not to occupy positions of privilege but to serve people. Because this spirit of service was hard to understand, Jesus enacted his message by washing his disciples' feet at the Last Supper.

Jesus Challenged the Law and the Religious Authorities

72 Jesus respected the Law of Moses, but he condemned excesses and misinterpretations of the Law and placed his own authority in opposition to such excesses. Frequently, the priests and scribes of Jesus' time allowed themselves to be guided more by the letter of the Law than by its spirit, pushing God's covenant with the people out of the center of religious life. At the same time, these priests and scribes demanded fulfillment of the many rules and rituals that had been added to the Law of Moses over time, some of which only further burdened people who were already struggling and marginalized, such as women, poor people, and sinners.

73 Some religious men and women used their time in the Temple to assuage their conscience. They felt consoled and confident in God's presence, but at times they paid no attention to the demands of the covenant. Certain priests, Pharisees, and scribes who worshiped at the Temple felt sure that they possessed truth and perfection, but they ignored the abuse of poor people and showed no mercy toward sinners. Many religious people so valued the Temple and outward signs of holiness that they forgot the real origin of people's basic holiness—their creation in the image of God.

74 At the same time, money changers even used the Temple for business. Jesus, in seeing these various people and situations, reacted angrily by throwing out the money changers, denouncing the

Pharisees' hypocrisy and neglect of justice, and exhorting people to be pure and clean within, not just in outward things.

75 Jesus knew that none of God's children should ever be manipulated, oppressed, or marginalized by the Law, for God's law is the law of love. So Jesus radically opposed laws that harmed humans or human solidarity. He also made his position clear through his actions: eating publicly with sinners; curing people on the Sabbath (the day consecrated to Yahweh); speaking with and physically touching outcast, "unclean" people (such as people with leprosy); and choosing simple, unassuming people as his disciples.

76 Jesus clarified both the Law and the Covenant for the Jewish people; he reordered the commandments and specified that the principal law is the law of love. He insisted that love of God be lived out in relation to one's neighbors—all one's sisters and brothers—and be made manifest in a life of justice, mercy, and faith. This new law aspired to and carried people toward the perfection of God.

Jesus Acted in Solidarity with Poor People and Sinners

77 Jesus proclaimed the Reign of God to all persons, especially to poor people and sinners, who were the least in the eyes of the religious authorities of the time but the greatest in the heart of God. From the beginning of his ministry, Jesus showed his solidarity with common people, such as farmers, fishers, shepherds, and other laborers, and with public sinners, such as prostitutes and tax collectors. In addition to treating all these people with care and dedication, Jesus so deeply identified with their needs and desires that he took up their cause and confronted priests, judges, tax collectors, teachers of the Law, and Pharisees.

78 Jesus did not tolerate discrimination of any kind. He ate publicly with sinners, and those who repented their sins and accepted the Good News were blessed in God's sight. Jesus did not neglect or ignore sin or human problems; instead, he dedicated himself to giving new life to people—loving them, healing them, forgiving them, and seeking justice for them. By acting in solidarity with poor and marginalized persons, with compassion toward those who suffer, and with mercy to sinners, Jesus moved against the current and challenged others to do so as well.

79 Jesus was not a smooth or diplomatic person. His denunciations and public accusations made those in power uncomfortable.

His demands caused some of his disciples to abandon him. Both his followers and his enemies knew that his death resulted from his identification with poor people and from the threat he posed to the Pharisees' interpretation of the Law. But Jesus' solidarity with poor people was not the only form of solidarity he lived out.

80 Jesus, God incarnate, God-become-flesh, lived a life of solidarity with all humanity, even to the point of death. As a human being, Jesus shared people's feelings and emotions. Thus, near the time of his death, Jesus cried out in a loud tone: "'My God, my God, why have you forsaken me?'" (Matt. 27:46). In his perfect humanity, Jesus gave himself over to God with complete abandon and absolute confidence. Jesus' last words give witness not only to his absolute confidence in God but also to his solidarity with all humans in accepting his death: "'Father, into your hands I commend my spirit'" (Luke 23:46).

Jesus Called and Sent His Disciples to Extend the Reign of God

81 Jesus began his ministry as a traveling preacher who announced the Reign of God from town to town, speaking to people in images that addressed the heart and in words understood by every person of goodwill. Very soon, a group of disciples began to form around him.

82 Jesus' teaching was creative and radical. His impact as a teacher remains so strong that two thousand years later, millions of people want to be his disciples. Jesus' only criterion in choosing disciples was to distinguish between those who heard and those who did not hear—in other words, between those who received his message and those who ignored it. Jesus did not care about the intellectual capacity or the socioeconomic status of his followers. His only concerns were their openness to the Reign of God, their loyalty to him as a teacher, their commitment to following his teachings, and their willingness to collaborate in his mission. Jesus' impact as a teacher resulted from his radical message and teaching methods.

83 From among his disciples, Jesus chose a group of persons called "the Twelve" and commissioned them to carry on his mission of proclaiming the Good News, teaching, making disciples of all nations, and baptizing and reconciling people. Because the Gospels frequently identify the Twelve as the Apostles, however, we

sometimes fail to recognize that the Christian Scriptures also speak of other apostles and disciples sent out to proclaim the Good News. In his writings, Saint Paul speaks broadly about the nature of the apostolate, which consists of being sent out to proclaim the victory of Jesus over death. The Gospel of Luke relates that the first persons to proclaim the Risen Jesus were women. Thus, the term *apostle* can be understood to mean disciples other than the Twelve, and it can be applied as fittingly to modern people as to the people Jesus himself commissioned.

84 The meaning of the term *apostle* is very similar to the meaning of the term *prophet.* Both terms refer to persons sent by God to proclaim the message of salvation and to call people to conversion. Today, pastoral agents and young people who are active members of the church are called as apostles to evangelize Latino young people and young adults.

Encountering the Risen Jesus

85 The foundation of Christian faith lies in recognizing Jesus as both truly human and truly divine. Jesus was far more than just a gifted prophet, leader, and teacher. His disciples, even his closest disciples, knew him first solely as a human person. Only after the Resurrection, after encountering the Risen Jesus and being transformed by the Holy Spirit, would the disciples truly know Jesus as God.

The Easter Experience

86 Jesus' disciples, the civil and religious authorities of Jesus' day, and the Jewish people as a whole believed that when Jesus died, his vision and mission died with him. Instead, a new life began, and Jesus' vision and mission were made more complete. Through his death and Resurrection, Jesus permanently reconciled human beings with God and established the Reign of God as a reality for all people.

87 Jesus' death and Resurrection are not two separate events, but two complementary realities of the one Easter mystery. The image of Jesus' Resurrection after his death on the cross can sometimes overshadow Jesus' glorification and his going to the Father, where he is seated at God's right hand. Seen together, these events show

that Jesus' rising was not a resuscitation, like the raising of Lazarus or the son of the widow of Nain, both of whom returned to life but would die again. Rather, Jesus, with his Resurrection, began a glorious new life that has no end.

88 The death and Resurrection of Jesus are two key moments in his mission of redemption. His death resulted from his action for the Reign of God, and his Resurrection was the firstfruit of the eternal fullness of the Reign of God. In writing the Gospels, the Evangelists did not try to explain the Resurrection, but to share the disciples' experience of the Risen Jesus. So powerful was the experience of the Risen Jesus that it transformed the disciples from a weakly joined, disillusioned, and fearful group into a community of courageous witnesses willing to continue Jesus' mission.

89 Just as the Reign of God lay at the heart of Jesus' Gospel, the Risen Jesus lies at the heart of the Good News proclaimed by his disciples. Without this conviction, the Christian message makes no sense. Saint Paul's image of the Mystical Body of Christ shows that Jesus, as a person, exists at the same time within God and within the Christian community. Paul's image also shows that there is an uninterrupted continuity from the Jesus of Galilee to the resurrected Christ to the church as the body of the living Jesus, who acts and is present in history.

90 In being baptized as Christians, we have been immersed in the paschal mystery. We have been made one with Jesus by the work of the Holy Spirit. By being buried with Jesus, we have died to sin; by being raised with him, we have been reborn to eternal life with God. The sacrament of reconciliation inserts us in this same mystery whenever we need to re-establish or revitalize our union with God and with our sisters and brothers. In the Eucharist, we celebrate the paschal mystery in a special way: we sacramentally commemorate Jesus' human life, his death, and his Resurrection. Also, we encounter Jesus alive in the Christian community united in the Spirit. By sharing Jesus' body and blood, the community is renewed and strengthened to continue its faith journey.

Jesus Alive in the Church Community

91 In the Gospels, the Risen Jesus brings inspiration and amazement to his disciples, whom he sends out to carry the Good News to others. The proclamation and spread of the Resurrection news by

eyewitnesses situates Jesus within history in a new way and forever authenticates his mission. And just as Jesus was sent to fulfill a mission of redemption, the Holy Spirit was sent to the Christian community to continue that mission in every generation—beginning with the disciples at Pentecost.

92 As the first Christian communities lived out and deepened their faith in the experiences of Easter and Pentecost, they deepened their relationship with God. They recognized that they related in distinct ways to three persons of a trinitarian God: the Father, the Son, and the Holy Spirit. Little by little, the first Christians realized that they related to the Father as their creator and destination in life; to Jesus Christ as a brother and as the way to the Father; and to the Holy Spirit as the One sent by the Father and Son to unite, illuminate, and support the Christian community in its task of extending the Reign of God on earth. In this way, the early Christians' daily lives were both an experience of and a preparation for the enjoyment of eternal life with God.

93 The early Christians' yearning to share their faith with all people led the disciples to develop a method of evangelization with five basic elements:

1. proclamation of the Good News, *kerygma* in Greek
2. profession of their faith, in a creed
3. baptism into the Christian faith, carried out in the name of the Father, the Son, and the Holy Spirit
4. celebration of the Christian experience in the Eucharist
5. the sharing and deepening of the theological and moral teachings of Christianity through catechesis

94 By about 70 C.E., the early Christian communities had collected various letters written by the Apostles, particularly by Saint Paul, in which the Apostles shared their experiences and reinforced their teachings about Jesus. In addition, the early Christians had traditions and written accounts of Jesus' words and actions, and of the various ways each community discerned Jesus' living presence. The writers of what today is known as the Christian Testament drew upon these communal memories in order to express Christian faith in Jesus and his mission.

Emmaus: A Way of Hope

95 Although during his life Jesus shared the meaning of his messiahship and mission with his disciples, his disciples did not fully understand or internalize this meaning. Thus, when Jesus was being crucified, the majority of his disciples abandoned him. When he rose again, believing in him was difficult—even for the Apostles. The Emmaus account in the Gospel of Luke (24:13–35), about the appearance of the Risen Jesus to two of his disciples, captures not only the essence of Jesus' Good News but also the essence of how Christians are to follow Jesus in this world.

Fleeing Away

96 In Luke's account, two of Jesus' disciples were traveling from Jerusalem to the village of Emmaus, on the first day of the week following Jesus' Crucifixion. For the disciples, Jerusalem symbolized failure and danger, the scandal of the cross, and the death of their hopes. Emmaus represented a return to a safe routine, which seemed boring and void of meaning. They walked along in sadness, sharing the frustration that resulted when their faith and hope in Jesus crumbled.

97 Then another traveler joined the two disciples and asked what they were speaking about. The disciples told the traveler about Jesus of Nazareth, his death, how their hopes had died with Jesus, and how they were confused by stories that some people had seen Jesus alive. The traveler responded that they were not understanding what had happened because of their lack of faith in what the prophets had proclaimed—that the Messiah would have to suffer before entering into his glory. Then the traveler began to interpret the Scriptures for the two disciples so that they might understand what had happened.

98 The traveler, of course, was Jesus, who had come looking for his disciples. Why did he look for them? Had they not doubted his Resurrection and decided to return to their previous lives? What good could it do to speak with them if they were so disillusioned that they had lost their trust in Jesus and his mission? Would it not have been better to leave them in peace and look for other, better disciples? In any case, why begin by asking them about their own

experience? Would it not have been better to explain to them their error and clearly tell them what they should think and do?

The Encounter with Jesus

99 Throughout his journey and conversation with the two disciples, Jesus offered neither directives nor sermons. And he treated the disciples as friends, listening to them and helping them to interpret their personal experiences and the signs of the times. The disciples in turn accepted the sincere friendship offered by this fellow traveler, even though he was a stranger, and they began to feel a new ***cariño*** toward this mysterious friend.

100 Thus, when evening approached and Jesus took leave of them, they insisted: "'Stay with us, because it is almost evening and the day is now nearly over'" (Luke 24:29). So Jesus stayed with them. The disciples showed Jesus the same welcome and receptivity to strangers that he had taught them long ago. Finally, when Jesus took bread, blessed and broke it, and offered it to them, the disciples recognized him. As soon as the disciples recognized him, Jesus disappeared.

The Way of Commitment

101 Jesus had left something new in the hearts of the two disciples. They were no longer sad nor empty. "They said to each other, 'Were not our hearts burning within us while he was talking to us on the road, while he was opening the scriptures to us?'" (Luke 24:32). Their encounter with the Risen Jesus had filled the disciples with his Spirit and so transformed them that they returned at once to Jerusalem to give witness to the living Jesus.

102 As pastoral agents and evangelizers, we need to have the same attitude that Jesus had. We must imitate Jesus when we encounter young people who have little faith and hope, whose hearts seem empty and whose lives seem meaningless, or who are closed up in self-centeredness or are prisoner to easy routine, vice, or corruption. We must see the good, the idealistic in young people, and speak to encourage that. We must seek young people out to dialog with them on the basis of their experiences. We must share friendship and the word of God with them, infusing their hearts with the life of God. And finally, we must leave them strong enough and committed enough to follow in our footprints as evangelizers.

103 It is true that this work requires organization, resources, and processes for evangelization. But above all, there is an urgent need for missionaries—young people and adults who, as Jesus' disciples, will go wherever young people can be found and who, through their Christian love, will awaken in young people trust in the Risen Jesus.

104 In finding happiness, peace, and inspiration in their encounters with God's missionaries, evangelized young people will then become new witnesses of Jesus, the risen fellow traveler. Their encounters with Jesus and the warmth of the Spirit of God in their hearts will lead more and more young people everywhere to cry out in hope, following the call of Jesus:

> "Go therefore and make disciples of all nations, baptizing them in the name of the Father and of the Son and of the Holy Spirit, and teaching them to obey everything that I have commanded you. And remember, I am with you always, to the end of the age." (Matt. 28:19–20)

5

The Evangelizing Action of God, the Evangelizers, and the Evangelized

5

The Evangelizing Action of God, the Evangelizers, and the Evangelized

The Church's mission is three-fold: to proclaim the good news of salvation; to offer itself as a group of people transformed by the Spirit into a community of faith, hope, and love; and to bring God's justice and love to others through service in its individual, social and political dimensions.

—United States Catholic Conference,
A Vision of Youth Ministry

1 This chapter focuses on the evangelization of Hispanic young people and young adults. It begins by presenting briefly some fundamental truths about evangelization. It then reflects on three necessary components of all evangelizing activities: the action of God's grace, the action of the evangelizers as members of the faith community, and the response of those being evangelized. It points out the most important elements and phases of evangelical action, suggests some practical steps for facilitating evangelization, and focuses on personal conversion.

Some Fundamental Truths About Evangelization

2 Evangelization is a continuous, mysterious, great—and yet humble—labor. Evangelization is rooted in the mystery of God. How and when God reaches each person lies beyond the knowledge of any evangelizer, for only God knows the day and time each person will come to know God. *Evangelization depends essentially on the grace of God.*

3 Through the church, the Mystical Body of Christ formed by Jesus' followers, God brings love and salvation to all people. God trusts that each community, as moved by the Spirit, will carry the Good News to all people. And as Mary and the other disciples experienced long ago at Pentecost, God fills people with the grace and the gifts that they need to fulfill their mission. All evangelizers

need to be part of a community of faith in which they are continually strengthened by the Holy Spirit. *Evangelization occurs only from within the church community.*

4 God works through normal, everyday people who, recognizing their faults and limitations, are humble and completely willing to collaborate with God. Such was the case of Peter and Paul, Francis and Clare of Assisi, Teresa of Ávila, Theresa of the Child Jesus, Ignatius of Loyola, Francis Xavier, Martin de Porres, and countless others—religious and laypeople alike—who have carried Jesus to the hearts of millions. *Action for evangelization occurs only when missionary men and women tenaciously dedicate their lives to proclaiming new life in Jesus.*

5 Evangelization is conditioned by the freedom to accept and respond to divine grace, a grace that is freely offered to us all as God's sons and daughters. God approaches people in many ways and asks them to respond in keeping with the grace that has been offered to them. Evangelizers do not know the manner in which God gives grace to another person, nor can evangelizers decide how another person should respond to God's gift of grace. Jesus instructed his disciples that if a house did not welcome them, they were to shake its dust from their shoes and continue forward in their missionary labor. *Evangelization does not exist unless the evangelized accept God's grace and experience conversion.*

6 For evangelization to be effective and to bring about justice, love, and peace in the lives of people, the positive aspects of the four preceding truths must be present within an overall framework of **inculturation.** When these positive aspects are present, people will be able to do the following: make use of all the gifts given by God to their culture; express and share their faith; question any cultural values, philosophies, and ideologies opposed to the Gospel; and be a transforming force within structures and institutions that impede the Reign of God. *All evangelization requires inculturation on the parts of the evangelizer and the evangelized.*

7 The action of God's grace reaches persons (the evangelized) through the evangelizing action of the church (the evangelizing community) and its members (the evangelizers). The circle becomes complete when the evangelized are converted, grow as members of the faith community, embody the Gospel in their culture, and carry out their own evangelizing mission.

The Action of God's Grace

8 God's life-giving and saving grace reaches people through the creative action of the Father, the redeeming action of the Son, and the unifying and liberating action of the Holy Spirit. God is a community of love between the Father, the Son, and the Holy Spirit; this love reaches out to people in many ways, especially through the church community. To these ways that God approaches humanity, there are corresponding evangelizing methodologies that lead to a profound conversion of the lives of the evangelized.

The Action of the Holy Trinity

9 The God of Christians is a communion of the essential and eternal love of the three divine persons. This love spills over from the internal life of God to human persons, generating in us an eager desire for communion within our families and within society. The love of this triune God is present in all individuals and peoples.

10 True evangelizers live consciously immersed in this communion with God and find there the reason and motivation for sharing the Good News of Jesus with other people. Indeed, as the Second Vatican Council concluded, the evangelizing mission of the church is an expression of God's love:

> The pilgrim Church is missionary by her very nature. For it is from the mission of the Son and the mission of the Holy Spirit that she takes her origin, in accordance with the decree of God the Father.
>
> This decree flows from "that fountain of love" or charity within God.[1]

11 Evangelizers look for signs of the presence of the Father, Son, and Holy Spirit in other people's lives and try to help people discover this presence. Among young Latinos and their families, God is present in many ways—in their communitarian spirit, in their yearning for love and understanding, in their desire to serve, and in their hope for a culture of sharing and peace. Evangelizers should help young people discover this presence of God in and among themselves, in order to constantly create more places of communion and participation for young people in the church community and to promote their equal integration into society.

The Action of a Creating God

12 God, who is life itself, is the source of life for the whole universe, with its great natural diversity, its evolutionary laws, and its reproductive processes. We human beings reveal, in a special way, the creative action of God. God created us so that we might be collaborators and cocreators with God; this divine action makes us givers of life—procreators of God's sons and daughters, who will continue God's work in the world. Thus, God's creating of us is a saving action, for by making us in the divine image, God makes us stewards of all creation. We are called to harness many natural forces to serve human needs and to alleviate the effects of catastrophes on humans and the rest of creation.

13 Young people receive God's creative grace from the beginning of their existence. But they become aware of God's action in their life only when they are evangelized. Evangelization of young people should awaken in them not only an awareness of the presence of God in their life and of their capacity and responsibility to be collaborators with God in God's creation, but also an awareness of their potential as procreators of new human beings.

The Liberating Action of the Holy Spirit

14 The Holy Spirit guides the course of human history, renews the face of the earth, and orients human life toward following God's will. The action of the Spirit continues Jesus' project over the course of history, making it possible for people to receive the Good News of salvation in their own language and according to their own need for liberation.

15 Wherever the Spirit is, there is freedom. This freedom is the gift of the Spirit to those who are oppressed or exploited by their own sins, by other persons, or by social institutions. The Spirit gives us light and strength for converting, resisting temptation, struggling against oppressive forces, being creative, and opening new paths toward God. Evangelizers facilitate the action of the Holy Spirit in and among young people to liberate in young people God's vitality, which is indispensable for people who want to give themselves to Jesus' mission.

The Action of Jesus, God Incarnate

16 God communicates love to people and makes it real among them through the Incarnation. The Word, eternal and universal, was incarnated in Jesus of Nazareth, who took on human nature and united the immanent (time-bound) dimension of human life and the transcendent (eternal) dimension of divine life. Through the Incarnation, God became visible, present "in the flesh," and active in human history. Jesus thus gave himself to all women and men, and he entered human history and culture so that we would be able to participate in God's love.

The Action of Jesus in the Evangelizers and the Evangelized

17 In imitating Jesus, those who evangelize young Latinos must do the following:

- proclaim that the Reign of God is among young people
- communicate the hope of eternal life with God
- make the Good News real by focusing on young people's concrete needs for justice, love, and peace
- generate a new way of life in which all people, including the young, are respected, valued, and treated with dignity
- struggle for a society in which young people and young adults will have real opportunities to attain their human and Christian development

All evangelization efforts must awaken young Latinos' awareness of the Incarnation, so that they recognize that God lives in them, that human experience and the life of God are not contradictory, and that God's fidelity asks for their fidelity as persons.

The Action of Jesus in the Church Community

18 God becomes present among persons of every time and place through Jesus risen in the church community. When young people feel the presence of the Risen Jesus and become aware that God is near to them, they discover their potential to be expressions of God's presence and to carry God to others. This occurs when young people encounter an evangelizing community in which Christians bear witness to Jesus as their friend, model, teacher, and center.

19 The Jesus of the church community is the Jesus who convinces and energizes young people, who helps them understand that they

cannot remain passive in the face of challenges. Welcoming, searching, uniting, committing—this is the Jesus who gives meaning to the sacraments and attracts young people and young adults to frequent participation in the Eucharist.

The Action of the Evangelizers as Members of the Faith Community

20 For young people to encounter Jesus and decide to follow him, they must hear others speak of him so that they can come to know and love him—not as an idea, but as a person. Young people need to identify themselves enough with Jesus that they can exclaim, with Paul: "It is no longer I who live, but it is Christ who lives in me" (Gal. 2:20). Making Jesus and his message this real involves two complementary kinds of action:

- presenting Jesus as a person who lives in the ecclesial community and acts through it
- using communication techniques that are adequate for effectively spreading the Good News

21 In the Gospel of John, evangelizers find a model for helping young people encounter Jesus:

- *They must proclaim Jesus* as John the Baptist did when Jesus passed by him: "'Look, here is the Lamb of God!'" (1:36). This proclamation should be made with clarity, directly naming Jesus and avoiding possible misinterpretation regarding the mystery of the Incarnation. The proclamation should also present Jesus without disfiguring, distorting, misrepresenting him; without converting him into a political leader, a revolutionary, or a simple prophet; without reducing him—the Lord of history—to a purely human level. At the same time, evangelizers should show Jesus sharing the life, hope, and anxieties of young people, thus emphasizing his solidarity with them.
- *They must stir up young people's enthusiasm for following Jesus,* as Jesus' cousin (John the Baptist) did:

> The two disciples heard [what John said], and they followed Jesus. When Jesus turned and saw them following him, he said to them, "What are you looking for?" They said to him, "Rabbi" (which translated means Teacher), "where are you stay-

> ing?" He said to them, "Come and see." They came and saw where he was staying, and they remained with him that day. (John 1:37–39)

To stir up young people's enthusiasm for following Jesus, evangelizers must help them encounter a living Jesus present and active in their personal and social lives.

- *They must help young people share the Gospel with others,* encouraging in all people the same enthusiasm the disciples showed:

> One of the two who heard John speak and followed [Jesus] was Andrew, Simon Peter's brother. He first found his brother Simon and said to him, "We have found the Messiah" (which is translated Anointed). He brought Simon to Jesus. . . . The next day Jesus decided to go to Galilee. He found Philip and said to him, "Follow me." . . . Philip found Nathanael and said to him, "We have found him about whom Moses in the law and also the prophets wrote, Jesus son of Joseph from Nazareth." (John 1:40–45)

The whole life of every Christian is essentially evangelical; in every moment, through their actions, attitudes, and words, Christians should make Jesus present and promote a culture of sharing and peace.

22 Like Jesus, the church offers the Good News in many ways, while also respecting the freedom of each person to give his or her own response to God. Jesus showed three different ways of evangelizing:

- carrying the Good News directly to other individuals through *interpersonal evangelization*
- inviting people to share the Reign of God in the community of Jesus' disciples through *communitarian evangelization*
- proclaiming the Good News to the multitudes through *evangelization of the multitudes*

23 Jesus combined all three evangelical styles: he directly addressed individual persons, he formed and taught a small group of disciples, and he preached to the multitudes. The parable of the sower (Matt. 13:1–23) is a good example not only of how Jesus evangelized people but of how he taught others about evangelization. Jesus told the parable to a large group of people, noted that

the seed must be sown through personal contact, and explained the meaning of the message in detail to the community of disciples.

24 In daily life, evangelization is achieved through personal contact, service, forgiveness, and compassion in the face of pain, as Christians share their faith and help their neighbors. In addition, evangelization happens through catechesis, liturgy, preaching, reflection sessions, and the media. Through whatever means, evangelization is intended to share, proudly and joyfully, the experience of God and the joy of being Christian.

25 Hispanic youth ministry should also use all three methods of evangelization. Certainly, evangelization in youth groups and in small communities of youth should be emphasized. Such groups are the heart that carries the Good News to the multitudes, the legs that go out to find young people who have not encountered God, and the arms that welcome into the Christian community those who seek the Reign of God.

Interpersonal Evangelization

26 A personal focus is essential in evangelization, either as the core of individual evangelization or as a dimension of communitarian evangelization. Interpersonal evangelization occurs first in the family, but it also occurs among friends, neighbors, classmates, coworkers, and whomever God places in our life path. Sometimes evangelization occurs by intentionally proclaiming the Good News; other times, perhaps more often, it occurs in a natural and spontaneous way as we share God's love and serve others.

27 The better we know people and their concerns, the easier it is to plant the seeds of the Gospel in their life; this "sowing" often happens among those who live near us. It is also easy to carry the Good News to people who need hope and help in order to move forward in their life. The evangelizer should approach those persons with the same spirit as Jesus, who treated people with love and tenderness, but who also respected their freedom. He did not prey upon their limitations or needs, nor did he manipulate or force them to follow him.

28 Interpersonal evangelization follows the model of the good shepherd, who knows his sheep by name and knows when they are hurt or have lost their way. When the good shepherd sees their ab-

sence, he goes to look for the lost sheep to bring them back to the fold and heal those who are hurt.

Communitarian Evangelization

29 The Christian community is the ideal place for fostering the human and religious growth of young people. The community is the fountain from which energy flows for building a world according to God's design. This community has various dimensions, from the great worldwide community of faith in Jesus Christ to the small cell of faith called the Christian family. The Catholic church recognizes many types of communities, among which the following stand out: the universal catholic community, dioceses, parishes, religious communities, **small ecclesial communities,** and families. Other ecclesial groups also exist, such as educational and social service institutions, apostolic movements, and groups of catechists and other ministers. The essential mission common to all these forms of ecclesial organization is to continue evangelizing their members and shaping their members as evangelizers. In addition, each group has its own particular function and goals, according to the nature of the organization.

30 To fulfill its evangelizing mission among young people, the church has created many kinds of organizations and communities. Currently, among Catholic young people in the United States, the following forms stand out for their numerical strength and their importance as sources of evangelization: parish youth groups, apostolic movements, **small communities of young people,** educational institutions, and campus ministry centers. Volume 1 analyzed the differences between a youth group and a youth community, and presented the characteristics and styles of evangelization appropriate to each of the five forms of youth organizations mentioned in the previous sentence. Here, the focus is exclusively on the dynamics common to all communitarian evangelization.

31 The first objective of communitarian evangelization is to facilitate young people's relationship with Jesus and to form a community among them. The second objective is to incorporate young people into the parish and diocesan communities. Within this framework, evangelizing action focuses on many interrelated activities:

- formation of Christian identity
- acquisition of evangelical attitudes and values
- education and maturation in the faith
- integration of faith with all of life
- discovery and strengthening of personal vocations
- active personal incorporation and participation in the different levels of church community
- promotion of Christian commitment
- development of spirituality

Without an active and ongoing process of evangelization, Catholics run the risk of being Christian in name only. No process of Christian maturation occurs, and evangelizing action by the church becomes more difficult.

32 Evangelization does not mean simply bringing young people and young adults into a group, movement, or community. Rather, it means facilitating the action of God's grace in all young people so that the Spirit can transform them into disciples of Jesus and prophets of the Reign of God. Through and within the community, young people can become instruments of God to create a culture of sharing and peace, and to become active agents of Hispanic people's liberation and development in the United States.

Evangelization of the Multitudes

33 Jesus evangelized massive groups of people on streets, in squares, out in the countryside, by lakes, and in the Temple and synagogues. Today, we need to carry the Good News to young people and young adults in parks, schools, stadiums, concerts, and theaters. Many young people experience God's love for them for the first time in mass events such as missions, encounters, and conventions; others hear about Jesus and his message through the media. Whatever the medium, young people's encounter with God's love helps them hear the liberating message of Jesus and experience for the first time the strength and unity of the Holy Spirit.

34 Mass evangelization usually occurs in three different forms: in liturgical celebrations, in ecclesial events, and in social events with evangelizing content. In whatever form it occurs, mass evangelization depends on five elements: the young people being open to receiving the message, the evangelizers knowing how to communicate the Good News, the environment facilitating the sharing of the

message, the content of the message being meaningful to the young people, and the experience being reinforced with follow-up evangelization.

35 **1. Young people's attendance at mass evangelization events:** Ensuring young people's attendance at religious events, whether these events are liturgical celebrations or large-scale gatherings, requires interpersonal or communitarian evangelization with young people before such events. It might be easier to present evangelizing messages to young people through mass communications without previous evangelization, but it would not be very effective. Young people will effectively hear these messages and be led to Jesus only if they have friends who guide them explicitly to Jesus and help them to internalize the messages. Otherwise, the messages fail to surpass the level of a vague humanism and probably do little more than create a corresponding vague religious restlessness.

36 **2. The communication of the message:** Successful proclamation of the Good News to the multitudes depends both on the talents and abilities of the speaker and on adequate and effective use of other means of mass communication, such as drama, group dynamics, and small-group reflections. The speaker's enthusiasm and speaking abilities count for so much in communicating a message to a large audience. On the other hand, a speaker's lack of enthusiasm or weak speaking abilities can create such frustration and boredom in young people that they avoid returning to any similar event. It is also very important for the speaker to avoid emotional manipulation of young people; this occurs with certain frequency in evangelistic congresses and concerts.

37 **3. A facilitating environment:** Establishing a favorable environment for a mass gathering is vital for two reasons: it creates a sense of welcome and it facilitates religious experience. Such an environment is achieved by using music, symbols, and rituals, and by creating a special spirit among the young people themselves. Like the speaker, the environment can be ill-suited or manipulative. If the environment is weak, young people lose interest in the message. If the environment is manipulative (amplified sound, music, and special lighting can have overpowering effects), a kind of mass psychosis may result; this can create exaggerated and false feelings of happiness, camaraderie, repentance, or fear among young people.

38 **4. A meaningful content to the message:** Although the content of the message is key in all types of evangelization, in mass evangelization the message's content plays an even greater role. The witness of Christian life that occurs in interpersonal or communitarian evangelization is far less existent in mass evangelization. As a result, stories or examples of instant conversions, miraculous healings, and other extraordinary interventions of God are often told in mass evangelization to awaken in young people the desire to follow Jesus. On certain extraordinary occasions, God clearly acts in miraculous or spectacular ways to give people new life, fortify their faith, or call them to a more authentic Christianity. But even these happenings require follow-up.

39 **5. Continuous evangelization:** The success of mass evangelization depends on its being continued and complemented by interpersonal evangelization and communitarian evangelization. Later accompaniment is indispensable to every mass evangelization effort. When unchurched young people attend a mass evangelization event, established members of youth groups and youth communities should be ready to invite them to a retreat or a youth encounter so that the new young people can join the group if they choose. In such groups and communities, new members can come to know Jesus and strengthen their beginning faith. Without follow-up, even an intense mass evangelization experience may become a moment that loses its impact over time.

Phases in Personal and Communitarian Evangelizing Action

40 Evangelization usually involves a process that follows certain phases, some of which overlap, imply one another, and continue throughout life. Evangelizers must be aware that not all young people pass through all these phases or do so in the same order or in the same way, because all young people are different and face life circumstances that affect them in different ways. In view of this, evangelizing action requires the evangelizer's special attention during the following phases:

41 1. **Giving testimony to the living presence of Jesus in the ecclesial community:** Giving testimony generally begins in childhood and intensifies in adolescence and young adulthood. The tasks of the ecclesial community are to draw in young people so that they feel part of the ecclesial community; to offer them a testimony of faith, hope, and love; and to establish a communitarian ethos in which ties of friendship, confidence, and mutual support can be forged.

42 2. **Establishing contact with young people:** To establish contact, the evangelizer must initiate a dialog with young people. This means seeking them out in the places where they live their daily lives, and gaining their confidence in order to establish a deeper relationship later. In seeking out these young people, the evangelizer must be motivated by a sincere interest in their lives and by a desire to find God in them.

43 3. **Developing a relationship as a companion or friend:** To achieve a relationship of companionship or friendship with young people, the evangelizer needs to speak personally with them about the things that interest them. Through these conversations, evangelizers must try to make possible a relationship that can grow and a dialog that can deepen, until it touches the most meaningful aspects of young people's lives.

44 4. **Inviting young people to get to know Jesus better:** The invitation to get closer to Jesus or to participate in the ecclesial community is usually accepted when companionship already exists between the evangelizer and the evangelized, or when the activity being offered is of interest to the one being evangelized. The invitation can be made through youth missions, home visits, or dialogs with young people in parks, schools, or workplaces.

45 Some young people and young adults want to attend Mass, participate in the sacrament of reconciliation, or speak with a priest; others get excited about attending a retreat, workshop, or conference; still others feel attracted to celebrations of **popular religiosity** such as the way of the cross, pilgrimages, or Ash Wednesday liturgies. Some youth want to explore the possibility of belonging to a youth group, and others are only willing to go to parties or to participate in sports or cultural activities.

46 In general, Hispanic young people will accept invitations to ecclesial events only if the person who invites them accompanies them to the event. Furthermore, young people's first encounter with the ecclesial community must be positive, or they will not return. Therefore, the youth community must maintain a strong spirit of hospitality and take care to provide a meaningful experience for prospective new members.

47 **5. Welcoming young people into the Christian community:** Hospitality provides the first experience of communitarian evangelization. Young people who attend a youth group or community for the first time hope to be received with enthusiasm, discover new friends, and experience a warm and trusting environment. Only when all members of the community make a new member feel at home can that person really feel part of the community.

48 Hospitality does not mean just having a reception committee that initially greets new members and then ignores them. All members of the group must display a welcoming spirit, and several group members should chat with the new members and then include the new members in group activities to help them see that they are important and that the group hopes they will keep coming. These actions should not be limited to new members' first meeting, but should continue until the new members themselves feel a part of the group and are comfortable welcoming those arriving for the first time.

49 **6. Incorporating and engaging young people in the community of disciples:** Young people experience God's call to them in many ways: through their desire to make good friends, to find a boyfriend or girlfriend, to have a place for healthy recreation, to seek support for living a Christian life, to satisfy their thirst for God and for better human and Christian formation. Whatever the reason, God's hand is at work in young people. Those who are drawn to the church know that they are going to a religious group and thus hope to find a sense of Christian community. When they encounter nothing more than a social group, they feel deeply let down.

50 Intense faith and authentic community in youth groups are vital for evangelization. Belonging to a group of young people committed to following Jesus and continuing his mission is the most important source of evangelization for many young people.

51 Young people's commitment to a community depends largely on their active participation in the group and on the quality of personal relationships that they form there. Therefore, young people must have opportunities to do the following:

- discuss their desires and concerns in an atmosphere of sincerity and trust
- reflect together on meaningful aspects of life
- work together to solve the problems they face, and offer one another adequate and timely advice
- accompany one another in their daily lives, especially as they struggle to achieve their ideals and as they share moments of crisis and joy
- help one another heal their emotional wounds and negative experiences, free themselves from oppression, and seek reconciliation with themselves, God, and others

52 **7. Encouraging young people to follow Jesus:** Evangelizers must help young people come to know the Gospels and discover Jesus—his mission, his message, and how he carries out his mission. Evangelizers must facilitate the Holy Spirit's work of giving birth to a faith that leads young people to Jesus, personal conversion, and a desire to share their faith journey with others. Young people need to learn from evangelizers what it means to live as disciples of Jesus. These goals are reached when pastoral work harmoniously combines prayer, catechesis, participation in the Eucharist, and moments of personal and communal reflection on life in the light of faith.

53 **8. Facilitating young people's growth into Christian maturity:** Christian maturity comes through a deeper and more complete knowledge of the faith and a more authentic living of Christian praxis. For young people to grow and mature as Christians, they must continuously deepen their baptismal commitment. Such a deepening occurs through these elements:

- catechesis that combines study and reflection on the faith tradition
- critical analysis of reality and continuous attempts to incarnate the Gospel message within that reality
- communal prayer and support for personal prayer
- spiritual direction or accompaniment
- reflection on experiences of evangelization and ministry

54 **9. Helping young people fulfill their mission:** Evangelizers have an important role in helping young people discover their own vocation, implement their life projects, and accept their communal commitment to the work of extending the Reign.

55 This dimension of evangelization focuses especially on young people's action in the world—through their daily lives, charitable activities, and participation in projects for social transformation. Some young people are further called to ecclesial ministry in addition to their mission in the world. Young people's experiences of mission and evangelization should be celebrated with commissioning ceremonies, liturgies concentrated on revitalizing pastoral efforts, and fiestas celebrating Christian action and commitment. These celebrations can be further ritualized by distributing crosses or other religious symbols that mark young people as missionaries among their peers.

56 **10. Motivating constant participation in eucharistic celebrations:** It is crucial that young people be encouraged to find meaning in the Eucharist, experiencing it as the following:

- the climactic moment in our celebration of the faith—that is, not as the only point at which we prayerfully, thankfully, and joyfully meet God acting in our life, but as the highest point in our broader encounters with God through daily prayer and celebration
- the center of our Christian life, which implies a Christian praxis in all areas of life (family, work, school, society, and church) before and after participation in the Eucharist

The Process of Personal Conversion

57 God's grace always respects our freedom to respond as we choose to God's love and calling to us. In the same way, evangelizers should respect the freedom of other people. Although evangelizers may introduce Jesus to young people and try to communicate to them the message of salvation, young people may not respond immediately to the Good News. This lack of response may result because it is not God's hour or because, making use of their freedom, young people ignore or reject the invitation to draw near to God. The responsibility of evangelizers is to sow the word of God as best they can and

to proclaim the Gospel always, for they never know when or how it will reach a person's heart.

58 How quickly and to what extent young people respond—that is, answer to the love of the Father, accept Jesus and his message of salvation, and try to make fruitful the gifts or **charisms** of the Holy Spirit—will vary from person to person. Conversion is a continuous and progressive process. Some young people are said to have had an instantaneous conversion when they have had an intense experience of God's love and salvation that leads them to radically change the direction of their life. But this is only the beginning of conversion. The process of conversion also has many later stages.

Holistic Conversion

59 For conversion to touch the whole person, it must gradually transform her or his entire being. Integral conversion helps young people transcend attitudes that keep them centered on themselves; get in the way of their accepting themselves, their reality, and their personal limitations; and impede their embrace of a life project that is consistent with Jesus' project of the Reign. Through continuous evangelization, conversion in these areas can touch all aspects of a person's life:

- *Relational conversion:* Young people discover Jesus as a living person who acts within history and within their own life, and they establish personal and communal relationships as friends and disciples of Jesus.
- *Conversion of the affective life:* Young people open themselves to God's love and allow this love to transform their affective life. They come to accept responsibility for their feelings and attitudes toward themselves, others, and God, as well as for how their emotional states influence their life and the lives of those around them.
- *Intellectual conversion:* Young people search for truth about the human person, the universe, and God, and they embrace the mystery of God revealed in faith.
- *Moral conversion, or conversion of lifestyle:* Young people shape their lifestyle and Christian practice under the guidance of Jesus' values, as oriented by the teachings of the church.
- *Ecclesial conversion:* Young people become aware that they are important members of the church and are responsible for seeing that the church fulfills Jesus' mission.

- *Societal conversion:* Young people recognize their responsibility to work for the Reign of God in society and to strive to shape social institutions and relations guided by the principles of love, justice, freedom, and peace.
- *Religious conversion:* Young people interpret their personal and communal experience in light of their relationship with God. And they see the mystery of life and death ever more fully from the perspective of Christian faith, intensifying their trust in God through prayer life, participation in the sacraments, and communitarian experiences.

60 Conversion in all these areas of life takes place slowly and unevenly. The conversion process follows no definitive order. Each person's life circumstances, interpersonal influences, personality tendencies, and experiences of church, as well as many other factors, intervene powerfully in initiating, facilitating, or impeding conversion in each area. Thus, to be successful, every youth ministry evangelization project must provide multiple processes and methods of evangelization that can touch the diverse areas of young people's lives.

General Stages in Holistic Conversion

61 In whatever way and at whatever moment young people begin their faith journey, the process of conversion passes through several natural stages. At times the individual person's disposition, God's grace, and the action of the evangelizing community accelerate the process of conversion or cause the individual to skip certain stages. Although the conversion process is different for everyone, it is possible to identify a broad pattern through which this process unfolds.

Searching for God

62 Young people look for God in many different ways. Some feel an emptiness, a need to relate to a supreme being or to transcend the limits of their materialistic life and daily routines. Some seek love, understanding, or forgiveness; others urgently need a friendly hand to help free them from the oppression caused by their own sins or by the social sins that affect them. Some seek a model to follow, a teacher to show them how to live in happiness, or a mentor to help them discern how to use their freedom and how to make decisions in critical situations. Still others eagerly seek a group of

friends with whom to share their yearnings, joys, and pains. Finally, some want to do good for humanity and thus seek a person or an institution to orient and support their efforts.

63 All these young people seek God, some consciously and others unconsciously. The majority of them, even if they are aware that they need God in their life, do not have the courage to go alone to church or to a Christian youth group. They need another young person to invite them specifically and to accompany them when they first attend.

64 Young people who are unaware of their deep longings, or who do not realize that only in Jesus will they find an answer to their aspirations, need someone to help them. They need someone to help them discover that their emptiness or their unsatisfied hopes in life are signs that they have not discovered God's saving presence. The evangelizer's challenge is to take on the longings and desires of young people's hearts and respond to them in a way that is meaningful for young people. Therefore, evangelizers need to be on the watch for the diverse ways young men and women express their need for God. Also, evangelizers need to speak with young people who are alienated from the church.

65 The living testimony of young Christians is a powerful evangelizing element in this first phase of conversion, the search for God. When young people who are seeking God recognize the mediocrity or incompleteness of their own life and contrast their life with the fuller life enjoyed by Christian young people they know, a restlessness is born in these young seekers. They ask: Why do these Christians seem to live with joy, but I cannot? How have they come to live that way? Can they help me? The young evangelizer who enters the life of a young seeker of God, when the seeker is asking these questions, finds fertile soil for sowing the seeds of the Gospel.

Encountering God Through Other Persons

66 God is present in the lives of all young people, but many of them are not aware of God's presence. The second phase of the conversion process consists of discovering God's presence. For this discovery to occur, someone must openly introduce young people to Jesus and communicate God's love directly to them.

67 Many young people have received God's love through the love, care, guidance, or service of their parents or other family members,

but have not recognized the hand of God in such loving acts. Evangelization with these young people begins by helping them discover God at work in their own life.

68 Some young people have lived in very unhealthy family situations, have been deeply hurt by someone or by their life circumstances (wars, poverty or misery, physical abuse, and so on), and have not found support from their teachers, friends, or even the church. For these young people, the proclamation of the saving love of God must be preceded and accompanied by a strong experience of Christian solidarity and love from the evangelizer. Otherwise, the proclamation of the Gospel will be just empty words that only create a deeper distrust of everything related to religion.

Finding Illumination in the Scriptures

69 Once young people have come to recognize that God acts in their life through other people—especially Christians who extend the work of Jesus in the church community and the world—they experience a desire to know more about the Jesus of history. They begin to ask questions about the mystery of God. At these moments, the process of conversion cries out for some initial contact with the Scriptures, especially the Gospels, in which young people find the good news of love and salvation that brought them to Jesus.

70 In this stage of conversion, young people yearn to draw from the word of God a new life, a different way of understanding the world around them, and a hope for the future. In these moments, they do not look to the Bible for information, nor are they interested in a systematic study of the books or themes of the Bible. What they want and need is to receive Jesus' life-giving message so that their life may be transformed and they can more clearly experience God's saving action.

71 For young people, finding illumination and inspiration in the Scriptures is decisive in founding a Christian life that follows the model shown by Jesus. This founding in turn depends on how evangelization is carried out. If Jesus' message is proclaimed to young people and the Scriptures illuminated for them exclusively as individuals (that is, focusing solely on God's action in their own life), the young people will acquire an egocentric vision of Christianity. They will think that everything revolves around personal

salvation. With this outlook, Jesus' mission of making real in society the Reign of God's justice, love, and peace becomes difficult to understand.

72 In contrast, when evangelization focuses both on Jesus' action in young people's lives and on their action as disciples of Jesus, their conversion rests on stronger foundations. With this balanced outlook, young people will continue acquiring new life to the extent that they continue following the way of true discipleship—considering Jesus not just as their personal friend and savior but also as the prophet of the Reign of God and as the one who teaches them how they should relate to others and act in history.

Choosing to Participate in the Church Community

73 From young people's perspective, wanting to follow Jesus and wanting to do good for humanity are not the same as wanting to participate in the life of the church. The "choosing to participate" level of conversion consists of understanding that God acts most effectively through Christians who are strongly active in the church community, where their faith is nourished, their will is strengthened, and where all can encourage one another in fulfilling their mission.

74 In this stage of the conversion process, young people begin to discover the meaning of the sacraments and to understand that the Holy Spirit keeps the church united so that it can continue Jesus' mission in history. This level of conversion depends greatly on the attitude of the church community. Often young people reach earlier stages of conversion through a retreat or a youth encounter, but if they do not find a youth community that embraces them, they will probably never become engaged in the life of the church. Thus, the previous stages may be left behind as passing experiences, without a serious impact in young people's lives.

Participating in the Mission of the Church

75 When Jesus has reached the deepest layers of young people's lives and is well inculturated, young men and women are capable of consciously taking on Jesus' mission. Through their words and deeds, they can become active promoters of the Reign of God among people, sources of renovation in the church, and agents of change in society. Youth ministers and pastoral agents should keep

in mind the different stages of the conversion process and not force young people into actions that do not correspond to their level of conversion and commitment. Many failures occur when the leaders of youth groups or youth communities are themselves young people in the initial stages of conversion—young people who lack the maturity and Christian commitment that are the fruits of later stages.

76 The evangelization process does not stop when a person becomes an active participant in the church's mission. In fact, it is from that moment on that the person becomes able to grow and mature as an evangelizer, while continuing to experience personal growth and evangelization. Becoming involved in the evangelizing mission of the church is the key to undergoing progressive and uninterrupted spiritual development.

Experiencing Continuous Spiritual Growth

77 People's personal conversion, like their personality, never truly reaches completion in life. There is always room for growth. And at its simplest, experiencing continuous personal growth is a process of learning to love as Jesus loves.

78 Nobody can love God without loving his or her neighbor. And nobody receives grace more than those who give away their egoistic life for the sake of following Jesus and continuing his mission. In Jesus' words: "'Just as I have loved you, you also should love one another. By this everyone will know that you are my disciples, if you have love for one another'" (John 13:34–35). Only those who bring salvation through love are truly disciples of Jesus.

Total Incorporation into the Love of God

79 Evangelization brings with it our incorporation into the Mystical Body of Christ, the church. In living out Jesus' commandment to love, we proclaim and announce the values of the Reign of God to other persons and to society. This life full of love gives us hope in the coming fullness of the Reign of God, in which we will participate when we are raised up in Jesus Christ.

80 Aware of the thirst for God felt by so many young Hispanics and of the ability that God has given them to be evangelizers of other young people, we join with the Hispanic bishops of the United States in this call:

We invite young men and women, especially, to place their enthusiasm, their sense of commitment and their sincerity at the service of the Gospel. May they be young apostolic bearers of the Gospel to the youth of today.[2]

6

Prophets of Hope: A Communitarian Evangelization Process

6

Prophets of Hope: A Communitarian Evangelization Process

For me, our meeting has been a deep and moving experience of your faith in Christ, and I make my own the words of St. Paul: "I have great confidence in you, I have great pride in you; I am filled with encouragement, I am overflowing with joy."

—John Paul II, World Youth Day 1993

1 This chapter refers to the practical dimensions of the pastoral-theological vision developed in the two volumes of Prophets of Hope. It presents the Prophets of Hope model for communitarian evangelization of young people and young adults.

2 The chapter is divided into five sections. The first speaks of young people in the church and in the world. The second presents the Prophets of Hope model. The third deals with the integral evangelization of young people in small communities. The fourth discusses the formation, enablement, and ministry of young ***animadores.*** The fifth discusses the enablement and ministry of ***formadores*** in Hispanic youth ministry.

Young People in the Church and in the World

3 The Second Vatican Council (1962–65), in its efforts to renew the church's faithfulness to Jesus and to respond more adequately to contemporary culture, returned to biblical sources and to the traditions of the first centuries of the church. In so doing, the council members realized that people's understanding of key aspects of the church had deteriorated over the centuries. The council members therefore dedicated several conciliar documents to clarifying the nature and mission of the church. Today, these documents fundamentally shape how the church sees itself and its mission. The following sections highlight some aspects of this ecclesial vision and how it relates to the evangelization of Hispanic youth.

4 Although today's young Latinos were born after Vatican Council II, post-conciliar renovation has reached only a small portion of them. Some young Latinos have received no pastoral attention, and others have received pastoral care informed by a preconciliar ecclesial vision. This chapter uses three conciliar themes from Vatican II documents to illuminate the evangelizing action of Latino youth: the Body of Christ, the pilgrim People of God on a journey, and the mission of the church to orient the world toward God.

The Church as the Body of Christ

5 *Lumen Gentium (Dogmatic Constitution on the Church)* begins by speaking of the mystery of the church, describing it as a sacrament, a sign and an instrument of the intimate union between people and God, and of the unity of the whole human family. This document emphasizes that the church is made up of *all baptized persons,* who are sanctified by the action of the Holy Spirit and journey toward God through Christ. God calls the whole church, including its young people, to love one another as Jesus loves us and to continue Jesus' mission of proclaiming and inaugurating the Reign among all people. In fulfilling its mission, the church becomes the seed and firstfruits of the Reign of God on earth.

6 After a brief review of various images of the church, *Lumen Gentium* dedicates an entire section to the image of the church as the Mystical Body of Christ, emphasizing once again that all baptized people are united with Christ, the head of the church, through the Holy Spirit. All Christians are transformed through baptism into new beings, united with Jesus and drawn together in the same Spirit. The Spirit gives to every Christian the gifts or charisms needed for the good of the whole Body, the ecclesial community.

7 Young people are members of the Body of Christ. United as an ecclesial community, they form a body that is full of vitality and oriented toward the future. In unity with adults, young people offer their gifts so that combined with the experience and charisms of their elders, the church may be constantly renewed and in search of creative ways to embody the Gospel within the culture of each new generation.

8 Small evangelizing communities act as the Body of Christ when their members live vigorously five dimensions of ecclesial life:

1. The *kerygma* is the "proclamation" that inaugurates the Reign in society by explicitly announcing the Good News, proclaiming Jesus' presence in current history, and bearing witness to the power of love in everyday life. Small communities of young people who live the *kerygma* are a source of liberation and conversion for one another and for many other young people.
2. The *koinonia* is the "communion" that builds up the ecclesial community, both within the small community itself and within the church as a whole. Evangelizing communities accomplish *koinonia* by watching over the well-being and unity of their members, by building ties with other ecclesial communities, and by joining in prayer and service with Christians of other churches.
3. The *didaché* is the "teaching" that imparts a solid catechesis so that young people learn the fundamentals of their faith and ecclesial life, embrace the values of the Reign, reinforce the Christian beliefs that give meaning and direction to life, experience deeply the mystery of God, bear witness to the faith, and defend the faith in the face of proselytizing religious sects and anti-evangelical ideologies.
4. *Diakonia* is "service" to others through a daily attitude of service and direct social and political action, both within the faith community and in the various settings in which young people live. This service focuses on meeting the material, emotional, social, and cultural needs of people, especially those who are poor and marginalized.
5. The *liturgia* is the "liturgy," in which young people communally celebrate their faith, offer thanks, seek forgiveness for their sins, and praise God—through both the Eucharist and the shared life of their youth community. In this way, the Eucharist truly becomes the center of a daily life of faith rather than an isolated event.

The Church as the Pilgrim People of God

9 In its second chapter, *Lumen Gentium* speaks of the church as the People of God, referring to what is *common in the whole of the church.* Only after discussing these two powerful images of the

church—as the Body of Christ and the People of God—does *Lumen Gentium* dedicate a chapter to specific sectors of the church, such as the hierarchy and laypeople. The introductory paragraph of chapter 2 states:

> At all times and among every people, God has given welcome to whosoever fears Him and does what is right. . . . It has pleased God, however, to make men holy and save them not merely as individuals without any mutual bonds, but by making them into a single people, a people which acknowledges Him in truth and serves Him in holiness.[1]

10 In the beginning, when God created man and woman, God established a covenant with them. This covenant was broken through sin. God established another covenant with the Israelite people. And later, through Christ, God instituted a new and perfect covenant with the new People of God.

> Christ instituted this new covenant, that is to say, the new testament, in His blood . . . by calling together a people made up of Jew and Gentile, making them one, not according to the flesh but in the Spirit.
>
> This was to be the new People of God. For, those who believe in Christ, who are reborn not from a perishable but from an imperishable seed through the Word of the living God . . . , not from the flesh but from water and the Holy Spirit . . . , are finally established as "a chosen race, a royal priesthood, a holy nation . . . who in times past were not a people, but are now the people of God."[2]

11 Young people fulfill their mission as the People of God by exercising their common priesthood and prophetic vocation, acquired through their baptism in Christ. This priesthood involves bearing witness to the reasons for Christian hope, offering to God their daily life, persevering in prayer, and celebrating the sacraments. Their prophetic vocation involves giving testimony to the Risen Jesus through a life of faith and charity, proclaiming the Gospel of Christ, and publicly praising God.

12 Young people—full of energy, ideals, and hopes, but also burdened by weaknesses, anxieties, and misjudgments—are in a continuous process of growth in their journey toward God. Jesus

accompanies them in this pilgrimage; he is Emmanuel, God-with-us. God's essential character is unchanging, but God is continually revealed in new ways that speak to changing cultures and new historical moments. Thus, God's liberating action remains meaningful for young people, no matter what their life circumstances are.

13 Small communities of young people are portions of the People of God that strive to be faithful to God. These communities also provide social settings in which young people support one another in their faith journeys and in their mission as prophets of hope. Like the Christian communities in the first centuries of the church, who lived in Jewish and pagan settings, small faith communities today find themselves surrounded by a culture that neither understands nor respects their faith experience. Today, young people's social environment is often secularized and sometimes paganized. As churches in diaspora (dispersed throughout the world), small communities of young people are a source of evangelization and ecclesial renewal.

14 In small communities, Latino young people sustain their identity as a doubly ***mestizo*** people—with the first ***mestizaje*** of indigenous, Spanish, Portuguese, and African blood and culture, and the second *mestizaje* happening now in the United States. Young Latinos in small communities live their covenant of love with God and open their hearts to other young people who need the warmth of authentic friendship and of God's presence. From their awareness of being part of a single People of God that is both divided and enriched by multiculturalism, young Latinos promote greater understanding and unity amidst diversity within the church and society. Through their Latino spirituality, these young people respond to the deep yearnings of their present reality and prepare for their journey into the future. Through their participation in the church and in society, Latino young people raise their prophetic voices and struggle for a more just society in the United States and throughout the world.

Young People, Placed to Orient the World Toward God

15 *Gaudium et Spes (Pastoral Constitution on the Church in the Modern World)* addresses not only Christians but the whole human family, with whom the church lives in solidarity. It begins:

> The joys and the hopes, the griefs and the anxieties of the men of this age, especially those who are poor or in any way afflicted, these too are the joys and hopes, the griefs and anxieties of the followers of Christ.[3]

16 The task of the church—in this case, its young people—begins with reading the signs of the times and interpreting them in light of the Gospel. Young people who do this can better respond to the uncertainties and challenges of modern living, the call to eternal life, and the relationship between the two. In this way, young people acquire a clearer awareness of the dignity and the vocation of the human person, which allows them to transcend modern society's excessive individualism, take responsibility for the common good, and live their lives according to Gospel values. Consequently, the chasm between religious faith and daily living gradually disappears among young Christians.

17 Young people bridge this chasm whenever they bring deep and well-informed religious faith to bear on contemporary challenges, such as shaping a civilization of love, promoting socioeconomic relations based on justice, encouraging political participation, struggling for human rights, building peace and a spirit of community among all people, and forming Christian marriages and families. These tasks must be pursued both through individual endeavors and through cooperative work with other young people to make a difference in contemporary society and to establish a better foundation for the future.

18 Small evangelizing communities give young people the space they need to critically analyze reality in light of their faith and to discern God's call for action within history. Small communities are privileged sites in which young people can discover their personal vocations and engage in communitarian pastoral praxis. In their efforts to establish the Reign of God in society, young people in small communities become the salt of the earth in their homes, neighborhoods, schools, factories, and offices; they become lanterns for other young people with whom they associate; and they become leaven in the dough of youth who have not found Jesus.

Young People, Apostles to Their Peers in Society

19 The decree *Apostolicam Actuositatem,* dedicated to the apostolate of laypeople, emphasizes the importance of young people's

work in the social, cultural, and political life of society. It stresses that efforts at ministry among youth and *by* youth must be redoubled so that they may offer to their peers the hope of life in Jesus. All apostles, as persons called to fulfill their vocation and mission, need communities to sustain them, to send them out to evangelize, and to which they can return to reflect on their mission. These communities must be open to receiving new members and willing to share their apostolate with them. Small ecclesial communities are apostolic because they have as a goal the evangelizing action of young people in the world.

20 In his apostolic exhortation *Evangelii Nuntiandi,* Pope Paul VI first insists that the church should pay special attention to young people. Then he emphasizes the need for young people who are well formed in their faith and well rooted in prayer to become apostles among other young people. Pope John Paul II, in his apostolic exhortation *Christifideles Laici,* ratifies these two approaches to action in the following way:

> Youth must not simply be considered as an object of pastoral concern for the Church: in fact, young people are and ought to be encouraged to be active on behalf of the Church as *leading characters in evangelization and participants in the renewal of society.*[4]

21 The church is called to carry the Gospel to the ends of the world. Young Latinos in the United States who enjoy great freedom of movement and action can be missionaries in their parishes and neighborhoods, in nearby cities, and in new areas to which they migrate. "'The harvest is plentiful, but the laborers are few'" (Matt. 9:37); the Latino youth population is so large and the number of pastoral agents so small that fertile ground for mission exists wherever Latino young people can be found.

22 To carry out their apostolic work in difficult environments and with young people who are passing through critical life situations, young apostles need a profound spirituality that gives them strength and courage to continue onward. Small communities are a source of deep spirituality; they foster communal prayer and nurture each members' personal prayer life.

23 Evangelization requires young missionaries. The Vatican II decree *Ad Gentes (On the Missionary Activity of the Church)* insists that

Jesus calls every disciple to evangelize, promote catechesis, form communities, and encourage others toward apostolic ministry. This work should always bear witness to the living Jesus and occur in union with the church. In general, young people who participate in small evangelizing communities are more motivated to missionary activity, more aware of the need for it, more inclined to discover and develop their God-given gifts for service, and more likely to receive the support they need to fulfill their vocations and missions as Christians.

24 In Roots and Wings, the first national congress held by the National Catholic Conference of Hispanic Ministry, in 1992, special attention was given to the role of youth and young adults in evangelization among Hispanics in the United States. This congress emphasized the need to relate Christian faith with the challenges and opportunities that young people find in their culture. The Fourth General Latin American Episcopal Conference in Santo Domingo specifically focused on the need to respond to the new situations emerging in Latin America and in the world with a **"New Evangelization,** Human Promotion, and Christian Culture." On World Youth Day 1993 in Denver, Pope John Paul II also emphasized the need for a New Evangelization in which young people play an important role as evangelizers.

The National Pastoral Plan for Hispanic Ministry

25 Hispanic people in the United States, through the general objective and specific dimensions of the National Pastoral Plan for Hispanic Ministry (1987), express the Vatican Council II vision of the church and its mission. The National Pastoral Plan proposes the following general objective:

> To live and promote by means of a *Pastoral de Conjunto* a model of church that is: communitarian, evangelizing, and missionary; incarnate in the reality of the Hispanic people and open to the diversity of cultures; a promoter and example of justice; active in developing leadership through integral education; leaven for the Kingdom of God in society.[5]

26 The specific dimensions of the National Pastoral Plan are these:

- ***Pastoral de conjunto:*** "To develop a *Pastoral de Conjunto,* which through pastoral agents and structures, manifests communion in integration, coordination, in-servicing, and communication of the Church's pastoral action, in keeping with the general objective of this plan."
- *Evangelization:* "To recognize, develop, accompany, and support small ecclesial communities and other church groups (e.g., Cursillos de Cristiandad, Movimiento Familiar Cristiano, RENEW, Charismatic Movement, prayer groups) which in union with the bishop are effective instruments of evangelization for the Hispanic people."
- *Missionary option:* "To promote faith and effective participation in Church and societal structures on the part of these priority groups (the poor, women, families, youth) so that they may be agents of their own destiny (self-determination) and capable of progressing and becoming organized."
- *Formation:* "To provide leadership formation adapted to the Hispanic culture in the United States that will help people to live and promote a style of Church that will be leaven of the Kingdom of God in society."[6]

In order to "guarantee the participation of Hispanic youth in the life and mission of the Church, [it is necessary] to identify existing, effective programs which can serve as models for reaching the most alienated youth and to assist in multiplying these programs in different dioceses and parishes."[7]

27 Accepting this vision is easy. The challenge lies in organizing and carrying out ministry so that young Latino Catholics can really become sacraments of Christ and instruments of evangelization for their peers. The model of communitarian evangelization that we present in this chapter offers some concrete suggestions for achieving this ideal. The model synthesizes in a practical way the pastoral-theological vision of the two volumes of Prophets of Hope.

The Prophets of Hope Model

28 The Prophets of Hope model focuses on forming small communities of young people and young adults who participate in a continuous process of integral evangelization that helps them become

prophets of hope in the varied settings in which they live. The following sections present the Prophets of Hope model, describe several of its elements, indicate the persons who bring it to life, and suggest some initial steps to implement it.

Elements of the Prophets of Hope Model

29 Two related processes make up the Prophets of Hope model for youth ministry: the formation of small communities and the process of continuous evangelization of young people and young adults.

1. The process of forming small communities requires the formation and training of young *animadores* and the preparation of ***asesores*** who support the *animadores* as they implement the Prophets of Hope model.
2. The process of continuous evangelization occurs in several phases. Each phase outlines a process and provides content for the evangelization of young people through Christian praxis.

Persons Who Bring the Prophets of Hope Model to Life

30 Implementing the Prophets of Hope model for evangelization of young people through small faith communities requires three groups of people:

1. All young Christians are called to live out their faith as individuals and in community. By promoting continuous evangelization and faith development in the personal and communal lives of every baptized person, the Prophets of Hope model helps young Christians respond to this call.
2. Among those young people who have accepted their baptismal commitment, some are called by God to exercise pastoral ministry within the church. The Prophets of Hope model needs these young *animadores* to form, encourage, and guide small communities of young evangelizers.
3. Young people who wish to serve as *animadores* of small evangelizing communities need training and pastoral accompaniment in this ministry. This training and accompaniment requires collaboration of *formadores,* persons who have been trained to run formation programs for *animadores.*

Suggestions for Implementing the Prophets of Hope Model

31 The following are several options for implementing the Prophets of Hope model, but many other options exist as well:

Possibilities Beginning with Formation Courses

32 The Prophets of Hope model can be implemented through formation courses for adults and young people.

1. Hold workshops for *formadores* and *asesores* of young *animadores* in small communities.
2. Offer formation and practical training courses for young *animadores* to help them begin to form their own small communities.

Possibilities Beginning with a Pastoral Experience

33 The Prophets of Hope model can be implemented through a communitarian experience for young people.

1. Bring together a group of young people who seek greater growth in their faith-life, serious pastoral involvement, a communitarian religious experience, or help to face life's challenges and develop personally and spiritually.
2. Take an already-existing large group of young people and transform it into a series of smaller evangelizing communities, or guide the evolution of a group of young people into a small community.
3. Begin intentional communities in diverse sectors of a parish, a university, or within a social group, a workplace, or an apostolic movement.
4. Form a new community by addressing the specialized pastoral needs of a particular group of young people.

Integral Evangelization of Young People in Small Communities

34 The process of evangelization of young people in small communities should be organized and focused in such a way that as young people move forward in personal and communal conversion, they gradually take on more responsibility in the church and in the world. The evangelization process achieves this by facilitating the

human and Christian development of young people; by using a communitarian, conscientizing, and liberating methodology; by offering integral evangelization; by encouraging personal and communal prayer; and by training young people for transformative action oriented to building the Reign in society.

Phases in the Evangelization of Young People

35 In the Prophets of Hope model, evangelization of young people generates a process of formation and deepening maturity within the youth community. The model identifies five basic phases of Christian growth at the personal and communal levels. The passage from one phase to the next is marked by a retreat and a special liturgical celebration. These phases focus on the following aspects of Christian life:

1. *God's self-communication in history:* The objective of phase 1 is that youth and young adults discover the presence of God in their life and hear God's invitation to live in God's love and to receive salvation through Jesus. This phase focuses on the Christian vocation from an **anthropological** perspective.
2. *Young people, followers of Jesus:* The objective of phase 2 is that youth and young adults know and relate to Jesus as his disciples. This phase focuses on the Christian vocation from a christological perspective.
3. *Young people's vocation and mission in history:* The objective of phase 3 is that youth and young adults discern their vocation, analyze the challenges they face in the environments in which they live, and become aware of their mission in history. This phase focuses on the Christian vocation from the personal perspective.
4. *Commitment with the church:* The objective of phase 4 is that youth and young adults get to know their church better, consciously assume their evangelizing mission, and commit themselves to the extension of the Reign of God in society. This phase focuses on the Christian vocation from an ecclesial perspective.
5. *Building a new world of hope:* The objective of phase 5 is that youth and young adults formulate a personal and communal life project founded on authentic discipleship of Jesus, on active participation in the life of the church, and on a free and conscious commitment to collaborate with God in human salva-

tion. This phase focuses on the Christian vocation from a sociological perspective.

Methodology for the Evangelization of Young People

36 The Prophets of Hope model uses a methodology of evangelization that is based on the lives of young people as members of small communities inserted in the world. It is an active methodology that emphasizes discipleship and missionary action on the part of young people. It includes the following processes.

Processes of Evangelization

37 The following are processes for evangelizing young people:

- Bring together the personal history of the youth involved, the history of the people of faith, and salvation history by promoting an ongoing encounter with Jesus in the Scriptures and in the young people's lives.
- Facilitate a continuous process of conversion by helping the young people discover God's call in the signs of the times, acquire a Christian vision of life, and make a free and proactive commitment to Jesus' mission.
- Foster a process of spiritual growth through personal and communal prayer, discernment of one's vocation and personal gifts, development of a lay spirituality based on the intimate relationship between faith and life, and celebration of the faith through the sacraments, especially the Eucharist.

Processes of Personal and Communitarian Promotion

38 These are processes for promoting individuals and communities:

- Assist young people in developing as whole persons by helping them know themselves, value their own dignity, and discern and build a life project, as well as by encouraging their interpersonal communication and personal Christian development.
- Help young people acquire the ability to live the faith within a community of faith through sincere dialog, Christian solidarity, an attitude of service and mutual support, and shared responsibility for the life of the community.

Processes of Pastoral Action

39 The following are processes for stimulating pastoral action:

- Train young people for their mission in the world through the testimony of their daily life, evangelizing action in the ordinary settings of life, organized apostolic activities, and transformative sociopolitical action.
- Form small communities of young evangelizers through which young people can grow personally, pursue their Christian vocation, and fulfill their mission in the world.

40 In summary, the Prophets of Hope model of evangelization strives to make Jesus the center of young people's lives. It strives to bring young people together in small communities so that they may become a source of renewal for the church. In this way, the church can become the sacrament of Jesus in society, effectively challenging our culture with the vision and mission of Jesus.

Formation, Enablement, and Ministry of Young *Animadores*

41 Young *animadores* of small communities can be either adolescents or young adults. These young people should be persons called by God to exercise this ministry and therefore have gifts that are useful for forming, facilitating, and guiding evangelizing communities. In no way does taking on responsibility for this ministry (or any other) negate young people's responsibility to live out their faith in the situations in which they live; that is the responsibility of every Christian. At all times and in all life's circumstances, *animadores* should live out the faith in ways that bear witness to and build the Reign in society.

Formation, Training, and Enablement

42 Young *animadores* need formation in several dimensions of their life:

1. Formation regarding the pastoral-theological vision that underlies the Prophets of Hope model
2. Practical training to develop their abilities as *animadores*
3. Integral formation in the following areas:

- *The human sciences:* anthropology, biology, psychology, philosophy, and sociology
- *Theology:* the Bible, **Christology, ecclesiology,** pastoral theology, and theology of the laity
- *Pastoral ministry:* methodology and techniques for pastoral action, with an emphasis on the apostolate among young people and on the evangelizing mission of the church

  This formation may occur as young people participate in the process of integral evangelization as *animadores* or as members of a small community. This formation may also occur through young people's participation in courses in faith formation, such as those offered for young leaders, catechists, or lay ministers.

4. Psychological and pastoral formation so that *animadores* can respond to the specific needs of adolescents or young adults
5. Specialized formation if a given *animador* plans to work with a specific group, such as farmworkers, university students, sick people, prisoners, gang members; or if the community needs him or her to develop special pastoral abilities for promoting social action, ministry to sick persons, peer counseling, retreats, and so on

43 Furthermore, it is vital for young *animadores* to make their experience a process of personal formation through *(a)* growth and deepening of their own faith-life; *(b)* professional supervision and guidance of their ministry; and *(c)* periodic pastoral-theological reflection on their ministry.

Methodology and Content in the Formation of Young *Animadores*

44 The specific objectives of the Prophets of Hope model are the formation of small communities of young evangelizers and missionaries, the Christian growth of young people, and an evangelizing pastoral practice. The *animadores* will accomplish these objectives in the small communities they serve, through the following:

1. Studying, reflecting on, and analyzing
   - their own pastoral experiences
   - the signs of the times
   - the qualities needed for a living faith community to truly promote evangelization and mission

2. Training for their task by offering theories, methods, and techniques to
   - form, lead, encourage, and coordinate young people within a small faith community
   - implement a process of continual evangelization using a focus that leads to Christian praxis
   - help the members of the small community fulfill their Christian mission
   - form new small communities of young evangelizers
   - identify and encourage the development of the gifts of other young people
3. Gaining knowledge of Jesus, his message, and his mission by
   - personally encountering Jesus in his role as founder and guide of a community of disciples
   - knowing the way Jesus evangelized people through personal contact
   - remembering Jesus' actions as a prophet who challenged the culture of death in his society, moved people to conversion, and offered them new life
   - appreciating Jesus' priestly mission and the way he sought people's reconciliation and union with God
   - discovering Jesus as servant to the poor and vulnerable
4. Reflecting alone and with others on
   - their personal experience as followers of Jesus
   - the kind of leadership they exercise among other youth
   - how to improve their ministry
   - their role as Hispanic leaders in the church and in U.S. society

45 Ideally, all young people who want to form a community, and especially *animadores*, should have the opportunity to participate in a formation program. If this is impossible, they can form a group for mutual reflection and self-formation, based on the Prophets of Hope model.

The Ministry of Young *Animadores*

46 Young *animadores* serve various simultaneous functions in small communities:

1. They guide the group toward forming a small community in which all members take responsibility for their communitarian life.

2. They coordinate a process of continual integral evangelization of all the young people in the small community, including themselves.
3. They motivate and help the young members of the community to fulfill their mission in the world and in the church.
4. They help other young people discover their vocation as *animadores* and develop the gifts that God has given them.

47 It is not necessary for one young person to fulfill all these functions all the time within a community. It works better to have a team of two or three young people who share the tasks of **animation.** In this way, more young people discover their vocation for this ministry, the accompanying responsibilities weigh less heavily on each person, and the team members bear witness to the value of shared work.

Enablement and Ministry of *Formadores*

48 In the context of the Prophets of Hope model, *formadores* are persons trained to form *animadores* of small communities of young evangelizers.

Enablement of *Formadores*

49 *Formadores* must share the underlying pastoral-theological vision of the Prophets of Hope model. They must also be trained to fulfill two key functions: form young *animadores* and serve as advisers for implementing the model. Fulfilling these functions requires the following:

- familiarity with the young people with whom the model is being implemented
- identification of the viable alternatives for implementing the model within their pastoral situation
- training in the formation of young *animadores* for small communities of young people
- identification of young people who have the gifts to minister as *animadores*
- training for implementing the model in a way that assures the formation, development, and multiplication of these small communities

- familiarity with the process of continuous evangelization so that they can advise the small community *animadores* on how to carry out their ministry

50 For a person to carry out the work of forming young *animadores* and of accompanying the young people who implement the Prophets of Hope model, enablement in the following areas is recommended:

- *Personal formation:* Adoption of the vocation and spirituality of *animadores;* an understanding of one's evangelizing mission and ecclesial role; and successful integration of one's personal life, ministry, and sense of profession
- *Spiritual-theological formation:* Foundational knowledge of the Scriptures, Christology, ecclesiology, Catholic doctrine, the sacraments, moral theology, Catholic identity, and **ecumenism.** Study, understanding, and application of Catholic theology as the foundation of a lay vocation to service
- *Leadership formation:* Knowledge and training for creating group environments that facilitate communication and foster the personal growth of young people; development of systems and processes that encourage group interaction; experience with integrating evangelization, catechesis, liturgy, and pastoral care in the life of the community; ability to administer programs and projects

51 Further, *formadores* of *animadores* require methodological training in different areas. For pastoral ministry they need training to work with adolescents and young adults according to their stages of development. For specialized ministries they need training in evangelization and catechesis, personal prayer and liturgy, and community formation. Also they need skills for youth ministry, including, among others, orientation techniques, methods for working for justice and social service, processes to facilitate personal development and faith maturity in youth, accompaniment and support techniques, and ways of bringing a family-centered perspective to youth ministry.

Pastoral Agents and the Prophets of Hope Model

52 Pastoral agents can collaborate in implementing the Prophets of Hope model in the following ways:

- by considering the formation of small evangelizing communities in their parishes as an alternative model for youth ministry
- by choosing this model for their evangelization and pastoral care efforts with Hispanic young people and young adults
- by adapting this model for different cultural settings so that multicultural parishes become large communities formed by many smaller communities—some made up of people from different cultures; others, by people who share the same language and culture
- by coordinating parish events so that all the small communities in the parish gather together periodically in ways that encourage their interaction and sense of belonging to the church
- by offering their pastoral service as advisers to the *animadores*

The Leaders of Apostolic Movements and the Prophets of Hope Model

53 Generally, the objective of Hispanic apostolic movements is to evangelize young people. Many of them offer only intense initial experiences of evangelization; others provide follow-up to these experiences through cell groups, small faith communities, or group reunions. Local leaders of apostolic movements can take advantage of the Prophets of Hope model in two ways:

- by helping the movement's central team develop as a small evangelizing community and not just as a ministry team interested exclusively in fostering the movement's growth
- by forming small communities as a way of offering ongoing Christian formation to young people who have shared a spiritual retreat or other intense religious experience

Asesores and the Prophets of Hope Model

54 Two groups of people can be called *asesores.* First are pastoral agents who work directly with young people but stay within their areas of expertise. These areas include leadership formation, **pastoral planning,** catechesis, school counseling, work with gang members, health and hygiene, developmental psychology, sexual formation, and marriage preparation. Second are lay adults who draw on their own Christian formation and pastoral experience to support, guide, and advise young people in their faith-lives and pastoral action.

55 The Prophets of Hope model will function well only if these advisers do *not* become *animadores* of the small communities. The advisers must remain clearly focused on formation and accompaniment of the young *animadores,* even when the *animadores* are adolescents. The materials for continuous evangelization that Saint Mary's Press will publish are being developed with this focus in mind. That is, the materials will rely on young *animadores* carrying out their *own ministry* of facilitating the integral evangelization of young people in their faith communities.

56 In this way, young people may fulfill their mission, as they were encouraged to do by Pope John Paul II in his visit to Denver for World Youth Day 1993:

> And to you, Latin American young people, what does Christ ask from you? He seeks collaborators in the New Evangelization. He is looking for missionaries of his word to all the countries of this continent of hope. He searches for builders of a new more just, more fraternal, and more warm society towards the "little" and the needy. Christ needs every one of you.[8]

7

Inculturation: A Challenge for Hispanic Youth and Young Adults

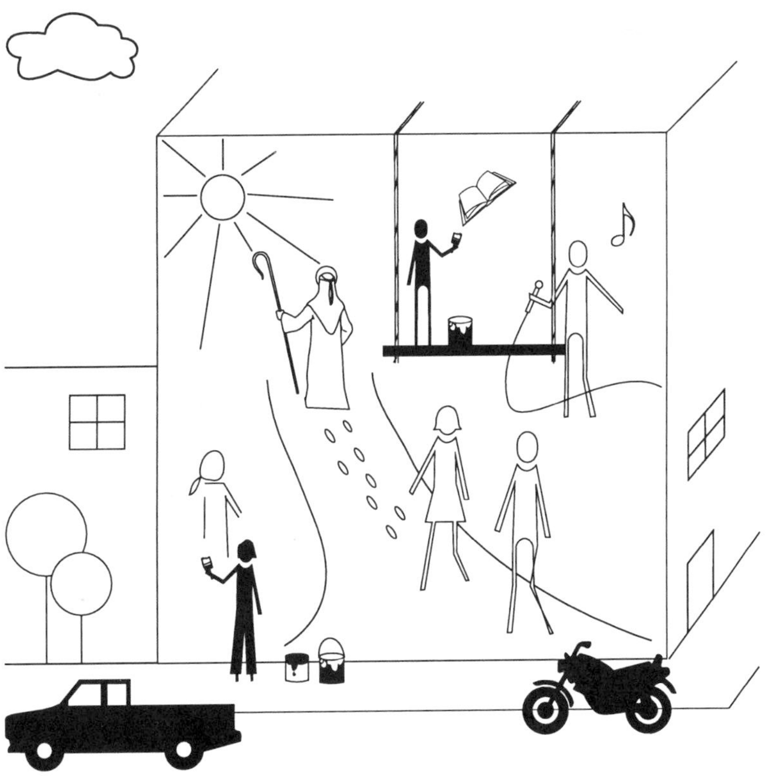

7

Inculturation: A Challenge for Hispanic Youth and Young Adults

> Through inculturation the Church makes the Gospel incarnate in different cultures and at the same time introduces peoples, together with their cultures, into her own community. She transmits to them her own values, at the same time taking the good elements that already exist in them and renewing them from within. Through inculturation the Church, for her part, becomes a more intelligible sign of what she is, and a more effective instrument of mission.
>
> —John Paul II, *Redemptoris Missio*

1 Beginning with the Second Vatican Council, the Catholic church has identified the lack of relationship between faith and culture as a key problem of modern times and has emphasized the need to relate them more successfully. To better understand the church's current teaching about the relationship between faith and culture, this chapter first outlines the principal ways the church has historically seen that relationship. Then it briefly analyzes the concept of inculturation and identifies five levels of cultural context that influence Hispanic young people. As the chapter points out, aspects of each level are especially significant for evangelization. Thus, some guidelines are provided for facilitating the incarnation of the Gospel in young people's lives and culture. Finally, this chapter offers a series of goals, criteria, themes, and processes necessary for achieving an inculturated evangelization.

The Church Relates Faith and Culture

2 Two thousand years ago God became flesh in Jesus, who was born in Bethlehem of Judea and educated within the Hebrew culture in the region of Galilee. Jesus adopted the culture of his time and used its methods and symbols to fulfill his mission of incarnating God within history and to show the way to God's paths of love, justice, peace, and truth. At the same time, Jesus gave a new meaning to some Jewish cultural and religious customs.

3 Jesus did not address only those who were faithful to Yahweh, but rather carried the Good News to Syro-Phoenicians, Samaritans, Romans, and Greeks. His Resurrection and the coming of the Holy Spirit on Pentecost opened new horizons for all cultures. Through Jesus, God's covenant with humanity took on a universal dimension and transcended all limitations of time, place, and culture. Jesus' final commissioning of the disciples specifies clearly God's will to be incarnated in the lives of all persons:

> The eleven disciples went to Galilee, to the mountain to which Jesus had directed them. When they saw him, they worshiped him; but some doubted. And Jesus came and said to them, "All authority in heaven and on earth has been given to me. Go therefore and make disciples of all nations, baptizing them in the name of the Father and of the Son and of the Holy Spirit, and teaching them to obey everything that I have commanded you. And remember, I am with you always, to the end of the age." (Matt. 28:16–20)

4 At first glance, this mission—left by Jesus to his followers—appears fairly simple, its greatest challenge lay in going out to the whole world to preach the Gospel, baptize others, and teach them to follow Jesus. But implementing Jesus' mission is complicated, and throughout Christian history it has led to serious theological and pastoral challenges. This complexity is greatest when evangelizing a society for the first time, but it also exists when pastoral workers and the people with whom they work come from different cultural backgrounds and have different expressions of Christianity. The latter is the situation for Latinos in the United States.

5 The following questions, which sometimes cause serious differences and even divisions within the church, make clear the seriousness of the pastoral-theological challenges to be faced and the complexity of fulfilling the mission Jesus gave to his disciples:

- Should evangelization concern itself with people's whole lives, including their cultural, social, political, and economic dimensions, or should it focus only on their spiritual lives?
- To what extent should the church demand that those receiving evangelization or catechesis accept the Christian tradition in the form in which the evangelizers learned it?

- What kinds of religious and cultural elements that differ from those of the evangelizer should be accepted and incorporated into the life of the local church, so that the Gospel can truly be incarnated in the lives of those being evangelized?

6 The following section strives to identify some of the most meaningful ways the church has related faith and culture, especially as this relationship has affected the evangelization of Hispanic people. To do this, key situations and themes in the history of the church have been chosen.

7 The relationship of the church to human cultures has always been marked by a certain degree of dialog, which has allowed many peoples being evangelized to receive and express the Gospel. At the same time, missionaries have almost always demanded that those being evangelized conform not only to the Gospel of Jesus but also to the way of life of the missionaries and to Western culture's way of living, expressing, and teaching the Gospel.

Various Emphases in the Evangelization of Peoples

8 Following the model offered by Jesus, the Apostles carried the message of salvation to persons within their life contexts. This helped the people embrace a new life within their hearts and in their culture. At the same time, the first Christians—who came from various cultures—brought into the church their own languages, values, philosophies, traditions, and customs.

9 Although the immense majority of Jesus' first disciples were Jews and kept the Jewish Law, the early church discerned that God did not want one culture to impose itself on another culture. Therefore, the church did not require non-Jews who converted to the faith to adhere to the Jewish law of circumcision. Also, the church allowed each community to express its faith in its own language and way of life. Thus, the early church placed before its followers a difficult lesson: evangelizers should discover what is essential to the faith and invite other persons to accept it, without imposing nonessential elements of this faith.

10 From then until now, the process of dialog and encounter between the church and the many cultures of the world has been carried out amidst diverse theological perspectives, which have influenced the methods and emphases of Christian evangelization. Some emphases and methods of evangelization have contributed to

the incarnation of the Gospel in various cultures by respecting each culture's own ways of life. Others have imposed the Western vision and way of life on other cultures, thus destroying to varying degrees the values and ways of life of native peoples.

Substitution of Religious Symbols

11 Substitution of symbols consists of giving a Christian meaning to non-Christian religious expressions. The church used this method with significant success in the first three centuries of the Christian era, when it carried out its missionary ministry in an environment of persecution. The success of this method is that as the meaning of the religious symbols change, the new way of seeing an old ritual or custom helps those being evangelized better understand the Christian message being transmitted intellectually. This new meaning begins to shape their hearts and transform their lives.

12 Jesus himself used this method. He preached in the synagogues and presented himself as a good Jew who went frequently to the Temple. At the same time, he gave new meaning to various traditional religious customs. For example, he adapted the Jewish Passover supper in instituting the Last Supper. This is a clear example of what today is called *inculturation,* that is, establishment of a dynamic relationship between the Gospel and human cultures.

Acceptance of Secular Symbols Foreign to the Gospel

13 The peace brought to the church by the emperor Constantine during his reign (306–337) created a positive atmosphere for the evangelizing mission of the church. The situation was so favorable that at times the church embraced the wider culture without exercising critical judgment in the light of the Gospel. Therefore, the church accepted into its interior life symbols of imperial culture that were contrary to the Gospel. For example, bishops adopted symbols of imperial royalty, losing the simplicity and freedom of lifestyle that characterized Jesus and the first disciples; priests functioned as authorities and lost their role as servants of the community; worship stopped being celebrated in homes and entered the basilicas, where it was celebrated with all the pomp of imperial ceremonies; sin stopped being understood as a violation of one's commitment to God and to the community, and began to be seen as the breaking of divine laws, which were understood and explained by

ecclesiastical laws. These two kinds of laws were gradually consolidated under the imperial court system.

14 By proceeding in this way, the church lost its evangelical flexibility, and missionaries lost their ability to distinguish between what belonged to the faith and what was simply a cultural expression. Unity began to be confused with uniformity, and Roman customs and rituals were imposed as new churches throughout the land came to be considered simple extensions of the church of Rome. This uniformity was carried so far that under the reigns of Popes Siricius (384–399) and Innocent I (401–417), the church taught that no one could embrace the faith of Peter if they did not embrace the customs and rituals of the city of Peter—Rome. This was taught in spite of the fact that Peter was a Jew and had evangelized Rome from a Jewish perspective—not from the perspective of the Roman Empire.

Consolidation of the Eurocentric Focus

15 The era of European colonial expansion between the fifteenth and twentieth centuries helped consolidate a Eurocentric focus in evangelization, and this strongly affected the missionary action of the church. The missionaries carried to native cultures and religions the arrogant attitudes of all conquerors, imposing their own culture on the native peoples even as they tried to offer them the Christian faith. Conversion to Christianity implied accepting the cultural forms of the European evangelizers. This contrasted with the practice of the early church after the Council of Jerusalem, which opposed imposing a vital aspect of Jewish culture (circumcision) on converts from Greco-Roman cultures.

16 The establishment of the Congregation for the Propagation of the Faith, in 1622, was an effort on the part of the church in Rome to end this cultural imposition. In 1659, the Congregation condemned European cultural and ecclesiastical ethnocentrism and asked explicitly that a true process of inculturation be implemented:

> Do not for any sense of zeal attempt to . . . persuade those people to change their rites, customs, and ways unless they are most obviously contrary to Faith and good morals. For what could be more absurd than to carry France, Spain, or Italy, or any other part of Europe into China? It is not this sort of thing you are to bring in but rather the Faith.

> Admire and praise the customs that merit praise. . . . Do not rashly and excessively condemn the unworthy. Let customs that prove to be depraved, be uprooted more by hints and by silence . . . gradually without jolting.[1]

But these words did not have the desired impact, as was evident in the condemnation by the Roman church (1742) of the Jesuit Matteo Ricci's efforts to establish a dialog between the Gospel and Chinese culture, and to accept some Chinese ritual expressions of faith.

The Individualist and Spiritualist Focus

17 In the earliest era of Christianity, evangelization was directed to persons within and through a community of believers; it was the community that nourished, sustained, and helped Christians mature in the faith. However, particularly in reaction to the Protestant Reformation, evangelization gradually shifted from this communitarian approach to an individualistic focus emphasizing salvation of souls. The church thus lost its focus on evangelizing persons within communities.

18 Over time, the goal of evangelization came to be twofold: to implant in a new setting the church as an institution, with its hierarchical and monarchical customs; and to promote evangelized persons' individual participation in the Catholic church as the only means to achieving salvation in Jesus. This model of evangelizing action saw only the soul as being important and understood salvation as coming only through initiation into the church through baptism. Within this model, evangelizers had little need to understand the culture of those being evangelized. Christians were expected to perform works of charity and to attend to the health and educational needs of others, especially the poor, but these actions were tied only to being a good Christian and were not seen as part of the process of evangelization.

Insufficient Efforts and Pastoral Flexibility

19 At the end of the nineteenth century and during the first half of the twentieth century, the church engaged in a lot of missionary activity, and also made some effort to replace the Eurocentric focus within evangelization, with its emphasis on the salvation of souls. Under Pope Leo XIII, the understanding of Saint Thomas Aquinas was reintroduced, with its non-Christian elements drawn from the

philosophy of Aristotle. People were invited to reflect on the nature of the human person and society as a means of discovering the relationship between human life, culture, and divinity. The need to see the human person as an integrated whole, with body and soul closely related, was emphasized. As a result of this more integral vision, the church began to generate its social doctrine. The first official document reflecting this vision was the encyclical letter *Rerum Novarum*, by Pope Leo XIII (1891).

20 If this focus had borne its full fruit, methods of evangelization would have changed. But the efforts of the official church had little influence in changing evangelization. Although the missionaries' exaltation of their own culture was strongly condemned, the education that priests received in seminary and that religious brothers and sisters received from their congregations kept a Eurocentric focus. This ambivalent relationship between ideas and practice led to three patterns of missionary practice: translation, adaptation, and indigenization.

21 None of these three patterns respects the culture and religious experience of the persons being evangelized.

- *Translation* presents the message of the Gospel in the local language, but with the vision of the dominant culture.
- *Adaptation* is a step forward in that it uses elements of the local culture to translate the Gospel message and present it more effectively. Yet adaptation still keeps the vision of the dominant culture.
- *Indigenization* follows the general approach of adaptation but has the advantage of promoting indigenous vocations to the priesthood and religious life. However, it leads indigenous candidates for ordination and religious life to abandon their customs by imposing upon them European ways of being, thinking, and acting.

22 In the first half of the twentieth century, understanding of missionary activity began to change and Pope Pius XII (reigned 1939–58) sketched the outlines of the idea of cultural pluralism. However, indigenization was still his predominant approach. In 1951, Pius XII wrote:

> The final goal towards which we must strive and which must ever remain before our eyes is the firm establishment of the Church among the peoples, each [local Church] having its own hierarchy chosen from the ranks of the native clergy.[2]

23 The maintenance of the Eurocentric and ecclesiastic focus contributed strongly to the church's failure to take advantage of advances in the social sciences. It also contributed to the failure of evangelization efforts to recognize either the needs of non-European cultures or the needs of modern culture. In this period before Vatican Council II, it became even more evident that an abyss lay between missionary rhetoric regarding the need to adapt the message of the Gospel to local cultures, on one hand, and Eurocentric pastoral practices, on the other. The consolidation of the Latin American countries, which had become independent from Europe a century earlier, and the growing nationalism of the African and Asian colonies as they gained their independence, made more evident the need to reconsider the Eurocentric focus.

24 Persistent use of the models of translation, adaptation, and indigenization made change difficult. Part of the problem was that missionaries generally considered their own culture superior in all ways to the local culture in which they worked. Many missionaries saw the native population as immature, ignorant, and in need of the missionaries' beneficence. Thus, the missionaries translated the "wisdom" of their own culture into the local language and culture, generally without taking cultural differences into consideration. Also, the missionaries treated those being evangelized paternalistically.

25 In this context, the enthusiastic optimism of Pope John XXIII (reigned 1958–63) seemed quite unrealistic. In his encyclical *Princeps Pastorum* (1959), John XXIII said:

> The [Church] does not identify herself with any particular culture, not even European and Western culture. . . . [The] Church is ever ready to recognize, to welcome and indeed to encourage all things that honour the human mind and heart even if they have their origin in places of the world that lie outside this Mediterranean basin.[3]

26 Not until after Vatican Council II (1962–65) did the church go back once again to renew energetically and clearly its efforts to inculturate the Gospel in different cultures. The next section of this chapter presents the process of evangelization of the Latin American people. The third section takes up the dialog between the official church and local cultures that followed Vatican Council II.

The Evangelization of Latin America

27 In the fifteenth and sixteenth centuries, European exploration began a period in which evangelization and political-cultural domination of conquered peoples occurred at the same time. The church awarded Spain and Portugal the double power of colonizer and missionary, thus mixing the temporal and the supernatural, the political and the ecclesial, the economic and the evangelical. This process produced something akin to the expansive military theocracies (forms of government directed by God in the name of God or through a priestly order) of the Middle Ages.

The Gospel Arrives in the Americas

28 Through the papal bulls *Inter Coetera* and *Eximiae Devotionis* (promulgated in 1493), the Catholic monarchs were given the newly discovered lands of the Americas. These documents gave to the kings, along with the land, the people who inhabited it, with the mandate to make these inhabitants participate in the benefits of the Gospel as members of the Catholic church. In their expansion as Christian kingdoms, Spain and Portugal had two inseparable goals: to conquer the lands and their inhabitants under the temporal power of the crown, and to evangelize the inhabitants by incorporating them into the church.

29 The missions in Latin America developed within an ambivalent context, framed by two institutions: a state that incorporated the goals of the church among its own means of expansion, and a church. The church gradually became aware of the need for freedom, for attending to the injustices committed against the conquered peoples, and for separating the goals of European political expansion from the missionary objectives of the church. Fray Bartolomé de Las Casas was the first missionary to propose that missionaries should go to the indigenous peoples peacefully and with exclusively evangelical goals. The Jesuits, due to their direct subordination to the pope and their relative independence from the crown, demonstrated a particularly unequivocal missionary commitment of this kind. Later, Latin American bishops also began to gain awareness of the need for freedom in order to evangelize, with Toribio de Mogrovejo, archbishop of Lima, leading the way.

30 Spain's decadence during the Bourbon reigns (1700–1808) led the church in Latin America into a crisis. This crisis resulted

primarily from the Americas becoming isolated from the rest of Europe, from the American regions being left with little contact among themselves, and from the lack of influence from new missionaries. Yet the missions continued during the eighteenth century, although they were less intense and fewer in number. For example, the Jesuits arrived in California in 1607, but only in the eighteenth century did the inspired Fray Junípero Serra (1763–1784) promote missionary action "like in the early days." In 1768, the Franciscans arrived in California. Little by little, with remarkable work and efficiency, they founded mission outposts and ***reducciones indígenas,*** beginning in San Diego (1769) and ending in San Francisco (1776). The Dominicans also founded Indian *reducciones* throughout California.

Early Efforts to Inculturate the Gospel in American Indigenous Cultures

31 It has been incorrectly said that Christianity in the ***Cristiandad de Indias*** was almost exclusively clerical. Much to the contrary, lay Christian conquerors—both Spaniards and Creoles—actively participated in the expansion of the Gospel, although always within the mold of Christendom. In addition, in relatively little time, indigenous converts began to accompany the missionaries in their travels, helping them as translators and evangelizing in their own tongue. In this way, the missionaries could write catechisms in the most common native languages. In some places, lay Christians who had already received instruction in the faith shared the catechism in their own language, even before the conquered peoples learned the language of the conquerors. Various indigenous laypeople died as martyrs at the hands of their fellow Indians, most outstanding among them the young people of Tlaxcala, Mexico, beatified by Pope John Paul II in 1992.

32 The early Christian church continued using many faith symbols of the Israelite faith, giving them new meaning. In the same way, it introduced into Christianity the symbols of Greco-Roman culture and civilization in order to try to communicate the message of the Christian faith. Similarly, missionaries in Latin America had the full right to choose from among the cultural expressions of pre-Hispanic civilizations those symbolic elements that would allow Indians to receive and communicate the essential substance of the faith being presented to them.

33 The evangelization of Latin America was based substantially on introducing Hispanic Catholic sacramentality into the lives of indigenous peoples while accepting into liturgical traditions and popular devotions many elements of pre-Hispanic religious practices. Given that missionaries could not sustain a constant presence in all the mission communities, nor change the liturgical calendar, they created countless paraliturgies. The great majority of these were directed by indigenous laypeople. This encouraged the transmission, expansion, and celebration of the faith even in the missionaries' absence, and gave rise to **popular Catholicism,** which is predominantly a lay practice.

Conversion to Cultural Christianity

34 An adequate inculturation of the Gospel requires, first, that missionaries know deeply the religious soul of those being evangelized and, second, that missionaries adopt methods of evangelization appropriate to the people being evangelized. Existential understanding of the pre-Hispanic religions presupposed identifying their **ethical-mythical nucleus,** which implied knowing indigenous consciousness, understanding the meaning of indigenous religious symbols, and observing the way indigenous cosmology and religious life interacted in the people's daily lives. In this respect, we can identify the following three stages in missionary work among Native American peoples:

- The first generation of missionaries identified the indigenous religions as intrinsically and absolutely perverse and, as a result, persecuted them and tried to eliminate them.
- The second and third generations of missionaries—including Acosta and Sahagun—understood that evangelization required knowing deeply the indigenous system of thought. So they carried out serious inquiries into what might be called the "soul" of the Native American.
- The fourth generation began the movements for indigenization, trying to evangelize and educate indigenous people by starting from their reality. But the truth is that the majority of missionaries remained unfamiliar with these inquiries and never put into practice the insights of the *indigenista* movement.

35 Several factors in Latin America led to the slowness of the transition from a pagan ethical-mythical nucleus to an understanding and acceptance of the Christian faith, as had occurred in

the Greco-Roman empire. Among these factors were the missionaries' lack of knowledge about the indigenous soul, the rapidity with which indigenous civilizations were destroyed, and the marginalization of indigenous people who kept their language and culture. Instead of a smooth transition, what occurred was a rupture, a radical break, the annihilation of the heart of ancient cultures. This impeded a more authentic and normal evangelization.

36 The immense majority of indigenous communities, denied the essential elements of their own culture, inevitably disappeared as cultural groups and became—sooner or later—assimilated into the dominant culture that had invaded them. In this context, evangelization occurred without interruption and almost by necessity from the sixteenth century until the eighteenth century. Indigenous communities passed, little by little, from one culture to the other and in doing so experienced an existential conversion to Christianity as part of the culture they adopted.

37 In general, the missionaries arrived too late, were too few, and brought methods of evangelization that were too ineffective to imprint the great foundations of the Christian faith onto indigenous peoples' awareness. The lack of a deeper stage of evangelization meant that a very large proportion of the Latin American people acquired and transmitted only a cultural Christianity, often without understanding the essential elements of the Christian faith.

Gradual Formation of a Christian Consciousness

38 Once the indigenous ethical-mythical nucleus had been destroyed, formation of the Latin American Christian conscience slowly began. The passage of time, the formation of the *mestizo* race, the work of new waves of European missionaries, and the maturation in the faith of persons and communities, have resulted in great variety among Latin Americans in their levels of acceptance and understanding of the fundamental mysteries of the faith. Throughout the history of the various Latin American nations, persons deeply convinced and committed to Jesus and his Gospel have existed alongside persons who call themselves Christians because they have been baptized, but know only vaguely what this means.

39 Some thinkers believe that because the indigenous population understood only the exterior dimension of religious worship without penetrating the mysteries that it symbolized, they continued

being fundamentally pagan and accepted Christianity only superficially and externally. Others believe that indigenous persons who call themselves Christians *are* essentially Christian, although they may have some deficiencies resulting from historical pastoral inattention. Still others maintain that two religions coexist in the lives of indigenous people, who try to blend them together.

40 Finally, some suggest that what actually exists is a **religious syncretism,** or "mixed religion," that has given rise to a true religious *mestizaje*. The message brought by the missionaries entered into the individual and collective consciousness of indigenous people, for whom the sacred penetrates all of life, every event is regulated by living gods who enter ordinary life, and all history carries theological meaning.

41 Confronting this religious clash, indigenous peoples often embraced Christianity to ingratiate themselves with the Christian God, to possess this new God and allow themselves to be possessed by God and by Mary and the saints, who took the place of the multiplicity of gods in their previous polytheistic religions. In this way, indigenous peoples formed a peaceful alliance with Christianity, accepting it from within their own mythical worldview and seeing it from a fundamentally pagan perspective. In these cases, the consequence was a fundamental paganism incorporating some Christian elements.

42 However, not all of Latin America is indigenous, nor have all Catholics inherited their faith from within paganized or only slightly Christian contexts. In addition to the variety presented by indigenous Christianity, Latin America always included groups of European Christians as well as Europeanized natives. The latter group gradually grew and included several groups: descendants of European immigrants; *mestizos* whose indigenous roots were remote; persons educated in Catholic schools and catechized by European religious congregations—many over the course of several generations; and Catholics committed to the congregations and apostolic works run by European missionaries.

43 The constant interaction between indigenous persons and communities, on one hand, and Europeanized persons and communities, on the other, led to a certain degree of mutual influence and a richness of Latin American expressions of Christianity. For the Latin American people as a whole, we can say that this slow

process of evangelization (sometimes unintentional and sometimes quite conscious) has been a true catechumenate that has not yet ended.

44 Since the beginning of Latin American evangelization, it has been difficult to discern the fundamental level of faith, that is, the degree of acceptance of the essential aspects of evangelization. This leads to the necessity for every evangelizer to avoid committing various mistakes, such as the following:

- confusing religious ignorance with fundamental paganism
- too easily affirming the Christian faith of people simply because they have been baptized or know something about Christian dogma
- thinking that no Latin American Catholics embrace Christianity authentically and deeply
- disparaging the depth and type of faith that people have
- measuring people's faith from one's own perspective, without knowing the depths of their religious reality

The Second Vatican Council and Church Renewal

45 In the middle of the twentieth century, Pope John XXIII initiated a period of renewal in the church. This renewal emphasized that to relate faith and culture, it is necessary to present the Gospel and church teachings in the language of the local people and in a manner that makes sense in their cultural context. The Second Vatican Council expresses the opening of the church to the modern world, mainly in three documents:

- *Gaudium et Spes (Pastoral Constitution on the Church in the Modern World)* clearly expresses the need to relate faith to culture. In this document, the church is considered a universal church that recognizes the presence of God in the plurality of people's experiences and concerns. The church tries to respond to the questions of life from a faith perspective, and it fosters a healthy promotion of cultural progress to respond to the most urgent problems of our time.
- *Sacrosanctum Concilium (Constitution on the Liturgy)* speaks of revising the liturgy in accord with specific situations and cultures; it also promotes the use of local languages and the adaptation of a culture's symbols, rites, and prayers into liturgical celebration.

- *Ad Gentes (Decree on the Church's Missionary Activity)* takes the Incarnation of Jesus as the model for missionary action, affirms that in every culture there are seeds of the word of God, and emphasizes that making the church present in societies and cultures is the responsibility of all Christians, particularly laypersons.

46 Pope Paul VI, who reigned from 1963 to 1978, emphasized the need to evangelize not only cultures but social systems and structures as well. Paul VI called the separation of faith and culture the great tragedy of our time. Since the Second Vatican Council, awareness has grown that the split between modern culture and faith has resulted from shortcomings on both sides. Modern culture's concentration on technology and individualism avoids facing questions of faith and shared meaning, and the church's slowness in responding to changing situations or new knowledge often leaves the church unable to present the Gospel in a way that is meaningful for modern life.

Post-Conciliar Renewal in Latin America and the United States

47 The church in Latin America, encouraged by developments at the Second Vatican Council and the General Latin American Episcopal Conferences (Río de Janeiro, 1955; Medellín, Colombia, 1968; Puebla, Mexico, 1979; and Santo Domingo, Dominican Republic, 1992), sought to implement a new evangelization of its people and promote a more just society. The church began to analyze both itself and its sociocultural context in light of the Scriptures. This analysis, made from the perspective of poor and oppressed people, *(a)* identified the causes and consequences of poverty and people's lack of power, *(b)* recognized the urgent need for social justice to be an integral part of the Gospel message, and *(c)* created processes of evangelization that were rooted in people's life situation.

48 Post-conciliar renewal in the United States has placed special emphasis on liturgical renewal and on the participation of laypeople in liturgy and in all ministries. In addition, this renewal has made great efforts to draw on the knowledge generated in the natural and social sciences, in order to deepen the church's understanding of human persons and their faith development, and to professionalize ministry.

49 The task of renewal faced by Latino young people today requires them to analyze their *realidad* in the United States, promote their effective participation in the church, gain solid formation in the faith, and effectively prepare for their mission in the church and in the world. This may happen as they assume the history of ecclesial renewal in Latin America and the United States, seek creative ways to respond to the challenges of contemporary culture, and prepare themselves to promote an inculturation process for the twenty-first century.

Inculturation, a Necessary Process in Evangelization

50 In his pastoral exhortation *Evangelii Nuntiandi,* Pope Paul VI pointed out the necessity of evangelizing the whole human person—filling all dimensions of life with the life of God and reaching the deepest levels of culture:

> What matters is to evangelize man's culture and cultures (not in a purely decorative way as it were by applying a thin veneer, but in a vital way, in depth and right to their very roots), in the wide and rich sense which these terms have in *Gaudium et Spes,* always taking the person as one's starting-point and always coming back to the relationships of people among themselves and with God.
>
> The Gospel, and therefore evangelization, are certainly not identical with culture, and they are independent in regard to all cultures. Nevertheless, the Kingdom which the Gospel proclaims is lived by men who are profoundly linked to a culture, and the building up of the Kingdom cannot avoid borrowing the elements of human culture or cultures. Though independent of cultures, the Gospel and evangelization are not necessarily incompatible with them; rather they are capable of permeating them all without becoming subject to any one of them.
>
> The split between the Gospel and culture is without a doubt the drama of our time, just as it was of other times. Therefore every effort must be made to ensure a full evangelization of culture, or more correctly of cultures. They have to be regenerated by an encounter with the Gospel. But this encounter will not take place if the Gospel is not proclaimed.[4]

51 Pope Paul VI's new way of seeing the relationship between the Gospel and culture gradually generated a new focus of evangelization that we call inculturation. Defined broadly, the term *inculturation* refers to the process by which the church tries to infuse a culture with the life and message of Jesus, so that the Gospel becomes incarnated in the soul of that particular culture, responds to its highest expectations, and reshapes the culture by making it grow in the Christian dimensions of faith, hope, and charity. Inculturation occurs when people and sociocultural groups welcome the Gospel into their total life or *realidad.* The process of inculturation has four dimensions:

1. the development of those values of a culture that are compatible with the values of the Gospel
2. the transformation of cultural aspects that are opposed to the Gospel through Christian praxis by the members of that culture; the task of the Reign of God becomes the principle that moves and guides the people's interpersonal relationships and their active participation in history
3. the growth and mutual enrichment of people and groups in a particular sociocultural milieu through the following of Jesus
4. the introduction of that culture, with all the gifts that God has given it for the benefit of humanity, into the life of the ecclesial community

52 The process of inculturation challenges the vision, methods, content, and objectives of all evangelization activity among young people. Inculturation takes place only when it takes into account the age, experience, language, and sociocultural reality of the young people being evangelized, and creates communal experiences that include proclamation of the Gospel, reflection, action, and celebration. Creating such communal experiences represents an especially strong challenge to the Catholic church, which is formed by people of diverse cultural traditions. This fact requires all evangelizers to give special attention to the way they promote inculturation in the ethnic and sociocultural group in which they work and to seek appropriate ways to foster a truly Christian communion among the different groups.

Inculturation at the Different Levels of a Culture

53 This section talks about the different levels that constitute a culture and that have to be considered in all inculturation processes. There are various ways of understanding and promoting inculturation. This book is based on an analysis that divides culture into five levels, according to its cultural content. The five levels interact with and influence one another, so the boundaries between one level and the next are flexible. The first level includes the external and easily visible elements of the culture; the second includes language, customs, and traditions; the third is made up of the social systems and institutions that structure a society; the fourth includes cultural values and the values of the Reign of God; and the fifth consists of a worldview that interprets and gives meaning to life. This section describes these five levels, examines how faith is immersed in each level, and offers some suggestions for achieving inculturation.

First Level: External and Easily Visible Cultural Elements

54 Material objects, pastimes such as sports and entertainment, and clothing fashions generally characterize the external and most easily observable level of culture. This level is present in all societies, and elements tend to spread from one society to another through commerce, transportation, and technological and social communication. Although external elements of modern culture facilitate the development of young people, these elements can also damage young people if they fall into consumerism, self-centeredness, competition, **materialism,** or **hedonism.** Because material or external elements appear simply to represent the material aspects of a culture, young people tend to accept them uncritically, without being aware of the influence these elements have on deeper levels of culture.

55 Evangelization at this level must encourage young people to reflect on their culture and consciously choose how and to what ends its benefits should be used. To make these conscious choices, young people need to develop their capacity for critical thinking. They also need to acquire an interior freedom that enables them to choose items and activities from this cultural level that promote personal dignity and foster personal development while avoiding activities, fashions, and technologies that dominate and manipulate.

56 When young people look only at the external cultural expressions among youth in the United States, they find many similarities because, in general, young people share similar tastes in fashion, electronic goods, and "pop" music. Remaining at this first level of culture makes it difficult for young people to consider deeper cultural aspects, in which the meaning of life is rooted, and where there are important differences such as language, ethnic culture, economic status, and social mores.

Second Level: Language, Traditions, and Customs

57 The second level of culture is made up of the language, social and religious traditions, and household customs through which people express their *idiosincrasia* and way of being. Among these elements, the following stand out: spoken language and body language; music, the visual arts, and literature; ways of reacting and adjusting to diverse life situations; and styles of celebration, relaxation, and expression. Also included in this level are a people's calendar of meaningful holidays, their tastes for certain foods, and their folkloric heritage.

58 All these elements are means by which people communicate and interact. They are the channels used to express the psychology and philosophy that give coherence and identity to a people. Therefore, people tend to adhere to them and make serious efforts to pass them on to subsequent generations. Parents tend to have strong cultural conflicts with their children when their children fail to respect the language, traditions, and customs of the parents' generation.

59 To evangelize this second level of culture, one must distinguish between tradition and traditionalism. In addition, young people must assume their role of building a new cultural synthesis.

Tradition and Traditionalism

60 Tradition conserves the roots and cultural elements that have a permanent value through history. Tradition is alive when people find creative and new ways of expressing their culture's roots and values, responding to new circumstances without losing the essence of those roots and values. Traditionalism tends to fixate on past customs, maintaining them in unchanging forms, without identifying their essential values or trying to relate them to new cultural

forms and historical contexts. Through traditionalism, customs can lose their meaning and reason for being.

61 Latino young people confront both Latino and Euro-American traditionalism daily, but they tend to reject Latino traditionalism and accept Euro-American traditionalism uncritically, thus abandoning values that they might appreciate and find important—if they were aware of them.

62 The relationship between faith and culture is stronger at this second level than it is at the first level. Language, household customs, and social traditions express and transmit the feelings and religious beliefs that are important to people. For example:

- Pilgrimages symbolize an arduous but joyful journey toward God.
- Family altars reinforce an awareness of God's presence in the home.
- Giving witness to miracles testifies to God's marvelous works in daily life.
- Music, song, dance, and other art forms arise from deep within a people's heart to capture and express their deep personal and communal faith experiences, their devotion, and their religious awareness.
- Rituals, gestures, and symbols signify people's union with God and the rest of the community.

63 Among the important social traditions that accompany and reinforce the ***religiosidad*** of Hispanic people are fiestas, ***compadrazgo,*** vigils, folkloric sayings, and myths. Hispanic young people frequently engage in these traditions without recognizing their meaning and value, thus running the risk of falling into meaningless traditionalism. Eventually, Hispanic young people may abandon their faith if they tire of or reject such traditionalism, or they may seek a different church, one that offers them socioreligious meaning in life.

Builders of a New Cultural Tradition

64 To become aware that they are active builders of a new tradition, young people need to know and analyze their present situation and the traditions of their culture of origin. They should be encouraged to find creative new ways to express their values and religious beliefs, according to their own way of life and cultural context.

65 Given the multicultural makeup of the Catholic church, young people should develop their capacity to dialog about the faith with people from other cultures and traditions. Generally, such dialog is best begun by sharing art, food, and folklore, because this sharing requires no profound change of attitude, it helps those involved shape a healthy pride in their cultural identity, and it promotes friendly relations and mutual respect among young people from diverse cultures. However, deeper intercultural dialog is necessary in promoting an understanding and appreciation of a culture other than one's own. Achieving a deeper intercultural dialog is often dependent on acquainting people with all five levels of one another's culture.

Third Level: Social Systems and Institutions

66 The third level of culture consists of systems and institutions (social, political, economic, educational, religious, and artistic) that structure society and embody the experiences and struggles of a people. Social systems and institutions generally reflect the culture in which they develop. Young people slowly become part of them, thus learning how to function in society. Young people need to learn the workings of these institutions in order to claim their own rights, fulfill their civic obligations, and transform those institutional elements that undermine their dignity, stand in the way of their human development, or impede their incorporation into society.

67 In the Christian vision, every social system and institution is to be a source of life for people, especially for the most defenseless and needy. The church has the mission of evangelizing all of society's institutions and structures—including the church itself—so that their goals and processes promote the common good. Furthermore, the church is committed to maintaining pastoral institutions that satisfy people's needs for belonging; identity; self-esteem; and socioeconomic, human, and Christian development. These pastoral institutions facilitate young people's participation in the church and in society.

The Church and Latino Young People

68 The church as an institution must embrace all its members, regardless of their race, language, or culture, in order to fulfill its

evangelizing mission with them. Latino people relate to the institutional dimension of the church primarily through pre-sacramental preparation and Sunday worship. The quality of this contact strongly influences Latino young people's faith-life and attitudes toward the church. When young people have positive church experiences and encounter a true community there, they generally open themselves to the Good News and accept their mission as Christians. On the other hand, when young people are not accepted, they have painful or destructive church experiences that affect them at a deep, meaningful, and personal level. To young people, rejection or belittlement by the church devalues them before God and their sisters and brothers. Young people who experience such devaluation normally become alienated from the church, and reconciliation requires special efforts on the part of the ecclesial community.

69 Parish groups, apostolic movements, and small communities are ecclesial institutions in which young Latinos can encounter God, express their faith, and give Christian meaning to their life. These groups should maintain communion with the rest of the church through structures that promote their participation in all important aspects of ecclesial life. This communion will help the church become a better sign and promoter of the Reign of God in the multicultural society of the United States.

Fourth Level: Cultural Values and the Values of the Reign of God

70 Values and value systems constitute the fourth level of culture. Cultural values are the beliefs and attitudes generated by the life philosophy and *idiosincrasia* of a people. Because values give direction to life, they are vitally important in forming the emotions, intellect, and will of young people. Values determine young people's attitudes, lifestyles, and ways of relating socially; they provide the perspective and viewpoint from which young people interpret life, set priorities, and make judgments; they provide the criteria for adapting to diverse situations and circumstances; and they help formulate, accept, or reject ideologies for confronting personal and social problems.

Values Formation

71 Both personal values and cultural values are acquired little by little, and they are formed and structured throughout life. Childhood, adolescence, and "youth" in general are the key stages of this process, first in receiving values from parents, and then in making choices oriented toward solidifying personal values. A family focus is vital in youth ministry. The family, as a domestic church, is the first level of ecclesial community, in which the values of the Reign of God should be lived out from day to day.

72 Young people need a formation based on free and well-informed choices about values. In order for young people to receive such a sound formation, pastoral ministry should supplement and support parents in their task as educators of the young. The process of values transmission and formation is achieved through three complementary types of action: witnessing of other people in the embodiment of a particular value, being motivated to embrace that value, and reflecting on how to live and express that value in one's own life. It is crucial that young people examine their values in light of the Gospel and through a critical analysis of their language, traditions, customs, and social systems and institutions. When these different cultural elements show no consistency in values, young people become confused and disoriented.

73 Positive experiences that affirm young people in their culture are essential for the formation of values and the acquisition of personal identity. During adolescence, when young Hispanics are searching and questioning prevailing values and the way to express them culturally, it is especially important that they recognize and experience traditional, positive Hispanic values. For example, personal relationships, cooperation, and community are highly valued; one's relationship with God is experienced and expressed in community; and religion and religious values are strongly connected to other aspects of life.

74 Values imposed on young people by the family or transmitted only through traditionalism are highly vulnerable to the negative impacts of modern culture and social pressure. Moralizing, imposing laws, and insisting on traditionalism—actions that are common among Hispanic families—only elicit negative reactions from young people and encourage them to reject Hispanic cultural values. Hispanic young people who associate their own culture with negative experiences may change their culture or turn to values—

materialism, individualism, and hedonism—that run counter to the values of the Reign of God.

Promoting the Values of the Reign of God

75 Being a Christian means taking on the values of Jesus as ideals and making those values a reality through a continuous process of conversion. This conversion should progressively touch all the attitudes and behaviors with which people respond to specific situations in their personal and social life. Youth ministry has the mission of shaping young people's values, for these values are the basis of every moral decision. Furthering values formation should promote a Christian vision of life while avoiding legalistic and overly intellectual positions.

76 Through his words, his actions, and his own person, Jesus clearly communicated the values of the Reign of God. Jesus' radical authenticity, love, service, commitment, courage, and faithfulness to God and to God's plan for salvation—all these values strongly attract young people, when these values are lived out. The scarcity of people living out these values results in a lack of models who can move and challenge young people. Young people need the Christian example of their parents, other young people, and the faith community acting responsibly and in a way consistent with the faith.

77 Given the cultural pluralism in the United States, young people should be offered opportunities to get to know the values of other cultures. By learning about other cultures' values, young people will not confuse respect for people of other cultures with indifference toward them. True respect for people different from ourselves implies building caring relationships with them, having an interest in knowing them, being sensitive to their needs, and making efforts to understand them and see life from their perspective. Valuing diversity enriches the process of affirming and living out Gospel values. Rather than experiencing divisions among themselves as a result of their differing ways of living the faith, young people can feel united and proud of the fact that in their church, unity in the Spirit is lived within a variety of expressions and complementary gifts.

Fifth Level: Personal Worldview and the Meaning of Life

78 A worldview, a way of understanding the world and of giving deeper meaning to life, constitutes the fifth level of a culture—a culture's very heart. At this level, people can seek and find the meaning and significance of life. It is at this level that young persons seriously ask and respond to the key and existential questions of life. A worldview includes a way of defining human nature, a perception of God, and a way of relating to God, oneself, other human beings, and the universe.

79 People throughout history have formulated worldviews expressed in various ways and founded on various systems of belief. Most of these worldviews recognize God's presence and action in all of creation.

80 The Incarnation of Jesus in the history of humanity liberates people from sin and death. This is the central axis of the Christian worldview that comprehends the truth about God the Father, Son, and Holy Spirit; about the human person created in God's image; and about the church and its mission to extend the Reign of God in society. This worldview gives Christian meaning and orientation to life. Also, it encourages every baptized person to journey toward God—following Jesus, animated by the Holy Spirit, and incorporated in the ecclesial community.

Expressing the Meaning of Life

81 Every culture creates its own unique way of expressing the ultimate meaning of life. Intimately connected to this level of culture is language—written, spoken, expressed through gestures, silences, tones, intensities, symbols, rituals, and so on. Language gives birth to ideas, concepts, and shared meanings that express a person's deepest and most intimate experiences. The language that carries the most profound meanings for a person is almost always the language originally spoken at home, the language of the heart, which shapes the experiences that forever mark a person's emotions, values, personal attitudes, and way of thinking.

82 People's values and attitudes are generally connected with their worldview and religious experiences and beliefs. Therefore, religious language tends to be a person's "mother tongue"—even when a person is bilingual or multilingual.

Transmitting the Faith

83 Every meaningful religious experience is rooted in this deep, worldview level of culture, this home of mystery where people confront the ultimate meaning of life and transcend human understanding and human action. Here the Gospel becomes incarnate, creating "new people" who can give Christian meaning and direction to their culture. From the worldview level, the destiny of persons and of whole cultures can be consciously directed.

84 Although the root and goal of religious experience lies at this cultural level, evangelization must occur through continuous and complementary experiences at all cultural levels, in order for the person and message of Jesus to reach young people's hearts. New creation in Jesus Christ requires that the Gospel, inserted at all personal and cultural levels, be able to clearly and decisively reach the deep realms from which young people's beliefs, ideals, and behavior emerge.

85 It is crucial that evangelization be carried out in the cultural language of the heart. Young people must be allowed to choose the language and cultural environment in which they can best relate to their sisters and brothers and to God, and best express their deep experiences. The majority of Hispanic young people have received the faith and learned to express it through popular religiosity and popular Catholicism. Evangelization among young people should take into account both of these ways of transmitting the faith, as well as the language—English or Spanish—of transmission. Only when these elements are taken into account will young people be able to identify with their religious experiences and base their hopes on the Reign of God.

The Inculturation Process in the Prophets of Hope Model

86 Nearly two thousand years ago, at the true founding of the church (Pentecost), the Holy Spirit flooded into the lives of people from diverse cultures, and Jesus' disciples began proclaiming the Good News "to all nations." Five hundred years ago, European missionaries brought Jesus' message to the ***indígenas*** of Latin America, giving new meaning and sense to their lives and history. Today,

Hispanic Catholics in the United States, moved by the spirit of the Risen Jesus, yearn to renew life and culture and to provide a Christian foundation for the new culture that is being born in the Americas. Hispanic young people carry a special role in this renewal and new birth, given their age, their cultural situation, and their large numbers in the church.

87 In the Prophets of Hope model, the inculturation process stems from small communities of young evangelizers. In this process, one may distinguish the following four phases, which are intimately related to one another.

First Phase: Formation of a Small Community

88 Small communities of faith are formed and developed when young people are doing the following:

- establishing friendships; developing understanding, trust, service, support, and respect based on their communion with Jesus; generating Christian love
- discovering the will of God for themselves as members of the church in a particular sociocultural environment and with a particular evangelizing mission
- knowing the meaning of the Christian message and living it in all areas of their life, with the support of community prayer and reflection

The formation of this type of small community requires use of the language, customs, and traditions that young people are most comfortable using in their relationships with one another and with God.

Second Phase: Evangelization of Culture

89 The evangelization of culture takes place as young people recognize God's presence in the values of their culture and learn to do the following:

- analyze and discern the signs of the times
- conduct their personal and social relationships based on the values of the Reign of God
- purify their cultural traditions and customs from elements that are contrary to the Gospel
- intentionally struggle to eradicate institutionalized sins in social organizations and systems

- consider history as the context in which Christ's liberation project takes place through Christian praxis

Achieving these goals requires an approach that promotes the incarnation of the Gospel in young people's own culture, and that nurtures a true Christian community among all ethnic and sociocultural groups in the church.

Third Phase: Transformative Christian Praxis

90 In the third phase, young people carry out intentional actions to bring about a new Christian cultural synthesis that affirms the positive elements of their culture as young Latinos in the United States, and that substitutes its negative elements with values, customs, and structures that promote the Reign of God. This implies a conscious and permanent option to live a continuous process of conversion that always seeks a greater coherence between Latino culture and the Gospel.

Fourth Phase: Celebration of the Life of Faith

91 The celebration of the life of faith takes place mainly in the sacraments, those special moments when young people experience the relationship between salvation in Christ and their life of faith incarnated in their culture. Thus, it is vital that young people celebrate the sacraments in their language, and that the sacraments have meaning in their life. Young people also celebrate their faith through community prayers that bind together their journey of faith and their efforts to live the Gospel, using a language, symbols, and signs that are meaningful for them.

92 Through these four phases, the Gospel gradually permeates young people's culture, which stems from the culture's vital nucleus and responds to the great challenges of modern society. The experience of the three central mysteries of salvation—the Incarnation of Jesus, Easter, and Pentecost—by young people who are aware of the need to foster an inculturation process is transforming

- their personal and collective history into a history of salvation
- their personal life into a project of evangelization
- their culture into an instrument that facilitates the life of people as daughters and sons of God

93 Through this process, young people may assume their Christian commitment, aware of their special role, as Pope John Paul II stressed it in his apostolic letter *To the Youth of the World:*

The future belongs to you young people, just as it once belonged to the generation of those who are now adults, and precisely together with them it has become the *present reality.* Responsibility for this present reality and for its shape and many different forms lies first of all with adults. To you belongs *responsibility for what* will one day become reality together with yourselves, but which *still lies in the future.*[5]

8

Toward an Evangelizing Praxis with Mary

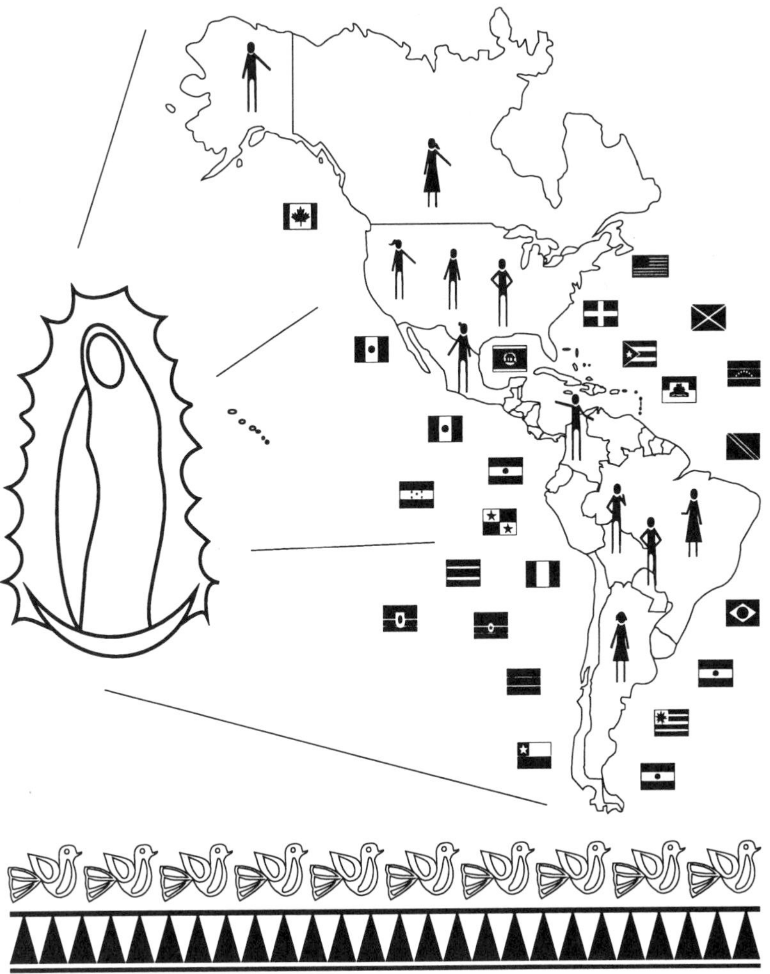

8

Toward an Evangelizing Praxis with Mary

We believe in Mary, our Mother, who has taken our Hispanic culture under her protection, and who has accompanied us and will accompany us always in our journey as she works to carry the message of Jesus to the whole world.

—Secretariat for Hispanic Affairs, *Prophetic Voices*

1 The Virgin Mary has long held a special place in the hearts of Latino people. Many aspects of Latin American life and culture testify to a profound devotion to Mary: the Latin American peoples' reliance on the Virgin as a symbol for unity and liberty during their wars of independence; their recognition of Mary as a patron saint in each nation; the large numbers of temples, sanctuaries, shrines, and chapels dedicated to her; and the many Marian devotions practiced throughout the region. The Latino people of the United States also feel a great love for Mary as their mother, and this love is one of the values Latino people most desire to pass on to future generations.

2 This chapter draws on Mary's example as a source of inspiration for evangelizing action. It offers a brief reflection on **popular Marian piety** and on Mary as a prophet and an evangelizer. Then it suggests the Guadalupan process of evangelization as a model that can bring coherence, *mística,* and direction to efforts for evangelization among Latino young people and young adults in the United States.

Popular Marian Piety

3 Popular Marian piety runs through all sectors of the Hispanic population, but it is most intense among poor and oppressed people. It is a lively and emotionally rich piety, charged with symbolism and strong religious meaning. In the United States, however, popular Marian piety tends to be weakened by the influence of **secularism,**

the Protestant vision of life, and the relative lack of enthusiasm for Marian piety among non-Hispanic Catholics.

4 The Marian experiences of young Hispanics vary with their culture of formation, their level of participation in a Hispanic church community, and the level of catechesis they have received. It would be fruitful to investigate the beliefs and feelings of young people regarding Mary, but such a study is beyond the scope of this book. Instead, this book offers suggestions regarding Mary's importance to the faith of Hispanic people in general, and encourages evangelizers to test out firsthand who Mary is for the young people with whom they work.

Mary as the Maternal Face of God

5 It is sometimes said that Hispanic people "put Mary in place of God" and consider her more important than Jesus. Many religious groups use this argument to attack Hispanic Catholicism and insist that being Christian does not require devotion to Mary, because Mary has a very limited role in the Bible. In evangelization with Hispanic young people and young adults, it is necessary to take these perceptions into account and help young people clarify their beliefs, strengthen their faith, and make sense of the confusion caused by people who judge Hispanic devotion to Mary from outside the Catholic Tradition and religious experience of Hispanic people.

6 In general, Hispanic people know that Mary is the mother of Jesus, the Mother of God, and our mother. Although Hispanics give Mary a very high status, they do not place her on the same level as God or Jesus. Pope John Paul II understood and articulated this in his homily in Zapopan, Mexico, in 1979:

> "Faith in and devotion to Mary and her mysteries are part of the identity of the people of Latin America and characteristic of their popular piety. . . . This popular piety is not necessarily a vague sentimentalism, void of a solid doctrinal base, nor an inferior form of religious experience. On the contrary, very often it is a true expression of the soul of a people, touched by grace and shaped by the fortuitous encounter between evangelization and the local culture."[1]

7 The great importance that Hispanic people give to Mary is based on their experience of her maternal love, which places her in close relationship to them and to God. This experience is deeply influenced by their pre-Hispanic religious roots. The idea of an exclusively masculine God was foreign to the experience and philosophy of the indigenous people of Latin America. Most groups and cultures had masculine and feminine deities. Others believed in a creator-God whose appearance, way of being, and way of acting were both masculine and feminine. In all cases, these two aspects interacted with and complemented each other to create and sustain life.

8 The Virgin Mary had a powerful impact on the indigenous people of Latin America, for to them she represented the maternal face of God. Through Mary's mediation, God was shown to stand with them as close and protective, compassionate and merciful, able to dignify, liberate, and reconcile them after they had been defeated in the European conquest of Latin America.

9 The indigenous people received Mary with open arms. They received her as the Virgin of Guadalupe, the heart of a whole system of evangelization in Mexico; as the Copacabana Virgin, who validated the religious experience of the "Indians" of Peru; as the Virgin de la Caridad del Cobre, who appeared in solidarity with the struggle of the native people and Africans in Cuba; and as other embodiments of the one Mary, Mother of God. Through these different advocations, Mary served and still serves as God's vital instrument for evangelizing indigenous people throughout Latin America.

10 Mary reflected the indigenous experience of a God who integrated the feminine and the masculine. Indigenous people deeply understood and venerated Mary's willingness to be the mother of Jesus. This understanding facilitated their acceptance of God as Creator and Father. Furthermore, Mary's femininity complemented the masculine attributes of God and helped the indigenous people see that God also has a feminine dimension. Through both Jesus and Mary, God encountered the indigenous people in the course of their history.

Mary, Mother of the Latino People

11 The focal point of Marian devotion for Latinos, both young and old, is Mary's role as mother. Mary's motherhood is expressed as a living, complex, and enriching role that adapts to the diverse situations of life. Her motherly love becomes apparent in many ways: in her understanding of and compassion for people's problems; in her protection during times of danger; in her blessing of children, projects, and undertakings dedicated to her; in her saving intercession throughout difficult and desperate situations; and in her faithful accompaniment during life's difficult journeys. Mary is a place of refuge for persecuted, defeated, and suffering persons. She is also the lap on which her children become reconciled to one another, a seat of peace and harmony amidst the violence and contradictions of life, and an understanding heart that pardons repentant sinners. In these ways, Mary as mother gives birth to and sustains faith in God and provides strength, hope, and liberation for Latino people.

12 At the same time, Mary's image as a fertile and generative mother of life is connected to the experiences of rural farming people who are tied to the land, and to the experience of mothers, for whom children are a blessing. Mary's motherhood, a suffering and painful motherhood, is also much like the motherhood of women oppressed by poverty and machismo.

13 Mary, like other mothers, is usually seen as a faithful presence inside the home, where the mother embodies the role of a pious, honest, strong, reconciling woman: a source of peace and union, the center of family life, and the person responsible for preserving the family, and cultural and religious traditions. This representation of Mary in a family setting tends to become a portrayal of the "ideal," self-sacrificing, and pure woman. Consequently, many people hold women up to this standard, while they pardon the rudeness and immorality of men's behavior toward women.

14 Mary's unifying power is a key element of the religious experience of Hispanic people. Marian fiestas are special moments in which all people are welcome, regardless of their moral behavior, social and racial differences, level of participation in the church, or political beliefs. Mary is the mother who unites the people, thus serving as an effective instrument of integration and identity. She also unites the people with the church, creating an expectation that the church should receive *all* of Mary's children whenever they

want to return to her, accepting them with the same mercy with which Jesus accepted sinners, the poor, and the needy.

15 In these various ways, Mary lightens the burdens that her children carry, makes their lives more bearable, and reinforces the faith of a people who live in poverty, oppression, and marginalization. Evangelization of young Hispanics should consider experiences that are deeply rooted in the Hispanic soul through personal devotions, family religiosity, and popular Catholicism. Evangelization should also complement these deeply rooted experiences with a more biblical and liberating image of Mary. In this way, the love shared between Mary and Hispanic young people will lead young people to a greater respect for and value of women, and will help instill in young people the social conscience needed for their integral liberation and for their becoming agents of change in history.

Mary: Prophetic and Evangelizing Woman

16 The sociocultural context in which most Hispanic people live makes their relationship with Mary at times rich and satisfying, at times impoverished and limited. It is rich and satisfying because Mary's understanding, security, protection, and intercession are treasured by those who live in uncertainty, misery, and institutionalized violence. It is impoverished and limited because these qualities of Mary are not enough for a people who yearn to be liberated and to enjoy a new and fuller life.

17 The New Evangelization to which we are called by Pope John Paul II provides an opportunity to re-examine the Marian experiences of Hispanic people. These experiences need to be illuminated with the light of the Scriptures. And Hispanic young people and young adults need to be offered a relationship with a prophetic mother who lives in solidarity with them in their struggle for personal development and liberation from oppression.

Prophet Among the Poor and Proclaimer of the Living God

18 Through the Magnificat, Mary's canticle of praise to God (Luke 1:46–55), we know Mary as a prophet among the poor. Mary appeared as a free woman, aware of the problems around her and knowledgeable about God's special care for the poor and the weak.

Far from being a passively submissive woman with an alienating religiosity, Mary was a woman who confidently affirmed that God overthrows the powerful from their thrones and brings justice to those who are impoverished and oppressed. A strong woman who intimately knew poverty and suffering, flight and exile, she felt like the most beloved daughter among the humble and poor children of the Lord. Mary thus stands as a model for all those who, with a Gospel spirit, want to engage in the liberating actions needed to promote justice.

19 In the Magnificat, Mary reinterprets biblical tradition and uses it to express her solidarity with a people who clamor for liberation. The Canticle of Mary should also be the prayer of every Christian, especially every evangelizer.

20 Mary's portrayal of God in the Magnificat makes it clear that God is a living God with a heart sensitive to misery, a God who stands with the poor and takes up their cause. Mary also shows us that God's mercy is not set aside for the end of life, that God does not tolerate the greed and egoism that cause impoverishment and humiliation of others, and that no agreement is possible between God's way and the way of oppression. God demands a conversion that brings with it a change in people's way of thinking, feeling, and acting, so that people's relationships are not guided by domination and the privileges of the strong.

21 In her canticle, Mary gives thanks to God for having remembered and saved her in her poverty and humility. She shows her indignation in the face of injustice and proclaims God's raising up of the humble and filling of the hungry with good things, the conversion of the so-called wise, the pulling down of the powerful from their posts of power, and the divestment of those who were rich. In the Magnificat, Mary—a young woman who had just begun her adult life—reveals herself to be the first Christian, clearly marking the new order that Jesus came to inaugurate.

Guadalupan Evangelization: God's Gift to the Poor

22 In 1531, at Tepeyac, a hill in the countryside north of Mexico City, the Virgin Mary appeared to a native peasant named Juan Diego. The Virgin told Juan Diego of her wish for a temple to be built on

that hill, and directed him to inform the bishop in Mexico City of her desire. Juan Diego did as he was instructed. After twice being dismissed by the bishop, Juan Diego conveyed to the Virgin the bishop's request for a sign; whereupon she bade Juan Diego to fill his cloak with flowers from the hilltop—Castilian roses blooming out of season. Rearranging the flowers in Juan Diego's cloak, the Virgin sent him back to the bishop. When Juan Diego opened his cloak and let the roses spill out, the bishop fell to his knees, for upon the cloak was a brightly colored image of the Virgin as she had appeared to Juan Diego—an image that has been preserved to this day, despite having suffered from poor care and inclement weather.

23 For nearly five hundred years, ever since her encounter with Juan Diego, the Virgin of Guadalupe has occupied a beloved place in the hearts of Mexicans, for whom she has been a continuous source of hope, love, and trust. She has been a mother to and a faithful companion of the Mexican people, accompanying them in their life of faith. However, perhaps because of the miraculous and still-present sign left by the Virgin at Tepeyac, most people, including many Mexicans, are unfamiliar with the depth of the Guadalupan event, its details, and its evangelizing potential. As a result, Guadalupan devotion usually fails to awaken in young people the missionary and prophetic spirit that characterized Juan Diego, and it fails to generate the evangelizing impact it had at the dawn of Christianity in America.

24 In addition to sowing the liberating seeds of the Gospel among the indigenous people in Latin America, the Virgin's encounter with Juan Diego established a model for evangelization. Looked at in its depth and details, the evangelization model brought by the Virgin of Guadalupe is integral, conscientizing, liberating, and inculturating. The Mother of God, under the sign of Mary of Guadalupe, carried the Good News to the indigenous people dominated by the Spaniards, and to the new *mestizo* people born in Latin America. And they in turn have brought her as a gift to the United States. Today, for young Latinos in the United States, Guadalupan evangelization can also serve as a source of inspiration.

The *Nican Mopohua:* Story of the Appearances

25 The *Nican Mopohua* (literally, "an account") is the original and most complete written narration of the appearances of the Virgin of Guadalupe. Written in Nahuatl, the native language of Juan Diego, the *Nican Mopohua* bears striking similarities to the Gospel narratives.

26 First, the Gospels narrate the action and message of Jesus among a people of faith, a people embedded in their history and culture. The *Nican Mopohua* narrates the action of the Virgin of Guadalupe with another people of faith, in a crucial moment in their history and culture. Second, in the Gospels, Jesus formed a group of disciples who transmitted his message and shared their own faith experiences with others, thus generating new followers. In the *Nican Mopohua,* Mary made Juan Diego a more fully evangelized disciple of Jesus, a disciple who transmitted the Gospel message and shared his own religious experience with others, thus helping to make possible the indigenous people's acceptance of Jesus Christ and his message of liberation. Finally, both the Gospels and the *Nican Mopohua* were written years after the events that inspired them, using rich and diverse literary techniques to express the experience of a people of faith.

Guadalupan Evangelization: Substance and Process

27 The Good News given to Juan Diego by the Virgin Mary echoed in the hearts of the indigenous people because it was transmitted through a context, a language, and a process that had meaning for them and could become a source of new life. The Guadalupan process includes a broad and significant set of facts, symbols, and messages. The Virgin of Guadalupe is ***mestiza.*** Her image contained a basic catechesis for the indigenous people, using their Nahuatl symbolism. She appeared in a rural area, not in the center of religio-political power in Mexico City; therefore, she is considered mother of the poor. The value and spirituality of the Guadalupan event are rooted in the totality of the event, not just in the image of Mary that came out of it.

28 The following reflection on the story of the Virgin of Guadalupe presents the *Nican Mopohua* in broad strokes. The story also explores the relevancy of the Guadalupan process in the evangelization of Latino young people and young adults today. This

story is interspersed, where necessary, with explanations of the symbolism of the Nahuatl people.

Encounter in the Everyday

29 In the year 1531 in Mexico, about ten years after Hernando Cortés had conquered Mexico for the king of Spain, the Virgin Mary appeared on a little hill outside of Mexico City and encountered Juan Diego on the path he followed on his daily walk to Mass. The story does not speak of an apparition, but rather of an encounter. There on a hill, in the everyday setting of his life, Juan Diego experienced a great and mysterious manifestation of God present for the indigenous people through Mary.

- Following Mary's example, evangelizers must go out to encounter young people in their everyday settings, in the places where they spend their time. It is in these places that evangelizers can be effective bearers of the message of God.

Languages for Dialog and for Faith

30 The Virgin spoke in the native language, Nahuatl, to communicate with Juan Diego. However, in speaking about God, the Virgin kept God's name in Spanish, thus preventing Juan Diego from confusing the God of Jesus with the native deities. In this way, she established a dialog between the two religious traditions and lay the foundation for inculturating the Gospel within the emerging *mestiza* culture.

- In order to dialog with young people, it is necessary to speak the language of youth. In evangelization with them, it is necessary to speak their language to reach their daily life. To help them know their faith, it is necessary to use the language and fundamental concepts of Christian faith and Catholic Tradition.

The Beginnings of the Guadalupan Evangelization

31 Juan Diego's first encounter with Mary is described as follows:

> It was very early dawn on Saturday. He was on the way to divine service and to do his errands. When he came to the little hill of Tepeyac, day was breaking. He heard singing from atop the hill. It was like the singing of various beautiful birds. At times the voices of the singers ceased and the hillside wilderness seemed to echo in response. Their singing, very soft and

pleasing, surpassed that of the *coyoltototl* and *tzinizcan* and other lovely song birds.[2]

32 Juan Diego's encounter happened in the early morning, when a new day was dawning; a better world was being illuminated by a fresh light. The Nahuatl people symbolized the wholeness of truth, beauty, and philosophy with "the flower and the song." For the indigenous people, songs were one of two symbols representing truth, beauty, and the profound philosophy of their culture. Here, the songs indicate a truth that the people were only beginning to glimpse. Only at Juan Diego's last encounter with Mary did the flowers appear; until then, the Virgin's message was incomplete. Juan Diego understood Mary's initial encounter with him as a truth from God, because birds symbolized the mediation between heaven and earth, and the word *song* (which occurs five times in the text) symbolized the crossroads of the path of God with the path of humanity.

33 Guadalupan evangelization is presented from the beginning as a moment of mediation: God encountered the indigenous people through the Virgin Mary and Juan Diego. Evangelization is the union of divine work and human work.

- Evangelizers among Latino young people have to be like Juan Diego—an instrument that God uses to enter young people's lives. As in the Guadalupan event, in which God acted through the Virgin and through Juan Diego's labor and effort, young people must discover that God acts through human effort.

The Relationship of the Evangelizer to the Evangelized

34 Juan Diego, the first person to see the Virgin, was a *macehual*. The *Nican Mopohua* uses the Nahuatl concept of *macehual* to intentionally identify Juan Diego as "socially poor," even though he belonged to the order of the Eagle Knights, who played the role of community mediators among his people. Juan Diego, a layperson and a "poor Indian," carried the Good News to the bishop. Only later did the bishop see the Virgin, thanks to the Indian who fulfilled the mission Mary gave him.

- Today, Latino young people are generally among the socially poor, and God wants to come close to them with a message of liberation and support. Along with God, these young people must be invited to be prophets who announce the Gospel, like

Juan Diego did, both to common people and to people holding positions of authority.

The Use of Symbol and Myth

35 The use of symbol and myth to express Juan Diego's faith and mission allows all generations to see that his religious experience was rooted in his past, has meaning in the present, and offers hope to future generations. As already noted, flowers and songs were two primary symbols for the Nahuatl people, and both played a significant role in the Guadalupan event. Throughout the *Nican Mopohua,* the use of symbolic language instead of historic-descriptive language makes it clear that we are encountering a faith experience. It is also clear that what happened at the dawn of the evangelization of the Latino people can happen as well through new evangelical efforts carried out throughout history.

- Today, it is necessary to discover and examine how and where the Virgin Mary enters the lives of Latino young people in the United States. What is her message, what symbols now accompany her message, and what language does she speak? Who are the Juan Diegos of today?

God Presented as the God of Life

36 In presenting herself to Juan Diego and in giving him an understanding of God, the Virgin did not use unfamiliar concepts or complicated mysteries to communicate who God is. Rather, she used a concept and "mystery" already familiar to Juan Diego through his Nahuatl heritage and his Christian conversion—that of life itself.

> "Be it known and understood by you, the smallest of my children, that I am the ever Virgin Holy Mary, Mother of the true God from whom all life has come, of the Creator, close to whom is everything, the Lord of heaven and earth."[3]

37 The Virgin introduced God as "the true God from whom all life has come," thus indicating that all life comes from God and that the new life offered by the Christian God does not interrupt the continuation of the people's lives.

- Young people today yearn for life and are open to sharing a new, more meaningful and intense life with others. So they are greatly attracted when evangelizers present God as a God who gives life and liberates them from the forces that inhibit life or take it away.

Importance of the Setting for Evangelization

38 Four places play important roles in the Guadalupan event: (1) the village where Juan Diego came from—*Cuautitlan,* which in Nahuatl means "place of the eagles," and to the Aztec people symbolically meant "a place of God's wisdom"; (2) *Tlatilolco,* the village in which stood the church Juan Diego attended to learn the Catholic doctrine, doctrine presented as abstract ideas and concepts foreign to the life experience of the indigenous people; (3) the hill of *Tepeyac,* where the Virgin Mary appeared and God was manifested in concrete ways. All hills carry powerful religious meaning, because hills were sacred places; it was there that the indigenous made pacts with God (this is why they built "artificial hills," erroneously called pyramids today); and (4) *Mexico City,* where the bishop resided, which was the political, social, and religious center of the invading people.

- Latino young people will receive the Gospel message and integrate it into their lives to the extent that evangelizers carry God's wisdom and present it in powerful and consistent ways that relate to young people's experience and perspectives about life. To do this, evangelizers must seek out young people where they live and reveal God's presence in their lives, filling them with the saving action of Jesus.

Respect, Correction, and Complementarity

39 Throughout her dialog with Juan Diego, the Virgin did not "attack" the polytheistic vision of the indigenous people. Instead, she described herself as the mother of all their gods—of God the Giver of Life, God the Great Truth, God the Creator, the Lord of Things Nearby, the Lord of Heaven and Earth. Thus, the Virgin interpreted the indigenous people's beliefs without denigrating the seeds of the Gospel that were already present in their religious life and beliefs.

- In evangelization with Latino young people, it is necessary to discover and respect the faith that they already have and through that faith present the Good News of Jesus.

A Gospel That Gives Life

40 Juan Diego was already accustomed to going to Tlatilolco for Mass and for instruction in religious doctrine. But the Virgin did not use this experience or routine in order to make Juan Diego a leader who would bring more people to Tlatilolco. Rather, she asked him to build a temple on the hill, close to where the native people lived:

> "I ardently desire that a temple be built for me here, where I can show and offer all my love, compassion, help and protection. . . . Here I wish to hear and help you, . . . to hear your complaints and remedy all your sorrows, hardships, and suffering."[4]

41 The Virgin wanted her son, Jesus, to be with the indigenous people, to participate in their life so that they would no longer have to look for him within a culture or a language that was meaningless for them.

- Evangelization following the Guadalupan style is done by participating in young people's lives—loving them, listening to them, feeling their joy and pain, helping them with their needs, healing their wounds, defending them from oppression and injustice, restoring their dignity, and strengthening their spirit so that they can build the Reign of God.

A Call to Conversion for Church Structures

42 The Virgin Mary did not act only for the sake of the indigenous people; she urged Juan Diego to go to the bishop and get the religious authorities to embrace a more appropriate method of evangelization for a people impoverished and oppressed by the colonial system. The bishop needed to be evangelized by the "poor Indian," for although the bishop believed in God, he was not aware that the Gospel message required liberation of the indigenous people.

- The evangelization of young people today depends both on direct pastoral work with young people and on work to transform church structures so that they respond to young people's pastoral needs.

Solidarity in Mission

43 After having encountered the Virgin, Juan Diego immediately went to the bishop's palace and told him what he had admired,

seen, and heard. Juan Diego was secure in his faith, knowing that his message was true. But the bishop, who was in charge of giving and teaching the faith, doubted him and asked him to return another day:

> "You shall come again, my son, and I will hear what you have to say at greater leisure; I shall look into the matter carefully from the very first and give much thought and consideration to the good will and desire with which you have come."
>
> [Juan Diego] left and started back sadly, for by no means had he accomplished the purpose of his errand.[5]

44 Juan Diego returned and sought out Mary. He explained to her what had happened, addressing her as "Lady, smallest of all my daughters." She had earlier addressed him in a similar way as "Juan Diego, the smallest of my children." Addressing an adult as "the smallest of my children" signified that the person had been belittled, humiliated, and oppressed. In the face of the bishop's rejection of Juan Diego, Mary, the Mother of God, joined in solidarity with Juan Diego. Humiliation of the "Indian" humiliated Mary.

- Christians need to show solidarity with all people who suffer from injustices done to them by other people and by systems that have institutionalized sin. Only through solidarity can evangelizers bear the Good News in a way that is meaningful to Latino young people.

A Rejected Prophet

45 When Juan Diego departed to give his message to the bishop, he went with great confidence. But by the time he returned, he had changed. Upon seeing the Virgin, he said clearly, "I went to fulfill your will," for he knew that he had not failed, that he had done what he was asked to do. However, the bishop had failed to trust him, and this had destroyed Juan Diego's self-confidence. Thus, when Juan Diego talked with the Virgin, he said the following:

> "[The bishop] thinks I may have made it up about your wanting a temple made for you here, and that it may not be an order of yours. So I earnestly entreat you, my Lady and Daughter, to entrust one of the important people with the message, someone well-known, respected and held in esteem, so that it will be believed; for I am a little man [somebody

> without status in society], a thin rope [tied and knotted, without a role in history], a little wooden stepladder [a trampled man], a tail [stinky and repulsive], a leaf [a dead man, detached from the tree of life], one of the little unimportant people [a man unable to stand by himself], and you, my Child, smallest of my daughters, my Lady, send me where I am out of place and have no standing. Forgive me if I cause you much grief and make you angry with me, my Lady and Mistress."[6]

46 The distrust of the bishop, who was the authority of the church, immediately undermined Juan Diego's self-confidence. Consciously or unconsciously, the bishop led Juan Diego, the "Indian," to accept domination, to assume that the powerful are responsible for acting, to feel incapable of achieving his own mission, and to try to escape his role in history. As a result, Juan Diego's position and attitude were exactly the opposite of what the Virgin Mary intended. His status as a person of dignity had been undermined. But Juan Diego could not see how this had occurred, so he felt guilty, as is clear from his way of addressing the Virgin.

47 The same kind of rejection has occurred for millions of indigenous people and *mestizo* Latinos; they have heard the liberating message of the Gospel, but have been personally mistreated and have seen their struggles reduced to ashes—sometimes by members of their own church.

48 In the United States, thousands of Latino young people have come to social institutions and parishes seeking a better life, and many young Latinos have tried to carry the Gospel to others.

- How many young people have been belittled or ignored by persons in positions of authority? How does the distrust and lack of understanding sometimes shown by pastoral agents deeply wound or weaken young people's faith?

Role of the Prophetic Poor

49 In spite of his being rejected, Juan Diego remained true to his Lady, though he felt downcast and defeated. The Virgin did not accept Juan Diego's change of attitude. Nor did she try to hide or minimize his feeling of oppression, but rather insisted:

> "Listen to me, smallest of all my beloved Children, and understand that my servants and messengers are many, and any of

> them could be ordered to take my message and do my bidding; but it is in every way necessary that you solicit my cause and help me and that it be through your intercession that my wish be carried out. My little son, I urge and firmly order you to go again to the bishop tomorrow."[7]

50 Although there were Spanish missionaries who could have carried the Good News to the indigenous people, the Virgin insisted in evangelizing through the work and mediation of Juan Diego, a "poor Indian." In the plan of salvation, poor people are the essential protagonists of liberation. So Juan Diego's mission was not optional, but rather obligatory: "'It is in every way necessary that you solicit my cause and help me. . . . I urge and firmly order you.'"

- Likewise, evangelization of young Latinos does not come from outside, but from within the heart of the believing young community that takes on a prophetic role and fulfills its mission. To form young evangelizers and missionaries is not an option, it is an urgent necessity!

Missionary's Confidence

51 Once the Virgin had restored Juan Diego's confidence and loyalty to his vocation, he returned to the bishop, sure of himself and of the message that he carried. The stark contrast between Juan Diego's experiences with the bishop and his experiences with the Virgin had helped him see that for the Virgin, he was a person of ability, dignity, and courage. The Virgin's trust bolstered Juan Diego through his second meeting with the bishop, which went no better than the first meeting:

> The bishop, in order to verify the matter, asked many questions. Where had he seen her? What was she like? And [Juan Diego] gave a full account of everything. But even though he recounted with great exactitude what she was like and all he had seen and marvelled at, so that in every way it should have been obvious that she was the ever Virgin, Holy Mother of the Savior, our Lord Jesus, even then [the bishop] did not deign to believe him. He said he could not carry out the order just on the basis of [Juan Diego's] account and at his request, but that it would be most necessary to receive a sign before he could believe that the message had come from the Lady of Heaven herself.[8]

52 Juan Diego's precise explanation of all that he had seen and heard testified to the authenticity of his encounter with the Virgin, the Mother of God and the mother of Jesus Christ, but still the bishop did not believe him. He could not see the authenticity of the "poor Indian's" faith or validate his religious experience. On the contrary, the bishop distrusted Juan Diego all the more:

> When the bishop saw that he confirmed everything without hesitation or retraction, he had him followed by members of the household whom he could trust so that they could watch and see where he went, and whom he saw and spoke to. This they did.[9]

53 Juan Diego's faith did not fail; he was sure he would receive a sign, and he went out to find it in his homeland. There, in the setting he was familiar with, he would find the means to fulfill his mission. The bishop's agents, the people whom the bishop trusted, followed Juan Diego, but they lost track of him when he arrived at Tepeyac, his homeland and place of liberation. When the bishop's agents reported back to the bishop, they tried to prejudice him against the "Indian," saying that Juan Diego was a liar who had fooled him. Also, they decided that Juan Diego deserved punishment.

54 Just as Juan Diego's faith was strengthened, young people's faith is strengthened in recognizing Jesus as God-become-human to give them new life. But too often, their faith is placed in doubt by their parents, religious authorities, or pastoral agents. So often we hear only about the defects and problems of youth.

- It is necessary to put more trust in young people's faith and sincere efforts to find a place in the church, improve themselves, and build a better world. It is also necessary to examine the tendency of adults to prejudge young people's intentions and abilities. Based on these prejudices, society and the church tend to abandon young people to their own struggles. Which is the position of evangelizers today—Mary's position or the position of the bishop and his agents?

Priority in Attending to Critical Needs

55 At the time that Juan Diego was looking for the sign required by the bishop, he found that his uncle, Juan Bernardino, had

become gravely ill with a pestilence brought by the conquistadores. Sure that he was going to die, the uncle asked Juan Diego to bring a priest to hear his confession and prepare him for death. For the Nahuatl people, uncles were extremely important figures: the title *uncle* was an address of greatest respect, children inherited from their uncles rather than from their fathers, and uncles played a central role in the life of the barrio and town. Juan Bernardino is key to the Guadalupan process of evangelization, because he symbolizes the desperate condition of the native people as a result of the conquest:

> On Tuesday before dawn Juan Diego was already en route to Tlatelolco for a priest. As he approached the road that passes at the side of the little hill of Tepeyácac toward the west, which was his usual route, he said to himself, "If I take the direct path, the Lady may see me and I must not be detained by the sign she is prepared to send the bishop. First I must hasten for a priest and get this anguish over with for my poor uncle is surely awaiting him anxiously."[10*]

56 The situation had changed dramatically. Juan Diego first encountered the Virgin in an environment of life; the sun was shining in the east. All of a sudden there came an atmosphere of death, which was indicated by the mention of the west (where the sun goes down or "dies") and which referred symbolically to the imminent death of Juan Diego's uncle, his people, and his native religion. Facing this situation, Juan Diego asked himself, For whom should I care first, the Lady of Heaven or my sick uncle? He decided to take care of his uncle first, without mistakenly thinking that to do so would be to leave his mission unfulfilled. His solidarity with his suffering uncle, the need to attend to his uncle's critical needs, was all part of the same mission—to be an instrument of God to bring a new life and new hope.

57 The Virgin worked through the sickness of Juan Diego's uncle. His healing unites the vertical dimension of faith in God and the

---

*Most translations of the *Nican Mopohua* include another appearance of the Virgin before Juan Diego goes to see his uncle. This section was added to the original text years later and breaks the symmetry of its symbolism. To understand the Guadalupan model of evangelization, we must omit this addition.

horizontal dimension of service and human liberation. The heart of the Guadalupan process of evangelization lies here, in the union of the social and religious dimensions of life.

58 The socioreligious reality in which many Hispanic young people live has certain parallels to the situation of Juan Diego's people. The majority of Hispanic young people are poor, oppressed, belittled, and marginalized in society. Their faith is doubted by Euro-American Catholics who do not understand them, and they are constantly confronted by the forces of secularism and by non-Catholic religious groups.

- Hispanic young people who are poor need to experience the Guadalupan process of evangelization, and those who live comfortably should be invited into solidarity with those who suffer poverty. Together, they can better strive for the integral liberation of Hispanic young people.

Faith and Hope in the Paschal Experience

59 When Juan Diego went to find a priest to take care of his uncle, he tried to avoid being detained by another encounter with the "Lady of Heaven." His route of avoidance was geographically complicated but symbolically simple and meaningful:

> So Juan Diego took another path around the hill which goes up and crosses to the other side toward the east so as to reach México more quickly, and not be detained by the Lady of Heaven.[11]

60 Juan Diego changed directions, climbed the hill (a sacred place) and headed east (where the sun rises), symbolically leaving the way of death and returning to the path of life. Thanks to his actions, Juan Diego "passed over to the other side," where he would find life. There, for the third time, the Virgin encountered him and spoke with him: "'What is the matter, my little son? Where are you going?'"[12] Juan Diego responded by greeting her and asking her about her health. Then he said that he was in a hurry to find a priest to assist his uncle on his deathbed. The trust that Juan Bernardino and Juan Diego held for the missionaries, who helped people pass from earthly life to eternal life, is clear here. But this concern—that Juan Bernardino should pass well to eternal life—was not Mary's intent. Guadalupan evangelization focuses on the

integral liberation of oppressed indigenous people, on liberation in all dimensions—physical, spiritual, political, economic, and so on.

> After hearing Juan Diego's words the Most Merciful Mother spoke. "Listen and understand well my son, smallest of all, that you have no cause to be frightened and worried. Let your heart be troubled no longer, have no fear of that sickness, nor of any other sickness or sorrow. Is this not your mother here next to you? Are you not here in the shelter of my loving shadow? Am I not your health? Are you not safe here within my loving bosom? What else hast thou need of? Let nothing worry or afflict you further, not even the sickness of your uncle, for he shall not die now. You may be sure that he is at this moment cured." (And at this instant the uncle was restored to health, as Juan Diego was to find out later.)
>
> When Juan Diego heard this from the Lady of Heaven, he was much consoled and became contented. He implored her to send him off without delay to the bishop with the token or sign to insure his belief.[13]

61 In this encounter, the Mother of God presented herself to Juan Diego as his own mother, the mother of the poor. In saying that he was in the shelter of her shadow, she showed her power to protect all people. She presented herself not only as the health that would heal his uncle at that moment but also as the health that would heal the sickness and anguish of his people in the future. Healing the uncle (the people) shows Mary's importance and helps us to recognize the truth of the Gospel. Mary is God's intermediary in giving new life to the indigenous people and to the new *mestizo* people then being born. The Guadalupan process happens in the midst of human history and transcends it; the process is valid today and will be valid always.

62 Juan Diego did not doubt Mary's saving action; he had no need to go see his uncle. He knew that if the Mother of God told him that his uncle was already healed, it was true. What concerned him was the bishop's unbelief. Juan Diego urgently wished to fulfill his mission.

63 Juan Diego embodies the figure of the prophet who carries the hope of his people while never ceasing to seek the conversion of structures and people in authority. Too often, people in authority

ignore the rights of native people and fail to consider the liberation of oppressed peoples as an essential part of the Gospel.

- Evangelizers must remember and live out the two dimensions of being a prophet—instilling hope and calling others to conversion. Each dimension requires the other. Latino young people—like young people of other ethnic groups—need both the direct work of evangelizers *and* a church that lives in solidarity with their struggle for liberation.

Messenger of the Truth

64 After speaking with the Virgin, Juan Diego showed his urgent desire to carry to the bishop the sign the bishop had demanded. Juan Diego did not ask Mary for the sign, for he knew that he himself had to find the sign. Mary, on her own initiative, sent him up the hill to look for and gather flowers to take to the bishop as a sign of the validity of his message.

> The Lady of Heaven bade him to go to the top of the hill, to the same place of the previous encounters. She said, "Climb my little son, smallest of all my sons, to the top of the little hill, there where you have seen me and received my orders and you will see many flowers. Gather them carefully and place them together, then bring them and show them to me."
>
> Juan Diego went immediately up the hill, and when he reached the top was greatly surprised at the number and variety of Castilian roses blooming out of season, that time of year being frosty and cold. They were very fragrant and covered with the dew which had fallen during the night. The dew drops looked like precious pearls.[14]

65 The Virgin sent Juan Diego up the hill, a place that symbolized the authority of the priests, for in the Nahuatl religious rituals only the priests climbed the temples on the top of the hills (the pyramids). The people remained below, on the flatlands. In this way, Mary indicated that the indigenous people were "a chosen race, a royal priesthood, a holy nation, God's own people, in order that [they] may proclaim the mighty acts of him who called [them] out of darkness into his marvelous light" (1 Pet. 2:9). Juan Diego, as a member of this people, embodied the role of the royal priesthood, a role that along with the role of prophet, helped him fulfill his mission in history.

66 The Virgin did not give the flowers to Juan Diego. He had to go look for them and cut them himself. When he finished gathering them, he carried them back to the Virgin. They were real roses, fragrant and covered with dew, even though it was not the season for their blooming. These roses indicated that the world had changed. A new and mysterious life was dawning, symbolized by the roses that had appeared where until that moment there had grown only weeds native to the arid hill of Tepeyac.

67 The flowers complete the Guadalupan framework. When Juan Diego saw the complete truth, when he knew that the Mother of God had come to bring salvation to his people, his "Easter experience" was complete. The roses helped a people of the Nahuatl worldview identify with and understand as truth the profound mystery of God-become-human to save them in the midst of oppression. The presence of "flowers and song" in the Guadalupan event facilitated the people's acceptance of the true God because, as previously stated, the Nahuatl people symbolized the fullness of truth with the "flowers and song." Through these elements, the people understood that God, through Mary, had come and encountered them to offer them salvation in Jesus Christ, using Juan Diego—an "Indian" like them—as the active agent of evangelization.

A Strengthened Evangelizer

68 The Virgin took in her hands the flowers that Juan Diego carried and put them back in his cloak, saying to him:

> "My little son these various roses are the sign and proof that you shall take to the bishop. You shall tell him in my name that these shall make him understand my wish and he must carry it out. You are my ambassador most worthy of confidence. I strictly order you not to unfold your outer garment or reveal its contents until you are in his presence. You shall tell him everything very carefully; that I sent you to the top of the little hill to cut and gather flowers, and of all you saw and marvelled at so as to convince him to give his help toward building the temple I want there."[15]

69 The flowers, not the image imprinted on the cape, were Juan Diego's sign for the bishop. The flowers symbolized work that had been blessed by Mary's hands as well as the total experience of faith

that had begun with the songs Juan Diego had heard when he first encountered the Virgin. Juan Diego was sure that with this sign he would convince the bishop, because he fully trusted the Virgin, who had confirmed his mission as her ambassador. He went to Mexico City contented and confident that everything would go well. He was careful of what he carried in his cape, being sure not to spill anything, in order to transmit the sign of his truth completely.

- If we take Mary's position and place our confidence and trust in young people's ability to fulfill their mission, we should also, like Mary, give them visible signs of our trust. We need to confirm and strengthen young people in their mission and in their experience of faith.

Challenges to the Poor Evangelizer

70 When Juan Diego arrived at the bishop's palace, he encountered opposition from some of the bishop's servants:

> [Juan Diego] implored them to inform the bishop of his presence, but they all refused, pretending they did not hear him, perhaps because of the early hour, or because they knew him from his other visits and felt he was giving them trouble with his repeated persistence. Also, they had already been informed by their companions of how he had slipped from their sight the time they had been ordered to follow him. After standing there a long time, head lowered and with nothing to do as if waiting to see if he might be called, they noticed that he seemed to be carrying something. They went over to him and tried to see what it was to satisfy their curiosity.
>
> Since Juan Diego saw that he couldn't hide what he carried from them, and fearing that they might tease, push or strike him, he opened the folds of his outer garment a wee bit.[16]

71 Facing domination by and disrespect from the bishop's servants, Juan Diego again lost his vitality and took on the traits of a marginalized person suffering discrimination. In his land and on the hill, Juan Diego was active and fulfilled his mission; in the bishop's palace, he was immobilized, unable to do more than wait. Even his body, able to rise early, walk long distances, and climb mountains, became downcast and defeated. Not wanting to risk a confrontation with the bishop's servants, and to keep them from

pushing, bothering, or beating him, Juan Diego showed them the flowers reserved for the bishop's eyes.

72 How often, as evangelizers, have we distrusted young people and failed to believe in them? How often have we, as evangelizers, felt like Juan Diego in the structures of our own church? How many young Hispanics have tried to follow their vocation to the priesthood or religious life in communities that lacked confidence in them or disrespected them because they are Hispanic? Yet how often we complain about young people's lack of initiative! Might it not be that their experiences at home, in school, and at work have drained their confidence in themselves and their ideals?

- When young people come to the parish with enthusiasm about some project, we can no longer leave them waiting and paralyze them by refusing to give them a chance to explain it.

Conversion of the Evangelized

73 Juan Diego let the bishop's servants see what he was carrying in his cloak, or *tilma:*

> When they saw that it contained roses of Castile, all of them different and blooming out of season, they greatly marvelled, and more especially so because they were so fresh and fully developed, fragrant and beautiful. They tried to grasp and take some of them away from him, but the three times they attempted they did not succeed, for when their fingers closed upon them they no longer saw real flowers but flowers which seemed to be painted, embroidered or sewn onto the inner surface of the cloth.[17]

74 The servants marvelled at what they saw and went to notify the bishop that the "Indian" had returned and wanted to see him, but that they could not understand the sign he brought. Juan Diego had prepared the bishop, but not the servants, so they did not recognize the sign when it arrived. Instead, they tried to strip the truth from Juan Diego. But they failed. The truth that Juan Diego carried was not made up of flowers; the flowers were only a symbol of the restored dignity and liberation given by the Virgin to Juan Diego, the representative of his people.

75 The Guadalupan story shifts easily from real roses to roses that had been painted, embroidered, or sewn onto Juan Diego's cloak,

thus indicating the symbolism at work. They were no longer loose flowers, but rather formed part of his *tilma*, and thus of his personality. That is, the flowers—the truth brought by the Virgin—were an integral part of Juan Diego, and no one could take them from him. Juan Diego had made his own the message Mary brought—her support in changing the world of injustice and meaninglessness in which the indigenous people lived. Hope for a new life had become part of this marginalized man's personality to such a degree that he could not shed that hope or abandon his mission. Juan Diego had been profoundly evangelized by Mary. As a result, even when he felt belittled, he knew that he had to fulfill his mission—to give the roses to the bishop as a sign that he was to construct a temple for the Mother of God at Tepeyac.

76 As people who have received the Good News, with whom do we most identify—the bishop's servants or Juan Diego? Are we insensitive to the clamor of young Latinos for a new life in the United States, to their cries for a good education, for a halt to drugs and violence, for work opportunities, for the chance to live in communities of justice, peace, and love? Are we ignoring the signs of the times reflected in the enthusiasm and faith of young people who yearn to fulfill their mission?

- If we are to be "light for the world" and examples to young people, we must truly integrate into ourselves the liberating message of Jesus that Mary brought to Juan Diego and to all dominated people. When we remain strong and secure in our mission, in spite of the weariness and frustration that come with the struggle for justice, young people can take the truth of our mission to heart and make it an integral part of themselves as well.

Conversion and Solidarity of Those in Authority

77 The bishop, hearing that the "poor Indian" had returned with some roses and that he had waited for a long time, understood that the roses were the sign he had asked for. The bishop immediately sent for Juan Diego, who told him once again what he had seen and then repeated the Virgin's message, emphasizing that although he knew it was not the season for roses, he had not hesitated to go for them because Mary had sent him:

> "She told me why I was to bring them to you, and this I do so that you may see in them the sign you asked for and comply

> with her wish, and also to make you see the truth of my words and the message. Behold them here: receive them."
>
> He thereupon opened his white mantle which up to then he had held close to his bosom. As soon as all the different roses of Castile fell and scattered out upon the floor, there suddenly appeared drawn upon the cloth the beautiful image of the ever Virgin Holy Mary, the Mother of God, just as she may be seen to this day in her temple at Tepeyácac under the name of Guadalupe. Upon seeing it the bishop and all those present fell to their knees regarding it with admiration for a long while, greatly moved and carried away with what they saw. They then grew sad and afflicted, which showed that they were contemplating her with their hearts and their thoughts.
>
> The bishop with tears of sadness prayed and asked forgiveness for not having set to work on what she wanted and had ordered.[18]

78 Juan Diego wanted the bishop to believe in Mary as he did; so he gave testimony to his faith. He wanted the bishop to believe in the truth of his word as an "Indian" and in his message of faith, for only by believing in Juan Diego would the bishop believe in the mission that the Virgin had given him. Only after establishing these foundations did Juan Diego give the flowers to the bishop. When he did, Mary's image was left imprinted on his *tilma*.

79 This fifth time that Mary appeared initiated a new epoch in the interweaving of human and divine paths. The bishop finally understood in heart and mind the clamor of the indigenous people. He repented and cried at his unbelief, coldness, and lack of action. He experienced a conversion, a new solidarity with the poor Juan Diego and his people. The bishop carried the image to his prayer room. Later, he invited Juan Diego to stay in his house for a day, thus showing his change of attitude toward him.

80 The following day, the bishop asked Juan Diego to show him where he was to build the temple. In asking for instructions, he was trusting the "Indian" and treating him as a person. The "Indian" now spoke in his own voice, telling the bishop what to do. Sent by Mary, Juan Diego, who knew his people's needs, was able to intercede for them. This layperson evangelized by Mary became conscious of his prophetic mission to the bishop.

- All of us laypeople who have received the Good News as a gift from God are responsible for building relationships with our bishops and priests so that together we can seek a better way of presenting Jesus to the People of God entrusted to us.

The Meaning of the Temple

81 As soon as Juan Diego told the bishop where to build the temple requested by the Virgin, he left to go see his uncle, Juan Bernardino. Juan Diego recognized that a temple serves as a place to adore God and gather strength, but that it loses meaning if we do not carry God's presence beyond the temple to our homes, neighborhoods, and people. So he immediately went to his uncle, accompanied by servants of the bishop, who now recognized his dignity as a person.

> Upon arriving they saw the uncle well and happy with neither ache nor pain. He was surprised to see his nephew arrive accompanied and much honored, and inquired to know the cause for so much honor and attention.[19]

Mediation by Mary and by the People

82 Juan Diego's uncle told everyone of his healing and of how the Lady of Heaven had visited him, appearing under the same form as she had to Juan Diego, and asking him to go to the bishop to give testimony of his healing. Now it was the task of Juan Bernardino (who also represented the people) to go to the bishop and give testimony to the new life he had received through Mary's mediation. The entire people now had a mission—to make real the Good News brought by the Virgin.

83 The presence of the Virgin has meaning only if it is a sign of new life for people. God's intention of using Mary as an intermediary was to bring liberation to the oppressed, dignity to those who receive no respect, comfort to the afflicted, protection to the vulnerable, peace to the anguished, reconciliation between enemies, justice to the exploited, health to the sick, and equality in place of domination. So while the temple at Tepeyac was under construction, the bishop hosted Juan Diego (the "Indian" missionary) and Juan Bernardino (the whole people) in his own house, as a sign of a new solidarity and a new attitude on the part of the conquering people. Despite the frequent failure of this new solidarity, the hope

and promise brought by Mary has been constantly renewed by people of prophetic faith.

84 Ever since the Guadalupan event, the image of the Holy Virgin Mary of Guadalupe has been a symbol of the incarnation of the Good News in the Mexican people, especially among *indígenas, mestizos,* poor people, and those who live in solidarity with their cause. Today, for the Virgin of Guadalupe in the United States to be more than just a decoration or an indication of Hispanic people's alienation from the dominant culture or of their conformity among themselves, she must become an effective sign of a liberating evangelization.

The Virgin of Guadalupe: Hope for a Transformed Society

85 The image of the Virgin of Guadalupe symbolizes the power and depth of the first evangelization of Latin America. This evangelization took the seeds of the Word, as well as the language and aspirations of the people, and gave birth to the Christian faith of millions of people. The Virgin of Guadalupe inspired the first pastoral letter of the Hispanic bishops of the United States (*The Bishops Speak with the Virgin*), in which the Hispanic bishops expressed the yearnings of their people in this country, gave thanks to the Virgin for the care she has shown for Hispanics, and asked her to continue bringing her son, Jesus, to the heart of their people. The model of evangelization used by the Virgin of Guadalupe provides hope for a transformed U.S. society and a renewed U.S. church.

86 Young people today may regenerate the enthusiasm, dedication, and trust of Latinos for the Mother of God, giving Mary her place as the prophetic and evangelizing woman she is. By taking on this task, young people will echo the words with which the Latin American bishops prayed to the Virgin of Guadalupe, in the prayer that closed their Fourth General Latin American Episcopal Conference in Santo Domingo:

> Lord Jesus Christ, Son of the Living God,
> Good Shepherd, and Our Brother.
> Our only option is for You.
>
> United in love and hope
> under the protection of our Lady of Guadalupe,
> Star of Evangelization, we pray for your Spirit.

Grant us the grace
so that, in continuity with Medellín and Puebla,
we may heartily carry out a new evangelization
to which we are all called
with special involvement by lay people,
and particularly youth,
committing ourselves to an ongoing education of faith,
celebrating your praise,
and proclaiming you beyond our own borders
in a firmly missionary Church.
Increase our vocations
so that there may be laborers for your harvest.

Encourage us to be committed
to promote a comprehensive development
of the Latin American and Caribbean people
out of a gospel-inspired and renewed
preferential option for the poor
and at the service of life and the family.

Help us to work
toward an inculturated evangelization
that may permeate the *milieux* of our cities
and may take flesh in indigenous and African American
cultures
through an effective educational activity
and modern communications.

Amen.[20]

Notes and Resources 

Chapter 1: Personal Development and Evangelization

Notes

Epigraph: John Eagleson and Philip Scharper, eds., *Puebla and Beyond* (New York: Orbis Books, 1979), no. 169; originally published as *Puebla: La evangelización en el presente y en el futuro de América Latina,* by Consejo Episcopal Latinoamericano (CELAM) (Washington, DC: National Conference of Catholic Bishops [NCCB], 1979).

1. NCCB, *Leaven for the Kingdom of God* (Washington, DC: United States Catholic Conference [USCC], 1990), no. 4.4.

2. NCCB Secretariat of the Committee for the Church in Latin America, *Santo Domingo Conclusions: New Evangelization, Human Development, and Christian Culture* (Washington, DC: USCC, 1993), no. 178; original Spanish-language text copyright © 1992 by CELAM.

Additional Resources

Acha Irízar, Félix. *Búsqueda de la propia identidad.* Bilbao, España: Mensajero, 1984.

Centro de Estudios a Distancia (CEVE). *Formación de catequistas.* Madrid, España: CEVE, n.d.

Erikson, Erik H. *Childhood and Society.* 2d ed. New York: W. W. Norton and Co., 1963.

Galilea, Segundo. *El alba de nuestra espiritualidad.* Madrid, España: Narcea, S.A. de Ediciones, 1986.

———. *El camino de la espiritualidad.* Bogotá, Colombia: Ediciones Paulinas, 1987.

———. *La inserción en la vida de Jesús y en la misión.* Bogotá, Colombia: Ediciones Paulinas, 1989.

Instituto Internacional de Teología a Distancia (IITD). *Curso de formación catequética.* Madrid, España: IITD, n.d.

John Paul II. *Redemptor Hominis.* Washington, DC: USCC, 1979.

Reed, Sharon. *Access Guides to Youth Ministry Spirituality.* New Rochelle, NY: Don Bosco Multimedia, 1991.

Roberto, John, ed. *Faith Maturing: A Personal and Communal Task.* Washington, DC: National Federation for Catholic Youth Ministry (NFCYM), 1985.

Shelton, Charles M. *Adolescent Spirituality: Pastoral Ministry for High School and College Youth.* Chicago: Loyola University Press, 1983.

Tonelli, Ricardo. *Una espiritualidad para la vida diaria.* Madrid, España: Editorial CCS, 1987.

Chapter 2:
The Path to Interpersonal Communion

Notes

Epigraph: USCC, *Human Sexuality: A Catholic Perspective for Education and Lifelong Learning* (Washington, DC: USCC, 1991), 7.

1. Ibid., 19.
2. John Paul II, *Familiaris Consortio* (Washington, DC: USCC, 1982), no. 14.
3. Paul VI, *Evangelii Nuntiandi* (Washington, DC: USCC, 1975), no. 71.

Additional Resources

Aguilera Titus, Alejandro. "Teens and sex: An adult decision," in *El Momento Católico.* Chicago: Claretian Publications, 1993.

CEVE. "Diálogo con las ciencias humanas. Psicología," in *Formación de catequistas* (Madrid, España: CEVE, Area Antropológica, Tema 5), 46–63.

Fromm, Erich. *The Art of Loving.* New York: Harper and Row, 1956, 1–5.

Galilea, Segundo. *El alba de nuestra espiritualidad.* Madrid, España: Narcea, S.A. de Ediciones, 1986.

———. *El camino de la espiritualidad.* Bogotá, Colombia: Ediciones Paulinas, 1987.

———. *La inserción en la vida de Jesús y en la misión.* Bogotá, Colombia: Ediciones Paulinas, 1989.

Kelly, Molly. *Chastity: The Only Choice.* Rocky River, OH: The Center for Learning, 1992.

Mejía Pereda, Alejandro, et al. *El misterio de la existencia.* México, DF: Editorial Progreso, Serie Christo-Kosmos, 1984.

Sánchez García, Urbano. *La opción del cristiano.* Vol. 3. Colección Síntesis. Madrid, España: Sociedad de Educación Atenas, 1986.

Shelton, Charles M. *Adolescent Spirituality: Pastoral Ministry for High School and College Youth.* Chicago: Loyola University Press, 1983.

USCC. *The Sexual Challenge: Growing Up Christian.* Washington, DC: USCC, 1990.

Valdez Castellanos, Luis. *Comunicación y manejo de sentimientos.* México, DF: CEB Cerro del Judío, 1994.

Vidal, Marciano. *Moral de la persona.* 6th ed. Moral de actitudes, vol. 2. Madrid, España: Covarrubias, 1990.

Whitehead, Evelyn Eaton, and James D. Whitehead. *A Sense of Sexuality.* New York: Doubleday, 1989.

Chapter 3: Toward Human Maturity

Notes

Epigraph: John Paul II, *Christifideles Laici* (Washington, DC: USCC, 1988), no. 46.

1. John Eagleson and Philip Scharper, eds., *Puebla and Beyond* (New York: Orbis Books, 1979), no. 1185; originally published as *Puebla: La evangelización en el presente y en el futuro de América Latina,* by CELAM (Washington, DC: NCCB, 1979).

Additional Resources

Acha Irízar, Félix. *Búsqueda de la propia identidad.* Bilbao, España: Mensajero, 1984.

Alburquerque, Eugenio. *Moral cristiana y pastoral juvenil.* Madrid, España: Editorial CCS, 1990.

Centro Nacional Salesiano de Pastoral Juvenil. *Juventud y Moral.* Madrid, España: Editorial CCS, Cuadernos mj de Pastoral Juvenil, 1985.

Checa, Rafael, et al. *Valores humanos, cambio social y civilización del amor.* México, DF: Centro de Estudios de los Valores Humanos, AC [CEVHAC], 1986.

Cooney, Nancy Hennessy. "Deciding for Oneself, Not by Oneself," in *Readings and Resources in Youth Ministry,* ed. Michael Warren. Winona, MN: Saint Mary's Press, 1987.

Ferrini, María Rita, et al. *Bases didácticas.* México, DF: Editorial Progreso, Serie Educación Dinámica, 1985.

Freire, Paulo. *Concientización.* Buenos Aires, Argentina: Ediciones Búsqueda, 1974.

———. *La educación como práctica de la libertad.* 17th ed. México, DF: Siglo XXI Editores, 1976.

———. *Pedagogía del oprimido.* 15th ed. México, DF: Siglo XXI Editores, 1976.

Gagné, Robert M. *The Conditions of Learning.* 3rd ed. Orlando, FL: Holt, Rinehart and Winston, 1977.

Galilea, Segundo. *El alba de nuestra espiritualidad.* Madrid, España: Narcea, S.A. de Ediciones, 1986.

———. *El camino de la espiritualidad.* Bogotá, Colombia: Ediciones Paulinas, 1987.

———. *La inserción en la vida de Jesús y en la misión.* Bogotá, Colombia: Ediciones Paulinas, 1989.

Mejía Pereda, Alejandro, et al. *El misterio de la existencia.* México, DF: Editorial Progreso, Serie Christo-Kosmos, 1984.

Nichols, C. H. "An Analysis of the Teaching Methodology of Jesus Christ and Its Relation to Adult Religious Education." PhD diss., University of Nebraska, 1984. Abstract in *Dissertation Abstracts International* 44A, 2329.

Sánchez García, Urbano. *La opción del cristiano.* Vol. 3. Colección Síntesis. Madrid, España: Sociedad de Educación Atenas, 1986.

Shelton, Charles M. *Morality and the Adolescent.* New York: Crossroads Publishing, 1991.

———. *Morality of the Heart.* New York: Crossroads Publishing, 1990.

Tonelli, Ricardo. *Una espiritualidad para la vida diaria.* Madrid, España: Editorial CCS, 1987.

Vidal, Marciano. *Moral de la persona.* 6th ed. Moral de actitudes, vol. 2. Madrid, España: Covarrubias, 1990.

Warren, Michael. *Youth, Gospel, Liberation.* San Francisco: Harper and Row, 1987.

Chapter 4: Jesus, Prophet of the Reign of God

Notes

Epigraph: Secretariat for Hispanic Affairs, USCC, *Prophetic Voices: The Document on the Process of the III Encuentro Nacional Hispano de Pastoral* (Washington, DC: USCC, 1986), 17.

Additional Resources

Bravo, Carlos. *Galilea, año 30.* México, DF: Centro de Reflexión Teológica, 1989.

———. *Jesús hombre en conflicto.* México, DF: Centro de Reflexión Teológica, 1986.

Castillo, José M., and Juan A. Estrada. *El proyecto de Jesús.* 2d ed. Salamanca, España: Ediciones Sígueme, 1987.

Díaz-Vilar, J. Juan. *El Dios de nuestros padres.* 3d ed. New York: Northeast Catholic Pastoral Center for Hispanics, 1985.

Echegaray, Hugo. *La práctica de Jesús.* 2d ed. Lima, Perú: Centro de Estudios y Publicaciones, 1981.

Equipo de Consiliarios CVX Berchmans. *Jesucristo: Catecumenado para universitarios-1.* 2nd ed. Santander, España: Editorial Sal Terrae, n.d.

Galilea, Segundo. *La inserción en la vida de Jesús y en la misión.* Bogotá, Colombia: Ediciones Paulinas, 1989.

González Faus, José Ignacio. *Acceso a Jesús.* 6th ed. Salamanca, España: Ediciones Sígueme, 1987.

———. *La humanidad nueva: Ensayo de cristología.* Vols. 1 and 2. 5th ed. Salamanca, España: Sal Terrae, 1974.

Jeremias, Joachim. *Las parábolas de Jesús.* 7th ed. Navarra, España: Verbo Divino, 1984.

———. *Rediscovering the Parables.* New York: SCM Press, 1966.

Kasper, Walter. *El Dios de Jesucristo.* 3d ed. Salamanca, España: Ediciones Sígueme, 1990.

———. *Jesús, el Cristo.* 7th ed. Salamanca, España: Ediciones Sígueme, 1989.

Lambert, Bernard. *Las bienaventuranzas y la cultura hoy.* Salamanca, España: Ediciones Sígueme, 1987.

León-Dufour, Xavier. *Resurrección de Jesús y mensaje pascual.* 3d ed. Salamanca, España: Ediciones Sígueme, 1978.

El mesianismo de Jesús, Hijo de Dios. México, DF: Centro Antonio de Montesinos, n.d.

Morales, H. Alfredo A. *Jesús: ¡El desafío!* Santiago de los Caballeros, República Dominicana: Hermanos De La Salle and Unión Nacional de Colegios Católicos, 1985.

Smith, Francis R. *The God Question.* New York: Paulist Press, 1988.

Sobrino, Jon. *Cristología desde América Latina.* 2d ed. México, DF: Centro de Reflexión Teológica, 1976.

Chapter 5: The Evangelizing Action of God, the Evangelizers, and the Evangelized

Notes

Epigraph: USCC, *A Vision of Youth Ministry* (Washington, DC: USCC, 1986), 3.

1. *Ad Gentes,* in *The Documents of Vatican II,* Walter M. Abbott, ed. (New York: America Press, 1966), no. 2.

2. *The Bishops Speak with the Virgin: A Pastoral Letter of the Hispanic Bishops of the U.S.* (Maryknoll, NY: Maryknoll, 1981), 29.

Additional Resources

Boff, Leonardo. *New Evangelization.* Maryknoll, NY: Orbis Books, 1991.

Boyack, Kenneth. *The New Catholic Evangelization.* New York: Paulist Press, 1992.

Carrier, Hervé. *Evangelizing the Culture of Modernity.* Maryknoll, NY: Orbis Books, 1993.

CELAM. *Pastoral juvenil: Sí a la civilización del amor.* 2d ed. México, DF: Comisión Episcopal Mexicana de Pastoral Juvenil (CEM), 1989.

Ekstrom, R. R., and J. Roberto, eds. *Evangelization.* New Rochelle, NY: Don Bosco Multimedia, 1989.

Fourez, Gérard. *Una buena noticia liberadora: Evangelio para un mundo en crisis.* Santander, España: Editorial Sal Terrae, 1987.

John Paul II. *Redemptoris Missio.* Washington, DC: USCC, 1990.

Paul VI. *Evangelii Nuntiandi.* Washington, DC: USCC, 1975.

Velasco, Juan Martin. *Increencia y evangelización: Del diálogo al testimonio.* Santander, España: Editorial Sal Terrae, 1988.

Chapter 6:
Prophets of Hope: A Commmunitarian Evangelization Process

Notes

Epigraph: John Paul II, Homily for World Youth Day 1993 in Denver, qtd. in "A Celebration of Life," *Origins* 23 (26 August 1993): 179.

1. *Lumen Gentium,* in *The Documents of Vatican II,* Walter M. Abbott, ed. (New York: America Press, 1966), no. 9.
2. Ibid.
3. *Gaudium et Spes,* in *The Documents of Vatican II,* no. 1.
4. John Paul II, *Christifideles Laici* (Washington, DC: USCC, 1988), no. 46.
5. NCCB, *National Pastoral Plan for Hispanic Ministry* (Washington, DC: USCC, 1988), 8.
6. Ibid.
7. Ibid., 51.
8. John Paul II, Address for World Youth Day 1993 in Denver, qtd. in "Young People of Many Nations," *Origins* 23 (26 August 1993): 190.

Additional Resource

NFCYM. *Competency-Based Standards for the Coordinator of Youth Ministry.* Washington, DC: NFCYM, 1990.

Chapter 7:
Inculturation: A Challenge for Hispanic Youth and Young Adults

Notes

Epigraph: John Paul II, *Redemptoris Missio* (Washington, DC: USCC, 1990), no. 52.

1. *Collectanea Sacrae Congregationis de Propaganda Fide,* qtd. in *Earthing the Gospel,* by Gerald A. Arbuckle (Maryknoll, NY: Orbis Books, 1990), 12.

2. Pius XII, *Evangelii Praecones,* qtd. in Arbuckle, *Earthing the Gospel,* 14.

3. John XXIII, *Princeps Pastorum,* qtd. in Arbuckle, *Earthing the Gospel,* 14–15.

4. Paul VI, *Evangelii Nuntiandi* (Washington, DC: USCC, 1975), no. 20.

5. John Paul II, *To the Youth of the World* (Washington, DC: USCC, 1985), no. 1.

Additional Resources

Ahumada, José E. "Inculturation Challenges Religious Education: Toward Faith Formation Programs Serving the Evangelization of Cultures." Master's thesis, Graduate Theological Union, Jesuit School of Theology, Berkeley, CA, 1991.

Azevedo, Marcello. *Vivir la fe en un mundo plural.* Navarra, España: Editorial Verbo Divino, 1993.

Dussel, Enrique. *Historia de la Iglesia en América Latina: Coloniaje y liberación 1492–1983.* Madrid, España: Editorial Mundo Negro, 1983.

Elizondo, Virgilio. *Christianity and Culture: An Introduction to Pastoral Theology and Ministry for the Bicultural Community.* Huntington, IN: Our Sunday Visitor, 1975.

———. *Galilean Journey: The Mexican-American Promise.* Maryknoll, NY: Orbis Books, 1983.

———. *Mestizaje: The Dialect of Cultural Birth and the Gospel.* Paris: Institute Catholique de Paris, 1978.

Flannery, Austin, ed. *Vatican Council II: The Conciliar and Post Conciliar Documents.* Rev. ed. Collegeville, MN: Liturgical Press, 1984.

González-Carvajal, Luis. *Ideas y creencias del hombre actual.* Santander, España: Editorial Sal Terrae, 1992.

Poupard, Paul. *Iglesia y culturas: Orientación para una pastoral de inteligencia.* México, DF: Librería Parroquial de Clavería, S.A., 1985.

Rokeach, Milton. *The Nature of Human Values.* New York: Free Press, 1973.

Rovira i Belloso, Joseph M. *Fe y cultura en nuestro tiempo.* Santander, España: Editorial Sal Terrae, 1988.
Schineller, Peter. *A Handbook of Inculturation.* Mahwah, NJ: Paulist Press, 1990.
Schreiter, Robert J. *Constructing Local Theologies.* Maryknoll, NY: Orbis Books, 1986.

Chapter 8: Toward an Evangelizing Praxis with Mary

Notes

Epigraph: Secretariat for Hispanic Affairs, USCC, *Prophetic Voices: The Document on the Process of the III Encuentro Nacional Hispano de Pastoral* (Washington, DC: USCC, 1986), 18.

1. John Paul II, "Homilia," Zapopan, México, 30 January 1979. In *María, evangelizada y evangelizadora,* Carlos Ignacio González, ed. (México, DF: CELAM, 1989), 382; translated by the authors.
2. *A Handbook on Guadalupe: Our Lady Patroness of the Americas* (Kenosha, WI: Franciscan Marytown Press, 1974), 146–147.
3. Ibid., 147.
4. Ibid., 147–148.
5. Ibid., 148–149.
6. Ibid., 149.
7. Ibid., 149.
8. Ibid., 150.
9. Ibid., 150–151.
10. Ibid., 151–152.
11. Ibid., 152.
12. Ibid.
13. Ibid., 152–153.
14. Ibid., 153.
15. Ibid., 153–154.
16. Ibid., 154.
17. Ibid.
18. Ibid., 155–156.
19. Ibid., 156.

20. NCCB Secretariat of the Committee for the Church in Latin America, *Santo Domingo Conclusions: New Evangelization, Human Development, Christian Culture* (Washington, DC: USCC, 1993), no. 303; original Spanish text copyright ©1992 by CELAM.

Additional Resources

Boff, Leonardo. *The Maternal Face of God: The Feminine and Its Religious Expressions.* New York: Harper and Row, 1979.

Carrillo Alday, Salvador. "El mensaje teológico de Guadalupe," in *Santa María de Guadalupe.* México, DF: Misioneros del Espíritu Santo, 1981.

Díaz-Vilar, J. Juan. *María: Canta la esperanza.* 2d ed. Elizabeth, NJ: Producciones Católicas Paz y Bien, 1989.

———. *Miriam: La mujer galilea.* 2d ed. New York: Northeast Catholic Pastoral Center for Hispanics, 1982.

González, Carlos Ignacio. *María, evangelizada y evangelizadora.* México, DF: CELAM, 1989.

González Dorado, Antonio. *De María conquistadora a María liberadora: Mariología popular latinoamericana.* Santander, España: Editorial Sal Terrae, 1988.

———. *Nuestra Señora de América.* Bogotá, Colombia: CELAM, 1986.

González-Medina, Salvador. "El acontecimiento del Tepeyac, mensaje de salvación," in *Santa María de Guadalupe.* México, DF: Misioneros del Espíritu Santo, 1981.

Siller A., Clodomiro L. "El método de la evangelización en el Nican Mopohua," in *Las apariciones de la Virgen de Guadalupe.* 2d ed. México, DF: Centro Nacional de Estudios Indígenas, 1981.

Glossary

Acculturation. A process that takes place when two or more cultures enter into direct contact; both the people involved and the cultures themselves are transformed, usually by adapting to or borrowing traits from one another, but without totally losing their own culture. *See also* **enculturation; endoculturation; inculturation; socialization.**

Agentes de cambio. Literally, "agents of change." Persons who, consciously and intentionally, display a lifestyle and act concretely to produce a specific transformation in society or church.

Animation, *animadores.* Animation describes the role and attitude of a leader in a small ecclesial community, apostolic movement, youth group, parish program, or specific ecclesial activity. Animation involves motivating each person and the whole community, facilitating the community's prayer life, nurturing hospitality and mutual care among members, and sustaining the community in times of difficulty. This role extends to the whole life of the community; it is not limited to meetings. People who fulfill this role are called *animadores* (animators) and are different from coordinators, whose role is to facilitate the meetings of the community. *Animadores* need a certain charisma and appropriate training to succeed in their role.

Anthropology, anthropological. The study of human beings—their origin; history; culture; physical characteristics; social, political, and economic dimensions; relationship with the divine; and so on.

Antivalues, disvalues. Concepts used in Latin American philosophy and in Spanish philosophy to identify values that are against the plan of God and the dignity of the human person.

Asesores. Christians who are mature in faith and are willing to share their life experience, their faith, and their professional and pastoral advice with young people and young adults.

Autonomy, autonomous. A person's capacity to assume responsibility for, and give direction to, his or her life. Autonomy does not imply separation or independence from one's broader community; rather, within a community, it implies respect for the self-direction and moral freedom of others, and a responsible interdependence.

Cariño. An affectionate feeling characterized by tenderness, empathy, caring, and warmth.

Catechesis. An educational process by which people are instructed in the Christian faith according to the Catholic Tradition and are assisted in reflecting on their life in light of their faith in order to mature as Christians, become authentic disciples of Jesus, and live the Gospel.

Charisms. Gifts of the Holy Spirit to be used for service to individuals and communities, in view of the formation of the Body of Christ and the building of the Reign of God.

Christian discernment. A personal or communitarian process of reflection from a faith perspective to discover God's will, used when facing various life situations that require decision making. *See also* **discernment.**

Christian utopia. The coming of the Reign of God here and now, on earth, as a result of the Spirit acting in collaboration with humanity throughout history, until the Reign of God is truly and fully an experience for all people, at the end of time.

Christology. The theological understanding, study, and interpretation of the person and mission of Jesus.

Common era. The common era refers to the period after the birth of Jesus. It is based on the calendar system used in most parts of the world. C.E. replaces the abbreviation A.D., *anno Domini,* which means "in the year of our Lord." Some non-Christians found this frame of reference offensive.

Communitarian. A description meaning "related to a community." For Hispanics, a community is always formed by persons and not by individuals. The community is not a simple accumulation of individuals, but a reality that exists as a result of the interrelationships among its members. In Hispanic conceptual terms, a person cannot exist outside of a community, because it is the community that validates a person as a human being. *See also* ***convivencia;*** **person.**

Compadrazgo. The relationship between the godparents of a child and the child's parents.

Compadres, comadres. People who form family-type social relationships in Hispanic culture by becoming godparents to people's children. A *compadre* is a godfather; a *comadre* is a godmother. *Compadres* and *comadres* are members of the extended family.

Compañeros. People joined to mutually support and assist one another, to accompany one another in certain activities, or to journey together in a particular aspect of life. *Compañeros* differ from friends in that *compañeros* do not necessarily forge strong personal ties or share their whole lives with one another. And they differ from *acompañantes* in that *acompañantes* usually have a higher level of maturity and experience than the person they accompany in their journey of faith. Loyalty, understanding, respect, and interest in one another's well-being characterize *compañeros.*

Conscientization. The process by which people *(a)* become critically aware of the cultural, social, economic, political, and religious aspects of their life, and *(b)* acquire a commitment to change those things that go against the dignity of the human person.

Consumerism. A viewpoint that considers individuals and communities as instruments of production and objects of consumption. Also, a strong tendency to always produce more, buy more, and have more.

Conversion. The answer, motivated by grace, to the merciful and benevolent love of God. Requires acceptance of Jesus Christ and his Gospel. Involves a continuous process of growth and development of one's faith, and also a Christian praxis.

Convivencia. In a general sense, sharing and celebrating life with other people. In pastoral ministry, events or meetings that build or strengthen friendship, understanding, and community among the participants. *See also* **communitarian.**

Cristiandad de Indias. A religious social and political system established by the Catholic church in Latin America at the beginning of the European colonization.

Discernment. A reflexive process with the objective of clarifying possible actions for facing a real situation in life. *See also* **Christian discernment.**

Disvalues. *See* **antivalues, disvalues.**

Divine Providence. Conception of God as the power sustaining and guiding human destiny.

Dueño de sí mismo. Literally, "owner of oneself," a concept that in English can have a business connotation. In Spanish, *dueño de sí mismo* corresponds to the psychological definition of freedom. The concept specifically encompasses self-knowledge, self-acceptance, and self-possession—three elements that form the foundation for a person's conscious and responsible exercise of freedom.

Ecclesiology. A branch of theology that studies the nature and mission of the church. *See also* **theology.**

Ecumenical councils. Worldwide official gatherings of church leaders. In the Catholic church, meetings of the bishops, summoned by the pope, to deliberate and decide on doctrinal, moral, or pastoral matters and to provide direction to the church. The Second Vatican Council (1962–65) marked the beginning of an era of strong church renewal based on the Scriptures and on efforts to relate faith to modern culture.

Ecumenism. Efforts of various Christian churches to find unity among all Christians. From the perspective of the churches, ecumenism involves a constant renewal in order to be more faithful to their vocation; a conversion of heart to heal and avoid further divisions; common prayer for the unity of all Christians; better mutual knowledge and dialog among theologians and the faithful; collaboration in the various fields of social service; and an ecumenical formation of all members of the church, especially ordained ministers.

Enculturation. The process by which people acquire their culture, both at home and in society. *See also* **acculturation; endoculturation; inculturation; socialization.**

Endoculturation. The process by which people acquire their culture at home through sharing the values, beliefs, and traditions that are lived and taught in the family, especially by their parents. *See also* **acculturation; enculturation; inculturation; socialization.**

Eschatological. Proclamation of Jesus concerning the time when the promise of salvation will be fulfilled—the Second Coming.

Ethical-mythical nucleus. A set of religious beliefs that finds its expression through myths, legends, symbols, and rites embodied in values that agree with the social institutions, tradition, and customs of a religious vision of life.

Evangelization. Implies a continuous, lifelong process of conversion by which a Christian makes an ever-deepening effort to establish a personal and communal relationship with Jesus and a commitment to live Jesus' message—the Gospel—and to continue his mission of bringing about the Reign of God. *See also* **New Evangelization.**

Existential. The word *existential* has a down-to-earth meaning among Hispanics. To speak about the existence of a person is to refer to his or her whole life, particularly as related to the circumstances in which he or she lives.

Formadores. Personnel trained to educate *asesores* and *animadores* of small communities of young evangelizers and missionaries, and to accompany young people on their faith journeys and in their ministries.

Fundamental option. A profound and radical response followed by a life commitment to matters of importance. In the Christian context, the fundamental option implies a conscientious and free decision to follow Jesus and continue his mission.

Hedonism. Doctrine that affirms that pleasure is the most important good or goal in life.

Hispanic, Latino. These two terms are being used interchangeably in this book to refer to people originating from Caribbean countries, Latin America, and Spain, where the Spanish language predominates, and their descendants in the United States, who may speak English or Spanish.

Holistic, integral. Terms that emphasize the totality of the human person and the interconnectedness of people's many dimensions—physical, psychological, religious, cultural, and so on.

Idiosincrasia. The psychological traits and culture embedded in the personality and "way of being" of a particular person or ethnic group.

Inculturation. The infusion of the Gospel within a culture to such an extent that the culture is reshaped and embraces Jesus' message and mission as its central guiding principle. *See also* **acculturation; enculturation; endoculturation; socialization.**

Indígenas. Indigenous or native people who lived in America before the arrival of Europeans; also, present-day descendants of the indigenous people who have not become *mestizos* in race or culture.

Integral. *See* **holistic, integral.**

Kerygma. The initial announcement of the mystery of Jesus and the salvation that he brings to people of all times and cultures. It implies a clear and direct proclamation that Jesus Christ is the definitive revelation of God, that he offers salvation, and that he invites us to conversion. *See also* **conversion; salvation.**

Latino. *See* **Hispanic, Latino.**

Liberation. A theological concept that emphasizes the human response to the offer of salvation in Jesus Christ, and to his call to love, justice, and peace. Liberation implies a personal and communitarian conversion that leads to the transformation of social institutions and structures, and to the extension of the Reign of God. *See also* **redemption; salvation.**

Materialism. A theory that physical matter is the only or fundamental reality and that all beings, processes, and phenomena can be exclusively explained as manifestations or results of matter. Also refers to assigning an absolute value or a very high value to material progress.

Mestizaje. The intermingling between people from two different races or cultures that gives birth to a new people. Usually, the Hispanic culture in Latin America is identified as the "first *mestizaje*" and the Latino–North American culture in the United States as the "second *mestizaje.*"

Mestizo, mestiza. These terms refer broadly to people whose parents or ancestors are from different racial groups. Used in a narrower, more specific sense, they refer to children of Spanish and *indígena* parents. *Mestizo* designates a male and *mestiza* designates a female. Used as an adjective, *mestizo* ("mixed") also describes the new people, and *mestiza* the new culture, formed from the intermingling of different races or cultures.

Ministry. Specific service to people and communities in response to a personal vocation on behalf of the church community, officially recognized and sponsored by the diocese or parish. *See also* **pastoral action; pastoral agents; *pastoral de conjunto;* pastoralists; pastoral planning; youth and young adult ministers.**

Mística. A set of ideals, attitudes, values, and feelings that enlighten and motivate individuals or groups in their faith journey, inspiring their response to God and producing a spirituality that animates their life and pastoral ministry.

Modern culture. In a strict sense, modern culture refers to the period between the eighteenth and twentieth centuries when the Industrial Revolution gave way to a new social, economic, and political order that affected all aspects of human life, especially through science, technology, democracy, capitalism, and secularization. In this book, modern culture is used in a broader sense to refer to the type of culture that is characterized by these traits. *See also* **traditional culture.**

Moral relativism. A view affirming that ethical truths depend on the preferences of individuals and groups, negating the existence of objective and general norms of behavior based on Christian moral principles.

New Evangelization. A call to conversion and hope by Pope John Paul II that rests on God's promises and derives from Christ's Resurrection, which is the primary proclamation and the root of all evangelization, the foundation for all human advancement, and the principle of all genuine Christian cultures. It is likewise the effort to inculturate the Gospel in order to respond to the new situation people are facing as a result of the social and cultural changes of modernity.

Noviazgo, novios. Men and women who are in a love relationship that they expect will lead to marriage in the future. *Novios* are in a particular stage in a love relationship, a stage called *noviazgo. Noviazgo* includes two phases: going steady with a commitment not to date other people, and being *prometidos* (engaged persons), with a set date for marriage and practical preparations to establish a home.

Pastoral action. Organized ecclesial activity to facilitate and nurture the Christian growth of persons and communities, promoting their missionary action to foster the Reign of God. *See also* **ministry; pastoral agents; *pastoral de conjunto;* pastoralists; pastoral planning; youth and young adult ministers.**

Pastoral agents. Persons who, in responding to their vocation and as members of a church community, have a commitment to the mission of the church in the area of pastoral ministry.

Pastoral de conjunto. The action of all pastoral agents, ministers, and committed Christians—each in her or his own specific ministry—animated and directed by a common vision and coordinated in a spirit of communion and coresponsibility. Broadly, the harmonious coordination of all elements, ministries, and structures of the local and universal church in their work of bringing about the Reign of God.

Pastoralists. Persons with professional formation, practical skills, and experience in the field of pastoral ministry who are capable of doing pastoral planning, conducting pastoral-theological reflections, and elaborating theories for the development of pastoral ministry.

Pastoral planning. Effective organization of the church's action in fulfilling the mission of being leaven of the Reign of God in the world.

Pastoral-theological framework. Theological and pastoral guidelines originating from a specific vision and understanding of church. In this series, the framework is based on the Second Vatican Council's vision of church and on the pastoral guidelines of the National Pastoral Plan for Hispanic Ministry.

Pastoral-theological vision. *See* **pastoral-theological framework.**

Person. In English, there is a frequent tendency to equate the words *person* and *personal* with the word *individual.* In the Hispanic philosophical framework, individual refers to the human characteristic of being a unique person; *individualista* (individualistic) refers to a human being in isolation, in himself or herself only. *Person* refers to the human being in himself or herself and in relationship with others.

Popular Catholicism. The set of Catholic beliefs and practices characteristic of the majority of Catholic persons in a particular culture. Hispanic popular Catholicism is usually influenced by either an indigenous or African religious perspective and culture. Most forms of popular Catholicism are complex and diverse in their expressions and have different levels of coherence with official Catholicism.

Popular (pop) culture. Refers to the general culture of modern times intentionally created by the media and economic forces *for* people in lieu of being the "popular culture" created *by* the people. It promotes values that degrade the human person and nurture materialistic, superficial, and changeable attitudes toward others.

Popular Marian piety. The religious feelings, expressions, and customs of a Catholic community that loves, respects, and venerates Mary as the mother of Jesus and their mother, who cares for the well-being of all her sons and daughters.

Popular religiosity. A set of religious beliefs, experiences, and celebrations that form the individual and collective consciousness with which a people perceive, feel, and live the mysteries of God. See also ***religiosidad.***

Positivism. A philosophical school of thinking based on the idea that knowledge of truth is based only on scientific proof verified by discrediting other means of acquiring knowledge of truth.

Praxis. A Latin word that translates literally as "practice" or "action." Christian praxis involves people's discipleship and their critical reflection about their actions—all in light of the Gospel.

Reality. A holistic concept that encompasses the life experience of a person, the concrete environment in which he or she lives, and the active influence of the economy, government, culture, religion, and educational institutions on the person.

Reconciliation. In a secular sense, reconciliation relates to overcoming difficulties or conflicts that have developed among peoples or groups, that is, reaching an agreement. From a faith perspective, reconciliation implies a re-establishment of the union among persons, and between persons and God, after there has been a separation as a result of sin. The church offers the sacrament of reconciliation to celebrate the repentance for the faults committed, the mercy of God, and a new life in Christ.

Redemption. A theological concept emphasizing the mystery of the Incarnation of God in Jesus Christ and the restoration of one's relationship in love with God, which was broken by sin. *See also* **liberation; salvation.**

Reducciones indígenas. Towns of indigenous people converted to Christianity. In broader terms, meetings of indigenous people, lasting several days, with the purpose of attending to an evangelizing mission.

Reign of God. Jesus' vision of God's primacy in people's hearts, minds, and actions; also, a state in which all personal relationships and social systems are guided by freedom, justice, peace, and God's love.

Religiosidad. A broad concept that includes the natural tendency of people toward the divine; their relationship with God and with the sacred world; the religious environment in which they live; and their religious beliefs and experiences. *See also* **popular religiosity.**

Religious syncretism. A process that combines two or more religious systems with the aim of uniting their doctrines, rites, and experiences to harmonize them with the life and culture of the group. This combination may range from a transition from one religion to the other, a juxtaposition of different religious beliefs and practices, or an integrated religious system.

Salvation. A theological concept emphasizing the history of the covenant between a faithful and merciful God and the human race. God always offers the re-establishment of the covenant when it is broken by the people. The history of salvation is fulfilled in the definitive covenant established by Jesus Christ. *See also* **liberation; redemption.**

Secularism. A philosophy that essentially separates human beings from God and sets up an opposition between them. It views the construction of history as purely and exclusively the responsibility of human beings. The world is explained solely on its own terms, without any reference to God. *See also* **secularization.**

Secularization. A process linked to the progress of science, technology, and urbanization, and to the advance of anthropological and social disciplines. It maintains that the material realities of nature and humanity are in themselves "good" and that their laws should be respected. Therefore, secularization poses a series of questions about human beings, God, and the world. It affirms the autonomy of science and art from religion, leads to sociocultural progress, and fosters the universalization of culture. The church views secularization as a process that challenges faith and pastoral ministry. *See also* **secularism.**

Signs of the times. Different situations that characterize the reality of life in a particular place and time and that challenge Christians to discern God's will and act accordingly.

Small communities of young people. Small ecclesial communities of young people and young adults.

Small ecclesial communities. A way of being and living as church in which small groups of people have direct interpersonal relationships, share their faith with a constant spirit of prayer, unite with other small communities, participate in their local church, and are signs of Christ in the world.

Socialization. Process by which persons acquire their culture through social institutions other than the family. *See also* **acculturation; enculturation; endoculturation; inculturation.**

Theology. The systematic study of God and of things related to the divine and religious. In broader terms, theology is the reflection made by persons and communities about the mystery of God and life, and about the involvement of God in history.

Traditional culture. Refers to the culture of a population segment or a particular person characterized for having a worldview, values, and ways of economic production and socialization that were typical before the generalization of modern culture in Europe, North

America, and more developed sectors of other countries. *See also* **modern culture.**

Volition, volitional. Use of one's own will in making a conscious decision and then carrying out that decision.

Voluntad. Faculty by which a person decides on and controls her or his own actions.

Youth and young adult ministers. Persons in a diocese or parish who are responsible for the pastoral care of youth and young adults. *See also* **ministry; pastoral action; pastoral agents;** ***pastoral de conjunto;*** **pastoralists; pastoral planning.**

 Index

D

R

S

Permissions

The excerpts on pages 61 and 248–249 are from *Santo Domingo Conclusions: New Evangelization, Human Development, and Christian Culture* (Washington, DC: USCC, 1993), numbers 178 and 303. Copyright © 1993 by the USCC, Washington, DC 20017. Used with permission. All rights reserved.

The excerpts on pages 65 and 77 are from *Human Sexuality: A Catholic Perspective for Education and Lifelong Learning* (Washington, DC: USCC, 1990), pages 7 and 19. Copyright © 1990 by the USCC, Washington, DC 20017. Used with permission. All rights reserved.

The excerpts on pages 143, 170, and 172 are from *The Documents of Vatican II,* by Walter M. Abbott (Boston: America Press, 1966), pages 585, 24–25, and 199–200, respectively. Copyright © 1966 by America Press.

The excerpts on pages 174 and 175 are from the *National Pastoral Plan for Hispanic Ministry* (Washington, DC: United States Catholic Conference [USCC], 1988), pages 8 and 51. Copyright © 1988 by the USCC, Washington DC 20017. Used with permission. All rights reserved.

The excerpts on pages 193–194, 195, and 196 are from *Earthing the Gospel,* by Gerald A. Arbuckle (Maryknoll, NY: Orbis Books, 1990), pages 12, 14, and 14–15, respectively. Copyright © 1990 by Gerald A. Arbuckle. Used with permission of the publisher.

Footnote numbers 2 through 19 in chapter 8 are from *Our Lady Patroness of the Americas: A Handbook on Guadalupe* (Kenosha, WI: Franciscan Marytown Press, 1974), pages 146–156. Copyright © 1974 by Marytown Press. Used with permission.

❦ Prophets of Hope ❦

Volume 1

Hispanic Young People and the Church's Pastoral Response

Contents